Spiritual
Formation
as if the
Church
Mattered

"For anyone who has ever thought that the way we 'do church' is missing something, this book is a godsend. Wilhoit reclaims the New Testament vision of local congregations being conformed to the image of Christ for the sake of others. In this second edition, Wilhoit has refined and strengthened his arguments—his wisdom—for how local gatherings of God's people are designed to be the nonnegotiable relational context for Christian formation and, thereby, mission. This book is my go-to for what Christian formation should look like in local churches."

—**Steve L. Porter**, Biola University; editor, *Journal of Spiritual Formation and Soul Care*

"Christian spiritual formation is often reduced to personal practices and individual faith without an awareness of its communal nature. Wilhoit provides a corrective by developing an ecclesiology that situates spiritual formation in faith communities and the broader social context. In a communal view of spiritual formation, Christians are not formed for themselves but for the sake of others, and are to engage in God's redemptive work in the world. I highly recommend Wilhoit's thesis of placing the church as the curriculum for spiritual formation because of its transformative power!"

—**Mark A. Maddix**, dean, School of Theology and Christian Ministry, Point Loma Nazarene University

"*Spiritual Formation as if the Church Mattered* is the mature fruit of a devout scholar. Here Wilhoit weaves theory, passion, and practice together into a rich re-presentation of the gospel for the local church. He takes the discussion about spiritual formation an important step forward, shifting the emphasis from private pursuit to corporate culture. Sensitive to the seldom-noticed dangers along the path of growth toward Christlikeness, this book is loaded with wisdom for those who desire to facilitate communities of formation."

—**Evan Howard**, author of *A Guide to Christian Spiritual Formation*

"Wilhoit has written a book of special urgency for our times. In it he addresses *the* central problem facing the contemporary church in the Western world and worldwide, the problem of how to routinely lead its members through a path of spiritual, moral, and personal transformation that brings them into authentic Christlikeness in every aspect of their lives. . . . He helps any serious person engage the project from where they are, discover what really works for Christlikeness and what doesn't, and assess outcomes realistically to make needed adjustments as they go."

—**Dallas Willard†** (from the foreword)

"From the first stunning sentence in Wilhoit's book—'The church exists to carry out Christ's mission in the world'—I was hooked. Wilhoit captures the journey and struggle of spiritual growth through the life and invitations of Jesus Christ. This lovely work nourished my heart, instructed my mind, and opened my spirit to the Spirit of Christ."

—**Adele Calhoun**, copastor of spiritual formation, Highrock Church, Arlington, Massachusetts

"The title of this tightly woven, consistently challenging meditation on Christian spiritual formation serves notice that this book is going to be more than another self-help manual. . . . This skilled writer uses many pedagogical tools to keep his audience focused. Clearly written from an evangelical perspective, this cogent and passionate book deserves to have wide appeal."

—*Publishers Weekly* (starred review)

SECOND EDITION

Spiritual Formation

as if the Church Mattered

GROWING IN CHRIST THROUGH COMMUNITY

James C. Wilhoit

Ⓑ
Baker Academic
a division of Baker Publishing Group
Grand Rapids, Michigan

Published by Baker Academic
a division of Baker Publishing Group
PO Box 6287, Grand Rapids, MI 49516-6287
www.bakeracademic.com

Printed in the United States of America

Library of Congress Cataloging-in-Publication Data
Names: Wilhoit, Jim, author. Title: Spiritual formation as if the church mattered : growing in Christ through community / James C. Wilhoit. Description: 2nd edition. | Grand Rapids, Michigan : Baker Academic, a division of Baker Publishing Group, [2022] | Includes bibliographical references and index. Identifiers: LCCN 2021033511 | ISBN 9781540963048 (paperback) | ISBN 9781540965387 (casebound) | ISBN 9781493435166 (ebook) | ISBN 9781493435173 (pdf)
Subjects: LCSH: Spiritual formation. | Communities—Religious aspects—Christianity. | Church growth. Classification: LCC BV4511 .W53 2022 | DDC 248.4—dc23
LC record available at https://lccn.loc.gov/2021033511

22   23   24   25   26   27   28   7   6   5   4   3   2   1

With gratitude to Evan B. Howard,
a good friend and companion in Christ,
from whom I have learned much

Contents

List of Figures

Foreword

BY DALLAS WILLARD

James Wilhoit has written a book of special urgency for our times. In it he addresses *the* central problem facing the contemporary church in the Western world and worldwide: the problem of how to routinely lead its members through a path of spiritual, moral, and personal transformation that brings them into authentic Christlikeness in every aspect of their lives, enabling them, in the language of the apostle Paul, "to walk in a manner worthy of the calling with which you have been called" (Eph. 4:1 NASB).

For most of the current century, we have been in a period of time when Christian churches have been distracted from the central task of teaching their people how to live the spiritual life in a way that would bring them progressively to enjoy the character of Christ as their own. But in the last few decades, a sense of spiritual shallowness and emptiness, in individual lives as well as in church groups and activities, has led to a renewed use of the ancient language of "spiritual formation." Spiritual formation (really, *trans*formation) is the process, in Paul's language, of "putting on the Lord Jesus Christ, and not organizing our lives around the satisfaction of our natural desires" (Rom. 13:14 author's trans.). In that process, we "put off the old self, which is corrupt according to the deceitful lusts, and are renewed in the spirit of our mind; and . . . put on the new self, which after God is created in righteousness and true holiness" (Eph. 4:22–24 author's trans.).

In the period we have recently come through, our church activities have simply had no serious intention of fostering the individual transformation of members of the group. Becoming the kind of person who routinely and easily does what Jesus told us to do has generally been considered out of reach and therefore not really necessary for what we, as Christians, are about. Paul, in conformity with the central teachings of the whole Bible, is referring to the type of life transformation from inside to outside—"first clean the inside of the cup and of the dish, so that the outside of it may also become clean," as Jesus said (Matt. 23:26 NASB)—that won the ancient world to Christ. If what we have more recently seen of Christianity in the Western world had been all there was to it in earlier centuries, there would be no such thing as Christianity today, or at best it would exist as a museum piece. How the church fell onto such thin times is, no doubt, a subject worthy of thorough examination. But the practical problem is this: How do we move back into the powerful form of life that won the worlds of the past and alone can meet the crying needs of our world today? Here is where this book comes in.

The answer to the question is that *the local congregations*, the places where Christians gather on a regular basis, *must resume the practice of making the spiritual formation of their members into Christlikeness their primary goal, the aim that every one of their activities serves.* Another way of putting the same point is to say that they must take it as their unswerving objective to be a body of apprentices to Jesus who are devoted to learning and teaching one another how to do, through transformation of the "inner self" (Eph. 3:16 NASB), everything Jesus said for us to do. That is what it means to "put on the Lord Jesus Christ" (Rom. 13:14).

Unless this course of action is adopted in the local or neighborhood congregations, the now widespread talk about "spiritual formation" and the renewed interest in practices of the spiritual life in Christ will soon pass, like other superficial fads that offer momentary diversion to a bored and ineffectual church *primarily* interested only in its own success or survival. But the church is the local group of apprentices whom God has chosen as his primary instrument in his redemptive work on earth. No doubt wisely, for only such a group is suited to be the place where humans learn to "love one another as I have loved you" (John 13:34 author's trans.). And as long as the local assemblies do not do this transforming work as their central business, everyone, church and world alike, will assume—as in fact they do now—that there is an acceptable alternative form of Christianity other than spiritual transformation into Christlikeness. Indeed, that is the assumption that produces the now standard form in North America of "nominal" Christianity: the curse of the valid aspirations of humanity and the perennial Golgotha of Jesus's trajectory across human history.

Currently, pastors and leaders of congregations do not seem to understand this. Their education, their models of success, and their understanding of what salvation or life in Christ is supposed to be like point them in other directions. The result is the absence of any overriding intention to devote their central effort toward constant transformation of all members of the group. Indeed, radical transformation is not what our folks are prepared for in "going to church." It is not what is in their "contract" with the preacher or the leadership. Thus you will find here and there congregations that spend months or years trying to develop a "mission" statement. Almost never—never, to my knowledge—do they come out at the point Jesus left with us: to be disciples (apprentices of Jesus in kingdom living) who make disciples and form them in inner Christlikeness in such a way that they easily and routinely do the things Jesus told us to do (Matt. 28:18–20).

In order to respond faithfully to Jesus's instructions, pastors, teachers, and leaders must form the intention and make the decision to live out the New Testament vision of apprenticeship to Jesus in the local congregation, as Jesus articulated it in his life on earth and as Paul articulates it in Ephesians 4:1–16: the vision of a body of disciples (not just Christians as now understood) building itself up in love and mutual ministry and life together. Then they can begin to think about what they do "in church" and in life that can effectively carry forward on a regular basis spiritual formation in Christlikeness in all the attendees. They will learn how to deal with the fine texture of relationships and events, within the redemptive body and beyond, in such a way that all might "grow in the grace and knowledge of our Lord and Savior Jesus Christ" (2 Pet. 3:18 NASB)—no hype!

It is hard today for pastors and leaders to form this intention and begin to put it into practice. Generally speaking, this is because they do not know how to make the group a context of honest spiritual formation, and they fear that, if they try to, they will fail by the current standards of "success." But there is a way forward, and it is *the details* that matter. That is where this book, *Spiritual Formation as if the Church Mattered*, is uniquely helpful. Dr. Wilhoit, with a warm heart and a gentle and intelligent manner, helps us see, in great detail, what we can do to relocate spiritual transformation to the center of *what we do* in gathering as disciples of Jesus. He helps any serious person engage the project from where they are, discover what really works for Christlikeness and what doesn't, and assess outcomes realistically to make needed adjustments as they go. No special equipment or ability—not even a budget—is required. As disciples, we learn what we need to know as we go. Remember, the churches have always been at their best when they had the least but were simply obedient to Christ.

Preface

This book had its beginnings in conversations with my students about the spiritual nurture they received in their families and churches. These conversations naturally arose during advising visits, over lunches, and in classes, and I soon became fascinated by the variety of formational practices that students had experienced. As I reflected on their stories, I began to look for the presence of formational principles. This led to a more intentional set of interviews with church leaders about patterns and practices of spiritual formation. I realized that some churches are marked by the presence of a "culture of formation," and while others may have many programs and much activity, they lack the presence of such a transformative culture. In the spring of 1989, I taught in a newly reopened seminary in Tallinn, Estonia, then still part of the Soviet Union, and I observed how churches had formed disciples who remained faithful even in a hostile environment. These churches all lacked the buildings and program structure that I had come to associate with Christian education and spiritual formation, but they had a definite culture of formation.

I write as an evangelical and one who is deeply concerned about the erosion of intentional practices of spiritual formation in many of our churches. My concern is that many of the formational patterns that served us well for several generations have quickly been set aside. To be sure, some of these practices of formation may have become stale and unattractive. But, tragically, it seems like we have often abandoned practices without adopting alternatives. Some practices that were common in evangelical churches for several generations and that have recently been set aside include an emphasis on systematic Bible teaching; Bible memorization and reading; Sunday evening services with an emphasis on testimonies, missions, and global Christianity; observing the Sabbath; sharing church-wide meals; practicing hospitality; attendance at nurture-oriented summer camps; pastoral visitation; and significant intergenerational socializing. These changes represent a sea change in our formational structures, and its effects will take a generation to fully manifest.

This book is not so much about reversing a trend as it is about a call to intentionality about our formation and to repentance about how we have tried to engineer formation more than prayerfully seek to open our lives and our churches to God's grace. I have sought to provide guidance on community-oriented and educationally based spiritual formation that has stood the test of time. I am grateful for the teaching and writing of Dallas Willard, who has reminded us that our spiritual formation must be grounded not merely in spiritual abstractions but in the life, teaching, and ministry of Jesus. I am distressed that so much Christian spirituality seems content to focus on a vague spirituality rather than on the life, teaching, and actual indwelling of Jesus.

I am grateful to those who have assisted me in this process. Faculty members from several schools have met under the leadership of Evan Howard for a gathering of Evangelical Scholars in Christian Spirituality. I am grateful for the comments on various chapters provided by members of this group: Paul Bramer, Klaus Issler, Michael Glerup, and Evan Howard. Tom Schwanda read the entire manuscript at an earlier stage and provided valuable comments. Portions of this new edition were worked on during a semester at Biola University's Center for Christian Thought, funded in part through a grant from the Templeton Foundation, and I am indebted to the Center for providing space for writing and intellectual engagement. The project was also made possible by the support of my family, who took an active interest it, listened to pieces over dinner, provided illustrations, and critically read portions. Thank you, Carol, Elizabeth, and Juliana.

ONE

Formation through the Ordinary

The Pathway to Flourishing in Christ

Therefore, go and make disciples of all the nations, baptizing them in the name of the Father and the Son and the Holy Spirit. Teach these new disciples to obey all the commands I have given you. And be sure of this: I am with you always, even to the end of the age.

Jesus (Matt. 28:19–20 NLT)

I know of no current denomination or local congregation that has a concrete plan and practice for teaching people to do "all things whatsoever I have commanded you."

Dallas Willard[1]

It takes time, and the penetration of the truth, to make a mature saint.

Richard F. Lovelace[2]

Spiritual Formation: The Task of the Church

The church exists to carry out Christ's mission in the world, and accomplishing this spiritual formation must be a central task of the church.[3] It represents

---

1. "Spiritual Formation in Christ: A Perspective on What It Is and How It Might Be Done," *Journal of Psychology and Theology* 28, no. 4 (2000): 256.
2. *Dynamics of Spiritual Life: An Evangelical Theology of Renewal* (Downers Grove, IL: InterVarsity, 1979), 143.
3. In the first edition I began with the more provocative statement "Spiritual formation is *the* task of the church. Period." I understand how that statement can be misunderstood,

neither an interesting, optional pursuit by the church nor an insignificant category in the job description of the body of Christ. Spiritual formation (hereafter referred to as Christian Spiritual Formation, or CSF) is at the heart of its whole purpose for existence.[4]

Christian Spiritual Formation is the pathway to flourishing in Christ. It is the way of rest for the weary and the overloaded. It is the way of Jesus's easy yoke and light burden (Matt. 11:28–30), of the good tree that cannot bear bad fruit (Luke 6:43), of building one's life on the foundation provided by Christ (1 Cor. 3:10–15), of "being rich in good deeds" (1 Tim. 6:18 NIV), of clothing yourself with love (Col. 3:14), of accepting the word planted in you (James 1:21), and of abiding in the vine and bearing much fruit (John 15). On this path, we discover that God's "commands are not burdensome" (1 John 5:3 NIV). We learn that Jesus, the Good Shepherd, "came that they may have life, and have it abundantly" (John 10:10). We see that in those who truly abide in God's love there indeed flow "rivers of living water" to a thirsty world (John 7:38). We are more inclined to do that which the Lord requires of us—namely, "to do justice, and to love kindness, and to walk humbly with your God" (Mic. 6:8) and to live so that "mercy triumphs over judgment" (James 2:13).[5]

The message we need to hear is not one of self-improvement but the good news of the gospel—the message that Jack Miller taught many of us: "Cheer up! You are worse than you think" and "Cheer up! God loves you more than you know!"[6] You couldn't be more loved than you already are. The Lord has already provided for us every provision that we need: "By his divine power, God has given us everything we need for living a godly life" (2 Pet. 1:3 NLT). You can't earn any more love and acceptance by your striving. So you are free to be your own person, the person you were truly meant to be. In seasons of self-doubt, I have taken great comfort from Revelation 2:17, which tells us that Jesus knows us so deeply that he will call us by name—a name we have

---

and I modified this sentence and was influenced in this rewording by John H. Westerhoff III, *Inner Growth, Outer Change: An Educational Guide to Church Renewal* (New York: Seabury, 1979), 54.

4. In this second edition I have elected to use the term *Christian Spiritual Formation* (CSF). I am increasingly concerned that "spiritual formation" is understood to be a generic human process marked by attention to the nonmaterial and the cultivation of spiritual practices with only passing reference to the work of God in our transformation. I use CSF to underscore the unique salvific component of true spiritual formation.

5. From James C. Wilhoit and Evan B. Howard, "The Wisdom of Christian Spiritual Formation," *Journal of Spiritual Formation and Soul Care* 13, no. 1 (February 5, 2020): 5–21. Used by permission. Material from this article is incorporated at several places in this volume.

6. C. John Miller, *Saving Grace: Daily Devotions from Jack Miller* (Greensboro, NC: New Growth, 2014), xv.

never heard—and we will immediately recognize it: "And I will give to each one a white stone, and on the stone will be engraved a new name that no one understands except the one who receives it" (NLT). God knows you fully, loves you, and calls you to rest in his love.

The church was formed to form. Our charge, given by Jesus himself, is to make disciples, baptize them, and teach them to obey his commands (Matt. 28:19–20). The witness, worship, teaching, and compassion that the church is to practice all require that Christians be spiritually formed. Although formation describes the central work of the church, and despite a plethora of resolutions, programs, and resources, the fact remains that spiritual formation has not been the priority it should be in the North American church.

Spiritual Formation Is Similar to Public Health

A safe food supply, clean drinking and recreational waters, sanitation, and widespread vaccinations have improved the quality of our lives. These interventions have eliminated diseases like smallpox and polio. These advances, and scores more, are part of the fruit of the public health movement that came to fruition in the twentieth century. I take many of these for granted, assuming they are just part of life, but in many parts of the world, they are not. Currently, 150,000 children die every year from measles, a disease easily prevented through vaccinations.[7] We take for granted public health initiatives of the last century that have had measurable, positive social benefits. In medicine, the two tasks of prevention and cure must work hand in hand. Cures may provoke media attention and buzz; however, the preventative measures and public health interventions generally provide the real "bang for your buck." Likewise, CSF makes its most significant contribution through quiet, hardly noticeable, behind-the-scenes work that places an emphasis on "prevention" and equipping rather than just on crisis interventions or headline-grabbing public conferences and programs.

Consider the effects of the painstakingly established public health infrastructure in the United States. According to the Centers for Disease Control and Prevention (CDC), "Since 1900, the average lifespan of persons in the United States has lengthened by greater than 30 years; 25 years of this gain are attributable to advances in public health."[8] The quiet and seemingly ordinary work of public health has made a tremendous difference in life expectancy

7. World Health Organization, "Measles" fact sheet, last modified December 5, 2019, https://www.who.int/news-room/fact-sheets/detail/measles.
8. Centers for Disease Control and Prevention, "Ten Great Public Health Achievements—United States, 1900–1999," *Morbidity and Mortality Weekly Report* 48, no. 12 (1999): 241–43.

and the overall quality of life. When one looks at the list of the CDC's "Ten Great Public Health Achievements," the achievements appear so reasonable that their implementation seems to be evident to all. The list includes now widely accepted "best practices" such as vaccination, motor vehicle safety, safer and healthier foods, and the recognition of tobacco use as a health hazard. Yet society implemented these strategies, which seem so commonsensical today, only after long struggles, careful science that established their efficacy, and the slow and ongoing work of public education.

Some years ago, a young physician summarized his medical-care trip to Central America by telling of the long days he worked caring for patients. He concluded his story by saying that he was convinced that he could have done more long-term good with one hundred meters of PVC pipe. So many of the people he treated suffered from medical conditions that were the result of the village's contaminated water supply—a problem that could have been easily remedied.

In this chapter, I want to begin to identify what the spiritual formation equivalent of safe drinking water and vaccinations might be. What are the patterns in Christian community life that make a positive contribution to CSF? What are the community practices that we can so easily overlook or underutilize but that help create a climate of formation in a church?

Methodology and Approach

For many years I have been listening to the stories of how faithful people have grown in grace. These accounts pulse with deep drama. I've realized that Paul was not using hyperbole when he told the Galatians, "I am again in the pain of childbirth until Christ is formed in you" (Gal. 4:19). These stories are unique—unique as the people who tell them—and I want to be careful not to simply reduce these amazing tales of grace to a few abstract principles. While themes and patterns do emerge when we look at the stories as a whole, there does not exist anything approaching a "technology of spiritual formation." Formation remains a messy and imprecise business in which character, wisdom, and faith play a far more significant role than theories and techniques. Ironically, one value of deliberate engagement in formation is that it drives us to prayer because it reminds us, more than popular how-to books do, that true formation comes from grace and by grace, channeled through our humble efforts. This is not to deny what others have observed, that "spiritual formation in Christ is an orderly process."[9] CSF is certainly a

---

9. Dallas Willard, *Renovation of the Heart: Putting on the Character of Christ* (Colorado Springs: NavPress, 2002), 10.

multifactorial process that requires us to continually ask God what we should be doing rather than rely on our power and skill.

C. S. Lewis famously set out in his World War II BBC "Broadcast Talks" to explain in a compelling way "mere Christianity," the beautiful and straight-forward core of the faith that has marked the church throughout the centuries.[10] In a similar vein, I am seeking to set forth "mere spiritual formation," which has characterized the best practices of the church from its founding. And so because I desire to be helpful to the various faith traditions of my readers, when we come to essential practices like the Lord's Supper, I am going to write in a general way; therefore, I will be less specific than if I were writing just for my church or tradition. However, unlike Lewis's popular theology, any applied writing on CSF needs to be placed in a specific context. For this book, that context is the evangelical church in North America.

In this book, I will suggest principles and patterns for communal CSF, and the reader will understandably wonder about my evidence: Why do I suggest that my approach is "the best way to do spiritual formation"? In response to that excellent question, I will demur and say my claim is more modest than that. I am not suggesting that I am setting forth "the best way," but I will identify patterns and practices that I discern to be compatible with the great pastoral tradition of the church, patterns and practices that are grounded in orthodox theology and informed by findings from contemporary studies of human flourishing and well-being.

I understand CSF to be, first and foremost, a theological discipline. The word *spiritual* has come to mean, in the broader culture, a positive, subjective experience of an interior/nonmaterial/sacred dimension. That is a far cry from the New Testament's understanding of the term *spiritual*, and yet this vague sense of spirituality has affected contemporary writing on spiritual formation. For example, at a recent conference, several prominent speakers on spiritual formation focused on spiritual formation as the process of shaping, healing, and forming one's interior through coaching and spiritual practices. There was virtually no reference to the work of the Holy Spirit. An interior focus is a necessary part of spiritual formation, but first and foremost, by CSF, we mean formation by the Holy Spirit. We are only facilitators for the work of the Spirit in CSF; all actual formation is the work of God.

Gordon Fee has persuasively argued that in the New Testament, *spiritual* (*pneumatikos*) "refers universally and unequivocally to the Holy Spirit" and

10. C. S. Lewis, *Mere Christianity* (New York: Macmillan, 1960).

"has to do with who the Spirit is and what the Spirit is doing."[11] He documents how English translations have consistently hidden the Holy Spirit's work by using the vague adjective *spiritual*. The foremost New Testament Greek lexicon makes a similar point that *pneumatikos* "in the great majority of cases . . . [has] to do with the (divine) spirit."[12] In writing about spiritual formation, we need to begin with an understanding of the person and work of the Holy Spirit and assume that the Spirit is the primary agent in the work of formation.[13] Throughout this book, there is an assumption that CSF describes processes, strategies, and practices we undertake to open ourselves and our faith communities to the presence and work of the Holy Spirit, who ultimately forms us.

In terms of the theological foundations for CSF, my reflections begin with Scripture. The Bible accurately describes the human condition, the nature of our redemption, and the work of the Spirit, who remakes us so that "you [plural] also, like living stones, are being built into a temple of the Spirit to be a holy priesthood, offering spiritual sacrifices acceptable to God through Jesus Christ" (1 Pet. 2:5 TNIV, marginal reading). The letters of Paul and the book of Acts directly address issues of spiritual formation through questions about discipleship and church life. This book will cite these sources regularly. I am grateful for the emphasis Dallas Willard places on learning from Jesus's program of spiritual formation. When I first heard Willard's lectures and read his *Spirit of the Disciplines*, I was struck by how a faulty Christology had led me to underappreciate Jesus's own spiritual formation. I implicitly acted as though he was a "little God" who did not need to develop as a person in his earthly life; I assumed that he pursued various spiritual practices because they just came naturally to him. Willard challenged my implicit Apollinarianism, my mistaken sense that Jesus's divinity had absorbed his humanity, and Willard showed me how Jesus underwent real spiritual growth and development. "Because of the contemporary bias with which we read the Gospels, . . . we have great difficulty seeing the main emphases in his life. We forget that being the unique Son of God did not relieve him of the necessity of a life of

11. Gordon Fee, "On Getting the Spirit Back into Spirituality," in *Life in the Spirit: Spiritual Formation in Theological Perspective*, ed. Jeffrey P. Greenman and George Kalantzis (Downers Grove, IL: IVP Academic, 2010), 39, 41.

12. "*pneumatikos*," in William Arndt, Frederick Danker, and Walter Bauer, *A Greek-English Lexicon of the New Testament and Other Early Christian Literature*, 3rd ed. (Chicago: University of Chicago Press, 2000), 837.

13. The use of the term *Spirit-ual* was suggested by Cherith Fee Nordling in "Practice Resurrection, Live Like Jesus," in *Tending Soul, Mind, and Body: The Art and Science of Spiritual Formation*, ed. Gerald Hiestand and Todd A. Wilson (Downers Grove, IL: InterVarsity, 2019), 122–33.

preparation that was mainly spent out of the public eye."[14] I also benefited from Gerald Hawthorne's cogent exegetical study of the Spirit's connection to Jesus: "God-in-a-body, as one might describe the Jesus of Apollinarianism, could never be called a human being in the true sense of the word."[15]

Many Christians do not think of Jesus undergoing spiritual formation. When they consider Jesus's spiritual life and development, they easily imagine that his spiritual life must have been largely baked in at birth and rather static. After all, he was the Son of God, and, as the creeds say, he was "very God of very God" and "of one substance with the Father." Yes, he possessed the divine nature fully, so one can wonder if there could be any real sense in which Jesus "developed" in his spiritual life. Yes, Jesus lived a sinless life, always did the will of his Father, and lived in intimate and unbroken union with his Father.

All true, but there is an important sense in which Jesus's spiritual life was anything but fixed and set at conception: constantly listening to and obeying the Father gave him a dynamic and growing spiritual life. The New Testament says of him that "he learned obedience through what he suffered" (Heb. 5:8) and "increased in wisdom" (Luke 2:52). His perfect obedience did not eliminate growth; it accelerated it. He aced every lesson, as it were, and was quickly immersed in advanced formation activities.

Jesus's spiritual growth was real. Luke tells us of Jesus's personal development, and the author of Hebrews goes to great lengths to emphasize the reality of Jesus's true humanity. He is "fully human in every way, so that he might become a merciful and faithful high priest in service to God, and that he might make atonement for the sins of the people. Because he himself suffered when he was tempted, he is able to help those who are being tempted" (Heb. 2:17–18 NIV). This text makes it clear that Jesus's temptations, sufferings, and resulting growth were genuine as could be and akin—not in magnitude but in kind—to our spiritual growth. In our study of CSF, we will examine time and again the life and formation of Jesus.[16]

There is a well-developed tradition of CSF that comes to us through various orthodox Christian faith traditions. Willard implores those seeking to practice CSF, "The Christian past holds a huge store of information on spiritual formation. It is a treasure—a God deposit—in Christ's people. We must

14. Dallas Willard, *The Spirit of the Disciplines: Understanding How God Changes Lives* (New York: HarperOne, 1988), 5.

15. Gerald F. Hawthorne, *The Presence and the Power: The Significance of the Holy Spirit in the Life and Ministry of Jesus* (Eugene, OR: Wipf & Stock, 2003), 201–2.

16. Bruce A. Ware, *The Man Christ Jesus: Theological Reflections on the Humanity of Christ* (Wheaton: Crossway, 2012), 59–72.

take the trouble to know it and to own it in ways suitable to today."[17] It is my sincere hope that I can honor the impulse of Thomas Oden, who teases out what he calls "Classical Consensual Ecumenical Teaching" in his *Classic Christianity*. He goes so far as to claim, "The only promise I intend to make, however inadequately carried out, is that of unoriginality. I plan to present nothing new or original in these pages."[18] In no small measure, the proper originality in CSF is not in the theory or theology itself but in the analysis of one's own cultural and ecclesiastical reality and the timely application of gospel-driven CSF to that situation. One of the ways I access this classic CSF tradition is through Adrian Van Kaam's formation science, as found in his eleven volumes on formation science, formation anthropology, and formation theology. His comprehensive work respectfully captures many of the contributions of a wide range of writers on CSF throughout church history.[19]

Guidance about how to conduct our CSF comes from a variety of sources. Historical, theological, and biblical resources offer or suggest specific practices and strategies. In the past forty years, a variety of wise, measured books on CSF have been published that emphasize specific ways to "do formation." I have read widely in these sources and used their wisdom and guidance throughout this book. The positive psychology movement has much to offer too in suggesting practices and strategies; some, such as Robert Emmons's work on gratitude, has clear application to CSF, while others apply less directly but are equally useful.[20]

God and Formation

The practices of faith are not ultimately our own practices but rather habitations of the Spirit, in the midst of which we are invited to participate in the practices of God.

Craig Dykstra[21]

The Bible opens with a description of God's formative work in creation: "In the beginning when God created the heavens and the earth" (Gen. 1:1). And

17. Willard, *Renovation of the Heart*, 249.
18. Thomas C. Oden, *Classic Christianity: A Systematic Theology* (New York: HarperOne, 2009), xv.
19. Van Kaam's theory of formation is well presented in this accessible volume: Rebecca Letterman and Susan Muto, *Understanding Our Story: The Life's Work and Legacy of Adrian Van Kaam in the Field of Formative Spirituality* (Eugene, OR: Wipf & Stock, 2017).
20. Robert Emmons, *Thanks! How Practicing Gratitude Can Make You Happier* (New York: Houghton Mifflin Harcourt, 2008).
21. *Growing in the Life of Faith: Education and Christian Practices*, 2nd ed. (Louisville: Westminster John Knox, 2005), 78.

creation, we read, involved a formation process. God created the stuff of the universe, but "the earth was formless and empty" (1:2 NIV). And God was at work, forming his creation. The image of God personally forming humankind furthers this picture: "The LORD God formed a man's body from the dust of the ground" (2:7 TLB). The personal creative activity of forming humankind established a bond between God and the first human, Adam. God deepened the relationship by preparing a garden, where "he put the man whom he had formed" (2:8). God also "formed every animal of the field and every bird of the air" (2:19). The creation—personally fashioned, crafted, and formed by God—pleased the Artist/Creator. "God saw everything that he had made, and indeed, it was very good" (1:31).

The contrast between the formless primordial cosmos (Gen. 1:2) and the harmony of the properly formed creative order (1:1–2:25) is an implicit reference point throughout Scripture. God established precedence for formation. Whereas other religions view good and evil as eternal constants, Scripture presents God as eternal, in contrast to sin, which is a parasitic, temporary condition bent on unraveling and destroying creation. I have found the term *spiritual entropy* helpful to describe our world's tendency toward spiritual decay, disunity, and dysfunction. God's love/grace acts powerfully against that entropy.[22] Love/grace is the powerful force that works against entropy.

In contrast to the formative work of God, chaos/entropy characterizes rebellion against his rule. Paul anchors his rebuke of the Corinthians for their disorderly worship in an appeal to God's character: "God is not a God of confusion, but of peace" (1 Cor. 14:33 NASB). Chaos and injustice mark any society, culture, or institution that divorces itself from the one in whom "all things hold together" (Col. 1:17). The connection between spiritual bankruptcy and the decay of the moral, spiritual, and civil order is a recurring prophetic theme. The biblical worldview recognizes an ever-present spiritual entropy at work in the fallen world. It is ceaseless because sin, the flesh, and our idols never rest in their battle against the human soul and God's kingdom claims on it. So we cannot accomplish CSF by merely setting up programs and writing policies. There is nothing "once and for all" about formation.

The difficulty of the divine work of formation is illustrated in the events of the exodus. We read that while Moses was on the mountain meeting with God, his brother Aaron "took the gold from them, formed it in a mold, and cast an image of a calf" (Exod. 32:4). The event represents a sad but constant reality in Scripture. God invites us to shalom, to peace, to wholeness, but

---

22. M. Scott Peck, *The Road Less Traveled: A New Psychology of Love, Traditional Values, and Spiritual Growth* (New York: Simon & Schuster, 1978), 268.

Our Aim: The Triumph of God in Our Lives

If all is not organized around God's plan for spiritual formation, what difference does it make if we regard some churches and ways of "doing church" as more "successful" than others? Biblical and historical "Christianity" has brought forth children of light to be, with Jesus Christ, the light of the world only in those times and places where it has steadily drawn people into his "kingdom not of this world" and taught them to live increasingly in the character and power of God.

No special talents, personal skills, educational programs, money, or possessions are required to bring this to pass. We do not have to purify and enforce some legalistic system. Just ordinary people who are his apprentices, gathered in the name of Jesus and immersed in his presence, and taking steps of inward transformation as they put on the character of Christ: that is all that is required.

Let that be our only aim, and the triumph of God in our individual lives and our times is ensured. The renovation of the heart, putting on the character of Christ, is the unfailing key. It will provide for human life all the blessing that money, talent, education, and good fortune in this world cannot begin to supply, and will strongly anticipate, within this present life, a glorious entry in the full presence of God.[a]

a. Willard, *Renovation of the Heart*, 251.

instead of accepting his transformative formation, we choose to form idols that meet our pressing needs. A theme running through the entire biblical narrative is humans' constant rejection of God and our ambivalence toward his grace-filled invitation for humanity to be formed—actually, transformed from our brokenness—into his beloved children. Humans generally select the expedient route of forming idols, whether actual or conceptual, instead of submitting to God's gracious formation.

All of our work in CSF must be set against the backdrop of the God who forms us in love. CSF is part of God's ongoing providential rule. God actively sustains the physical world through Christ, who "sustains all things by his powerful word" (Heb. 1:3). Thus God's love gives the world the only deep and true order we know. As we think about CSF, we must remember that all positive formation in the world has its origin in God's love for humanity. CSF has a specific goal and unique means provided by the cross and the incarnation. Still, it shares with all positive formation the power of love overcoming spiritual entropy/decay. "Let us love one another, for love comes from God" (1 John 4:7 NIV).

In What Sense Is Spiritual Formation Universal?

Every person is being shaped spiritually: their heart or spirit (the core of their being) is undergoing formation. Willard describes the universal nature of formation as "a process that happens to everyone. The most despicable, as well as the most admirable of persons, have had a spiritual formation. Terrorists as well as saints are the outcome of spiritual formation. Their spirits or hearts have been formed. Period."[23] The formation may be in either a positive or a negative direction. It may involve the cultivation of virtues that promote social harmony and care or may leave persons wary, self-protective, and unable to promote the welfare of society.

Christians have frequently concluded that since the presence of social virtues does not necessarily indicate a sustaining faith in God, their cultivation is of little spiritual value. This belief has contributed a sad chapter to our social witness and downplayed some essential strategies for personal growth. All persons of goodwill, Christian and non-Christian, should celebrate the presence of virtues that promote a society of shalom and justice. I recall a conversation I had with a missionary couple who were distressed by fellow Christians who made an effort to recycle household waste. To this couple, it seemed pointless because it had no direct salvific benefit and promoted the idea that we could improve society apart from God; they thought that such labor was being "wasted in non-kingdom work." While they represent a small minority, this couple illustrates a tendency to bifurcate formation into that which is radically Christian and beneficial and that which is ordinary and of little importance. Such orientation comes very close to Gnosticism.

We need to see that all true formation has its origin in God, who through Christ is reconciling the world to himself (2 Cor. 5:18–20). We must be very sober about the power of sin, and we need to see Christ, who "sustains everything by the mighty power of his command" (Heb. 1:3 NLT), as being behind the growth in virtue, in love, and in justice. This has a very practical implication. It means that Christians may avail themselves of ordinary avenues of change that promote the presence of virtues. Our change does not come in two forms: good Christian church-based change and ordinary secular change. All true formation has its origin in God, and we must humbly receive it as a gift. I have sat with several well-meaning Christians who

23. Willard, *Renovation of the Heart*, 19.

were hesitant to participate in physician-recommended programs designed to help address their debilitating anxiety because the programs were "not Christian." The irony is that the most frequent command in Scripture given "again and again, by God, by angels, by Jesus, by prophets and apostles" is *"Don't be afraid! Don't be afraid! Fear not. Don't be afraid."*[24] Reducing one's anxiety is part of Christian discipleship. We must be discerning, but much of what contributes to our positive spiritual formation may be ordinary activities that, when humbly received, are used to weave the beautiful tapestry of our formation.

All persons have their hearts deeply formed through both the ordinary events of life and intentional processes. In his *Confessions*, Augustine uses an illustration drawn from ancient physics in which objects were thought to have a "weight" or affinity. Rocks fall and fire rises, the thinking went at that time, because their weights bring them to their sources: rocks fall because their weights draw them to the earth, where they originated, and sparks rise from the fire because their weights draw them to the stars. "A material object works its way toward its own place by means of its own weight. A weight doesn't simply direct its course to the lowest level, but to its own proper place. Fire moves up, stone down. These things are in motion through their own weights, and they seek their own places. . . . My love is my weight. I'm carried by it wherever I'm carried."[25]

> All hearts are formed. It may be in either a positive or a negative direction. As Christians, we uniquely undergo the Spiritual formation of the Holy Trinity designed to reshape us and conform us more and more to the ways of Jesus as we seek to live out in our churches the reality of the unity we have in Christ.

For Augustine, the critical questions of CSF are about our loves, and especially about what we are learning to love more and more. This emphasis is captured in two questions that Steve Garber poses: "What do you love, and what are you learning to love?"[26] Every human follows their deepest loves, and these loves are formed throughout our lives. That there is a universal formation of our loves is captured well in the phrase "you are what you love."[27] We should not confuse the Holy Spirit's unique spiritual formation of Christians with the universal shaping of our loves that every human being undergoes.

24. N. T. Wright, *Following Jesus* (Grand Rapids: Eerdmans, 2009), 68.
25. Augustine, *Confessions*, trans. Sarah Rudin (New York: Modern Library, 2017), 436.
26. Steve Garber, "Learning to Love What God Loves," *Boundless* (blog), September 7, 1998, https://www.boundless.org/faith/learning-to-love-what-god-loves.
27. James K. A. Smith, *You Are What You Love: The Spiritual Power of Habit* (Grand Rapids: Baker Academic, 2016).

What Spiritual Formation Is and Why It Is Corporate

The Gospel orients us not so much to an object as to a person. The Gospel, then, is not so much belief *that* as it is belief *in*.

Kenneth J. Collins[28]

CSF refers to the intentional communal process of growing in our relationship with God and becoming conformed to Christ through the power of the Holy Spirit. This is the definition that captures what I see as the essential features of CSF, and here I will highlight a few implications in the definition.

First, my description of CSF as an intentional process that requires our engagement is intended to distinguish it from the broad sense in which heart formation refers to all the cultural forces, activities, and experiences that shape people's spiritual lives. In this book, I am interested in exploring the intentional and deliberate side of CSF—what is taught and sought rather than merely caught. With that said, those of us involved in the study of CSF should have the humility to admit that much of the most effective formation takes place through the quiet care extended by godly Christians who simply extend love, grace, and personal interest to those who cross their paths. A friend recently recalled how my mother welcomed him into our church as a new Christian more than fifty years ago. My mother's hospitality was born out of her simple desire to "make people feel at home" in church.

How do we know it is a process that requires our engagement? Jesus's parting words to his followers are to "make disciples" and teach them "to obey everything I have commanded you" (Matt. 28:19–20 NIV). Paul calls his audience to "redouble your efforts. Be energetic in your life of salvation" (Phil. 2:12 Message). In this book, I will make it clear that the grace of the gospel does not preclude our active engagement in our sanctification; it should engender gratitude and eliminate any sense that we have earned our growth in holiness.

Second, I have described CSF as communal—occurring in and through the church. God intends for the church to be the place of formation, worship, and mission, and Kevin Vanhoozer rightly asserts that, in part, "the church exists as a place to make disciples."[29] The outcome of CSF is both personal and corporate; it affects the person and the church. Spiritual transformation must extend beyond the individual to the church, the family, and society. In

28. *Soul Care: Deliverance and Renewal through the Christian Life* (Wheaton: Victor Books, 1995), 110.

29. Kevin J. Vanhoozer, *Hearers and Doers: A Pastor's Guide to Making Disciples through Scripture and Doctrine* (Bellingham, WA: Lexham, 2019), Kindle Loc. 1463.

God's gospel, the outcome is not merely sanctified individuals but a holy people, the bride of Christ. As a *means* of CSF, the body of Christ is a primary vehicle through which the Spirit of God guides and matures us. Together we hear the Word preached and share the body and blood of Christ, and in this common celebration of the resurrection, we are ourselves raised as a people of God. We bear one another's burdens, offer a prayer for healing, or share what we have with those who have need, and in this fellowship of heart and body, we encourage individuals and equip the body of Christ. The gifts and the fruit of the Spirit all are part of a vibrant, formative interaction of person and community.

Third, we can never accomplish CSF through our own power; we need the empowering of the Holy Spirit. CSF emerges from our saving experience of Christ. It is an appropriation of Christ's work as we "contemplate the Lord's glory," thus "being transformed into his image with ever-increasing glory" (2 Cor. 3:18 NIV). Our salvation is grounded in the work of Christ. Consequently, our participation in ongoing formation is working out what God has worked in us (Phil. 2:12–13). We live out the reality of our being "in Christ" (Eph. 2:10), our life "hidden with Christ in God" (Col. 3:3 NIV). Thus CSF is an expression of *faith*. It is the Christian believing in and responding to God's work in Christ and the Spirit, giving assent to the truths of the gospel and trusting in the God who gave the Spirit, the church, and the means of grace as vehicles of ongoing salvation.[30]

> CSF (1) is intentional, (2) is communal, (3) requires our engagement, (4) is accomplished by the Holy Spirit, (5) is for the glory of God and the service of others, and (6) has as its means and end the imitation of Christ.

The Gospel and Spiritual Formation

Paul uses five key words to describe Christianity—grace, truth, faith, love, and hope.

Klyne Snodgrass[31]

The Message version of the Bible begins Ephesians 4 with this call: "In light of all this, here's what I want you to do" (4:1). And that raises the question "In light of what?" As in many of his letters, Paul has spent the first half of this one discussing matters of faith and belief. He has laid the foundation

30. Kevin J. Vanhoozer, "Putting on Christ: Spiritual Formation and the Drama of Discipleship," *Journal of Spiritual Formation and Soul Care* 8, no. 2 (2015): 147–71.

31. *Ephesians*, NIV Application Commentary (Grand Rapids: Zondervan, 1996), 59.

of the Christian faith in God's grace and our union with Christ. The second half of the letter more directly concerns conduct issues, which flow directly from our new identity and the reality of Christ's reign.

The introductory section, Ephesians 4:1–16, forms a hinge between the two halves of the letter. This passage contains themes that need to be present in CSF programs in our churches. The passage begins with a call "to walk in a manner worthy of the calling to which you have been called" (4:1 ESV). We are to walk according to the way of the gospel, meaning that we are to be grateful each moment for the gospel's reality and we are to continuously give our loyalty to Christ. We can do this by acknowledging the reality of the Christian unity given by Christ and the Holy Spirit and maintaining and guarding it diligently. Protecting, maintaining, and treasuring our unity is both a means and a fruit of formation. And our desire for unity flows out of our marveling at the gospel. "If God's love is so great, if his salvation is so powerful, if God has granted such reconciliation, then believers should live accordingly. They should value God's love enough to be shaped by it."[32] This unity reflects the very nature of God, as Trinity, and reconciliation is at the heart of God's redemptive work. The extent of this undergirding unity is seen in Paul's sevenfold description of the unity believers experience: one body, one Spirit, one hope, one Lord, one faith, one baptism, one God and Father of all (4:4–6).

Living in true unity enables the church to become a mature body. One reason this passage is so crucial in CSF is that it speaks of maturing individual Christians and also of a maturing body. Becoming a mature body is not just about "producing a bunch of mature Christians." The body's maturity finds expression through the practice of corporate virtues, especially those that promote and protect the unity of the church in gospel truth.

The body is to grow up into maturity as its leaders equip each member to exercise their spiritual gifts for ministry—"to knit God's holy people together for the work of service to build up the Body of Christ" (Eph. 4:12 NJB). The ministry of God's redemptive work was revealed to Paul to unify all things in Christ, "to gather up all things in him, things in heaven and things on earth" (1:10). The church participates in this work of uniting as we live out the reality of our unity in Christ. We do this by cultivating the virtues of humility, gentleness, patience, love, and peacekeeping and by training God's people to do the work of ministry. CSF is a way we operationalize the calling in Ephesians 4:1–16 to live worthy of the gospel as we seek to make our unity a lived reality through the formation of gospel virtues in the context of leadership that equips the church to minister in love.

32. Snodgrass, *Ephesians*, 196.

CSF has a rich history with remarkable texts and well-honed practices to support it. Yet we must always remember that at its heart, it is about our being transformed through our union with Christ mediated by the Holy Spirit that is made available through the gospel of Jesus Christ. That may seem obvious, but I was nurtured in programs that tended to regard Christian education, discipleship, and spiritual formation as things that happened after the gospel was preached and believed. The diagram below captures how my mentors related the gospel and patterns of Christian nurture.

Figure 1. Gospel as pre-discipleship

In this view, the gospel contained both the indictment of our sin and the announcement of hope through the cross—a message that unbelievers certainly need to hear. This "gospel as pre-discipleship" was vividly set forth in a sermon I read recently. The pastor described the gospel as the sure foundation on which we are to build our spiritual house through discipleship and learning. There is a good measure of truth in this, but what is dangerous is when we think the gospel is merely the door by which we enter Christianity, something we leave behind as we grow spiritually. The other disturbing element of this sermon was its emphasis on "my building my house," while little emphasis was placed on grace. Like so many sermons, it seemed to say, "God saved me (gospel); now I need to make myself holy (discipleship)."

The gospel must permeate any program of CSF. Returning to the cross in awareness of our sin, rebellion, and brokenness is the bedrock of CSF. CSF's relation to the gospel looks more like figure 2.[33]

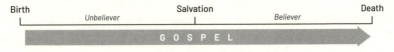

Figure 2. Gospel for spiritual formation

Much of our failure in conceptualizing CSF comes from our inability to keep the gospel central to our ministry. Too often, people see the gospel as merely the front door to Christianity or, worse, "heaven's minimum entrance

33. Patric Knaak, whose clear gospel teaching has helped me immensely, suggested the diagrams on the gospel and spiritual growth.

requirement."[34] A bifurcation of salvation into a grace-filled regeneration followed by sanctification through human striving leads to so many spiritual sorrows. The gospel is the power of God for the beginning, middle, and end of salvation. It is not merely what we need to proclaim to unbelievers; the gospel also needs to permeate our entire Christian experience.

> The gospel is the power of God for the beginning, middle, and end of salvation. It is not merely what we need to proclaim to unbelievers; the gospel also needs to permeate our entire Christian experience.

The Gospel and the Christian

When I was a young adult, the gospel was explained to me in terms of a bridge diagram. In this diagram, a chasm separates God and humankind. This gap is the result of sin and is so enormous that humans cannot bridge it through their efforts and good works. The person who presented this diagram to me did so with great enthusiasm and drew various human bridges (e.g., morality, religion, piety, and good works) on the blackboard, showing that all fell short of crossing the gap.

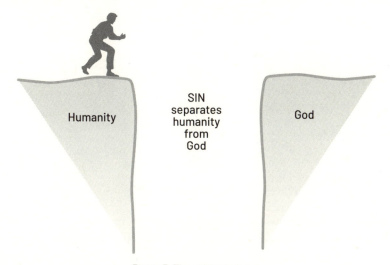

Figure 3. The spiritual chasm

I came to believe that the gospel was chiefly about bridging this gap. The cross fills the gap entirely and provides a way to traverse the great chasm. This is undoubtedly true, "For there is one God; there is also one mediator

34. John Ortberg, "True (and False) Transformation," *Leadership* 24, no. 3 (2002): 102.

between God and humankind, Christ Jesus, himself human" (1 Tim. 2:5). Part of the glorious news of the gospel is that we do have a mediator, and peace with God is possible through the cross of Jesus Christ. God, in his love, has bridged the gap fully and invites us into fellowship with him. In figure 4, however, the person who has crossed the spiritual gap is still running. The cross seems to become a means of transportation rather than God's means of transformation. That was my story: running, doing, serving, but thinking very little about the cross on a daily basis. In Richard Lovelace's words, I was one of those Christians who did not "know enough to start each day with a thoroughgoing stand upon Luther's platform: *you are accepted*, looking outward in faith and claiming the wholly alien righteousness of Christ as the only ground for acceptance, relaxing in that quality of trust which will produce increasing sanctification as faith is active in love and gratitude."[35]

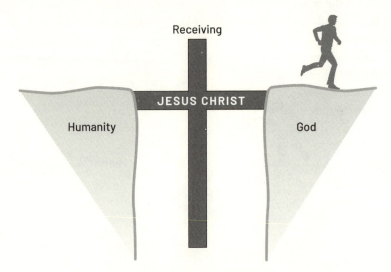

Figure 4. Bridging the gap

What I did not know then is how hard it is to live with a sense that the cross fills this gap. The person who showed me this diagram said something like, "Jim, this is true, just like 2 + 2 = 4. It's not about emotions, and you just have to believe it." Not quite. All of my observed reality supports the fact that 2 + 2 = 4. Yet much in my life does not seem to support "Jesus paid it all." My inborn pride rebels at this. The pain and guilt that are bitter fruits of my sin mock the atonement. Our society, which increasingly ties our worth to

35. Richard F. Lovelace, *Dynamics of Spiritual Life: An Evangelical Theology of Renewal* (Downers Grove, IL: InterVarsity, 1979), 101.

productivity, trains us to deny the cross. Learning that the cross is big enough is a lifelong vocation.

From personal brokenness and reflection, I have come to see that the gospel is not merely the door of faith: it must also be a compass I daily use to orient my life and a salve I apply for the healing of my soul. It is in returning again and again to the cross that we receive the grace that transforms us.

The metaphor of a gap between God and humans that needs to be bridged is surprisingly widespread. For instance, the chief priest of ancient Rome was called *pontifex maximus*—literally, "the chief bridge builder." The sense of a divine-human gap is a universal spiritual intuition; even when people deny having this sense, they live as though they must bridge the gap. However, we must be careful to express the reality of this gap in deep spiritual terms. I have sat with people who had little sense that they were sinners but felt deep agony over their inability to walk free from addictions. A gap was present in their lives, but they did not understand it as the classic "sin gap." To them, it seemed more akin to a hunger for true freedom.

Many Christians have learned the right answer, "Jesus paid it all," yet still live with a nagging sense of shame and guilt. In times of spiritual counsel, I frequently listen to persons who can declare in abstract terms the power of Christ to forgive, heal, save, and restore but who are ravaged with guilt and have no perception of God's love. Such people need to learn to rest in their identity as a child of God.

I remember hearing as a child about a single woman who had adopted an orphan boy from Germany after World War II. His parents had been killed during the war, and his postwar experience was horrific. While the woman loved her son deeply, it was only in adulthood that he finally began to love her as a son should. His adolescent years were marked by detachment and rebellion that brought his long-suffering mother great pain and embarrassment. The death of his birth parents and the betrayals his family had experienced made it so hard for him to live as a son rather than as an orphan. We, too, are beloved children who regularly "don't get it" and live instead as spiritual orphans, constantly trying to earn God's love and establish our worthiness.

For years, when I read a passage like Romans 1:15—"I am so eager to preach the gospel also to you who are in Rome" (NIV)—I assumed it meant that Paul wanted to come and hold an evangelistic campaign in conjunction with the church in Rome. Indeed, he was an evangelist, but he also had a deep burden that those who were already believers should hear and live by the gospel. He goes on to say that the gospel "is the power of God for salvation to everyone who has faith" (1:16). Salvation describes the complete process of redemption

Paul on Preaching the Gospel

To all God's beloved in Rome, who are called to be saints: Grace to you and peace from God our Father and the Lord Jesus Christ. . . . For God, whom I serve with my spirit by announcing the gospel of his Son, is my witness that without ceasing I remember you always in my prayers, asking that by God's will I may somehow at last succeed in coming to you. For I am longing to see you so that I may share with you some spiritual gift to strengthen you. . . . Hence my eagerness to proclaim the gospel to you also who are in Rome. (Rom. 1:7–15)

Who do we usually think about preaching the gospel to?

- Non-Christians

Who is Paul writing to?

- Roman Christians: "To all God's beloved in Rome, who are called to be saints. . . . Your faith is proclaimed throughout the world" (1:7–8).

Who is Paul eager to preach the gospel to?

- He wants to preach the gospel to the Christians in Rome: "Hence my eagerness to proclaim the gospel to you also who are in Rome" (1:15).

What is surprising about this?

- We tend to think that the gospel is just for non-Christians.

(beginning with turning to Christ and proceeding through our sanctification to eventual glorification).

It is clear from the book of Acts and from Paul's letters that Paul was committed to the ministry of the gospel in his work. An essential part of CSF is presenting the reality of the gospel as a way of life and discerning the cultural patterns that work against our trust in God's love and grace as our sure foundation. What was true for Paul—"You are so quickly deserting the one who called you to live in the grace of Christ and are turning to a different gospel—which is really no gospel at all" (Gal. 1:6–7 NIV)—is also true for us: the gospel is under attack.

True CSF will always carry out a twofold task in relation to the gospel. One task is preaching and teaching the gospel to promote a depth of understanding, greater trust, and spiritual cleansing and healing. This is the work of actively presenting the gospel so that people can engage it and use it in their lives. Paul describes the effects of this ministry when he says that as the gospel "is bearing fruit and growing in the whole world, so it has been bearing fruit among yourselves from the day you heard it and truly comprehended the

Why do Christians need to hear the gospel?

- Over time, we simply tend to wander from the truth. As God said to his people through Jeremiah, "You love to wander far from me and do not follow in my paths" (Jer. 14:10 NLT).

- All of us have idols at hand, which we use as substitutes for the cross to gain divine favor. The problem of the Galatians is a problem all of us face: "I am astonished that you are so quickly deserting him who called you in the grace of Christ and are turning to a different gospel" (Gal. 1:6 ESV).

Why does Paul want to preach to Christians?

- He wants to encourage them and strengthen them spiritually: "I can share a spiritual blessing with you that will help you grow strong in the Lord. I'm eager to encourage you in your faith, but I also want to be encouraged by yours. In this way, each of us will be a blessing to the other" (Rom. 1:11–12 NLT).

What is the gospel?

- The power of God for salvation (1:16). "It may well be said that, in Paul's view, Jesus Christ is the gospel."[a] The gospel is the source of grace/power needed to live the Christian life.[b]

a. Millard J. Erickson, *Christian Theology*, 2nd ed. (Grand Rapids: Baker, 1998), 1072.
b. Questions adapted from *Discipling by Grace* (Jenkintown, PA: World Harvest Mission, 1996), 1.3. Used by permission.

grace of God" (Col. 1:6). The language shows that we do not merely learn the gospel when we are converted and then move on from there. Paul asserts that the gospel continually works in us as we understand more and more of its truth and respond to it. We encourage the gospel's work as we seek to live out its teaching about speaking the truth, turning away from lust, diminishing racially biased judgment, and reaching out to serve with the bold love and grace nurtured in the soil of the gospel. The gospel calls us to discipleship and contains the power to enable us to follow Christ.

The second task of CSF is to confront the false gospels and idols that are always present in our lives. In Galatians, we see an example of this. Peter and the apostles had insisted that Gentile believers adopt Jewish cultural forms to be "real" Christians, thus maintaining their attitudes of racial superiority. As a result, evangelism, worship, and fellowship suffered. Paul confronted Peter and the apostles about this, calling them to repentance. But when Paul rebuked Peter, he did not say, "Your attitude of racial superiority is immoral" (though it was). Instead, he said that the apostles "were not acting in line with the truth of the gospel" (Gal. 2:14 NIV). The gospel was not growing and bearing fruit in the church because on this issue they had not understood God's grace in all its truth. The doctrine of grace should end the self-justifying behavior of cultural pride, a form of works righteousness in which the human heart seeks to use cultural differences as measurements of personal worth. Paul applied the gospel, and the result was a renewal, a great leap forward for the church.

In much of the popular writing on CSF, there is a tendency to convey a stunted view of the gospel. We get the idea that what unbelievers need is the gospel. Then, once they accept Christ as Savior, they move on to "needing discipleship," which consists of learning about Christ, developing the fruit of the Spirit, learning how to have a quiet time, and practicing spiritual disciplines. However, the New Testament paints a remarkably different picture. We must remember the description of the gospel as the power of God for the beginning, middle, and end of salvation. Often we do not understand all the vast implications and applications of the gospel. Only as we apply the gospel more and more deeply and radically—only as we think through all its truth—does it bear fruit and grow. The key to continual and deeper spiritual renewal and revival is the persistent rediscovery of the gospel. *So many of our spiritual problems come from a failure to apply the gospel.* This is true for us both as a community and as individuals.

In our culture of self-improvement, which at times has turned spirituality into a narcissistic pursuit, it seems vital that we do not see CSF as just another route to personal empowerment. CSF is first and foremost about the gospel. As Peter reminds us, we are to "grow in the grace and knowledge" of the gospel (2 Pet. 3:18), not sit passively in it or take it for granted. Let the power of the gospel transform God's church and his people.

Spiritual Formation Often Happens Quite Naturally

I am encouraged by George Gallup's survey research that finds that a sizable group of persons in the United States have been so transformed by the gospel that others can notice their constructive behavior. Gallup observes that these "highly spiritually committed" people not only pursue the spiritual practices of prayer, forgiveness, and Scripture reading but also exhibit laudable social virtues. "These people are much more concerned about the betterment of society. They're more tolerant of other people. They are more involved in charitable activities. And they're far, far happier than the rest."[36]

---

36. George Gallup, "Vital Signs: An Interview with George H. Gallup," interview by Jim Berkley and Kevin Miller, *Leadership* 8, no. 1 (1987): 15, https://www.christianitytoday.com /pastors/1987/fall/8714012.html.

Imagine the benefits to a society and to the witness of the reality of God's kingdom if there were more of these people.

Since I first read Gallup's observation some thirty-five years ago, I have been engaged in a quiet "saint hunt." I am looking for people whose spiritual practices and gospel virtues are patently evident. Part of my purpose in writing this book was to report patterns of formation I have observed in what often appeared to be haphazard, messy, real-life spiritual development. I have asked, "What consistent circumstances, patterns of communal nurture, and experiences helped produce many of these genuine, godly folk I have met?" I have sought to learn what contributed to the transformations of the people who have grown in grace.

Meanwhile, I have also witnessed a disquieting trend. So many initiatives aimed at spiritual formation seem to have lost their bearings and have settled for secondary goals. We've learned new terminology while maintaining the old lack of healthy spirituality. Sadly, many of these spiritual formation programs remind me of third-rate manufacturers that crank out mediocre products and never seem to catch on that their manufacturing processes will consistently produce shoddy goods. As Dallas Willard reminds us, "Your system is perfectly designed to produce the results you are getting."[37]

In summary, real spiritual formation is taking place all around us. Yet most of our Christian peers are not being profoundly changed by the gospel in ways that result in Jesus's promised lifestyle of peace, service, and spiritual authority. Our culture—and, sadly, many churches—seek to squeeze us into the mold of a sensible, consumer-oriented faith that meets our needs, asks us to be nice, and avoids offending anyone else.

For Further Reading

Boa, Kenneth. *Conformed to His Image: Biblical and Practical Approaches to Spiritual Formation*. Grand Rapids: Zondervan, 2001. A thorough survey of twelve key dimensions of spiritual formation.

Brother Lawrence. *The Practice of the Presence of God; and the Spiritual Maxims*. Mineola, NY: Dover, 2005. A brief, classic presentation on keeping the presence of God in mind and heart.

Chandler, Diane J. *Christian Spiritual Formation: An Integrated Approach for Personal and Relational Wholeness*. Downers Grove, IL: IVP Academic, 2014. A clearly written and careful integrative approach to CSF.

37. Dallas Willard, *The Divine Conspiracy: Rediscovering Our Hidden Life in God* (San Francisco: HarperSanFrancisco, 1998), 308.

Dykstra, Craig R. *Growing in the Life of Faith: Education and Christian Practices.* 2nd ed. Louisville: Westminster John Knox, 2005. A comprehensive treatment of community spiritual formation.

Howard, Evan B. *A Guide to Christian Spiritual Formation: How Scripture, Spirit, Community, and Mission Shape Our Souls.* Grand Rapids: Baker Academic, 2018. A comprehensive overview of spiritual formation that is grounded in a mature reflection on Scripture and the great tradition of Christian Spiritual Formation.

Mulholland, M. Robert. *Invitation to a Journey: A Road Map for Spiritual Formation.* Downers Grove, IL: InterVarsity, 2016. A book that defines formation as "the process of being conformed to the image of Christ for the sake of others" and provides sensible guidance on personal formation. A modern classic on spiritual formation that, as the title suggests, invites the reader to a deeper, transforming walk with Christ.

Palmer, Parker J. *Let Your Life Speak: Listening for the Voice of Vocation.* San Francisco: Jossey-Bass, 2000. A reminder that we are most authentic when we understand and honor our sense of self and calling.

Taylor, Jeremy, and Thomas K. Carroll. *Selected Works.* Classics of Western Spirituality. New York: Paulist Press, 1990. A masterpiece on how to live well and die well.

Thompson, Marjorie J. *Soul Feast: An Invitation to the Christian Spiritual Life.* Louisville: Westminster John Knox, 2005. A rich exploration of spiritual disciplines applicable to lay groups seeking spiritual formation.

Willard, Dallas. *Renovation of the Heart: Putting on the Character of Christ.* Colorado Springs: NavPress, 2002. An accessible and comprehensive call for spiritual formation as a way of becoming more like Christ.

TWO

Curriculum for Christlikeness

Imitation of Christ
as the Means and Glorious End of Formation

> Be imitators of me, as I [Paul] am of Christ.
> 1 Corinthians 11:1

> Therefore be imitators of God, as beloved children.
> Ephesians 5:1

> Let the same mind be in you that was in Christ Jesus.
> Philippians 2:5

When I first looked over my notes about the faithful people whose stories I had heard, I was tempted to say that spiritual formation simply comes from responding well to pain, suffering, loss, and prejudice. That would be an overstatement, but we do need to understand the environment in which spiritual formation takes place. Spiritual formation does not take place primarily in small groups and Sunday school classes; instead, it mostly takes place in the well-lived and everyday events of life. Our small groups, retreats, and studies should help us respond wisely to the events of life that form us.

In this chapter, we will look at a curriculum for Christlikeness. While Jesus was a teacher, he did not teach in a school or publish a formal curriculum. Jesus was a great and captivating teacher who understood that the teaching is worked out not in the classroom but in everyday life.

Designing a Curriculum for Christlikeness

The idea of constructing a "curriculum for Christlikeness" probably seems jarring to some. And for good reasons, if it implies that Christlikeness is automatically achieved by going through specific steps or applying a kind of technology. Years ago, I came across a comprehensive lesson plan that included twenty-five pages of behavioral objectives that defined "Christlikeness." I was struck by how reductionistic it seemed in thinking that the wisdom, love, virtues, prayerfulness, curiosity, and Scripture-saturated thought of Jesus could be reduced to a series of behavioral outcomes. Yet to be suspicious of thinking we can socially engineer Christlikeness is not to claim that the process of growing in Christlikeness cannot be comprehended. The great tradition of CSF has long suggested that formation can and should be conducted systematically.[1]

When we talk about a curriculum in this context, we mean a course of study that will enable the learner to gain the desired knowledge, skills, dispositions, and virtues through instructional practices, learning experiences, and participation in the work of the Holy Spirit. In Latin, *curriculum* means "the course of a race," and it has long been used in education to describe a plan for systematic instruction in a subject. The main aspects of the content of CSF have long been agreed on. For example, the Lord's Prayer, the Apostles' Creed, the Ten Commandments, and the sacraments and worship form the "core" of this curriculum. The question of what to teach has long been settled. Still, perennial, nagging questions persist about how to teach, who should teach, and how to respond to our unique cultural situation so that we "don't let the world around [us] squeeze [us] into its own mould" (Rom. 12:2 Phillips).

When we think about a curriculum, we do well to remember that in any educational enterprise, there will be multiple levels of curricula present. There is an explicit curriculum; this is the intentional instructional plan of CSF, which might be found in a formal curriculum plan or just something that is agreed to by the leaders. There is also the hidden curriculum that comes from the messages and values that are embedded in the organization of the educational program; as we put it earlier, these are things that are "caught rather than taught." We can sometimes also identify a null curriculum, a term that refers to those things that are not explicitly taught, giving the learner the impression that they are not essential to the enterprise. For example, a friend reflected on her seminary experience and said, "The Holy Spirit and spiritual practices were part of the null curriculum—by not talking about them, I learned that they were not essential to ministry." Finally, we can speak of the social curriculum. What are the messages related to CSF that come through the culture? For example, the dominant culture might push one toward thinking

---

1. For an example of the systematic approach to CSF in earlier ages, see Richard J. Foster, *Streams of Living Water: Celebrating the Great Traditions of Christian Faith* (San Francisco: HarperSanFrancisco, 1998); Evan B. Howard, *The Brazos Introduction to Christian Spirituality* (Grand Rapids: Brazos, 2008), 267–95.

that "spirituality" must be entirely self-constructed and me-centered, or that the goal of religion should be material prosperity, or that prayer is primarily a quasi-magical way of getting things from God.

The emphasis in this section will be on developing an explicit curriculum for CSF. Still, one of the most important things leaders can do as they foster spiritual formation in their churches is to look hard at the hidden curriculum: "that which is already *in* leaders and teachers, *in* structures, and *in* processes."[2] From the deportment of church leaders, learners may get the message that discipleship is viewed as highly optional or that personal holiness is merely a matter of personal preference. The church culture will teach and shape in ways that run counter to our best-laid formational plans. The hidden curriculum often shows itself in youth programs; as youth workers seek to connect with the "cool kids" or seem relevant, they often telegraph messages to the youth about what they see as really important, which may be at odds with the explicit message they claim to teach. On a more positive note, the hidden curriculum can also quietly support the work of formation

> The hidden curriculum deeply affects what is actually learned and sincerely believed. Prayerfully discern the patterns, leaders, and priorities that your formational ministries subtly communicate to the participants. Ralph Waldo Emerson has said, "That which we are, we shall teach, not voluntarily but involuntarily. Thoughts come into our minds by avenues which we never left open, and thoughts go out of our minds through avenues which we never voluntarily opened. Character teaches over our head."[a] This also means that "do no harm" by seeking to have our churches be a safe space is an essential aspect of community formation.
>
> a. Ralph Waldo Emerson, *Essays & Lectures*, Library of America (New York: Literary Classics of the United States, 1983), 395.

through the integrity and joyful discipleship that learners see week in and week out in the lives of church members who honor Christ in their various callings.

Step 1: Establish the Prerequisites for Cultivating a Climate of Formation

Years ago, Lawrence Kohlberg developed a theory of moral development that fit his cultural moment and received considerable attention.[3] School administrators were interested in Kohlberg setting up programs in their schools to

2. Susanne Johnson, *Christian Spiritual Formation in the Church and Classroom* (Nashville: Abingdon, 1989), 132.
3. Lawrence Kohlberg, "The Development of Modes of Thinking and Choices in Years 10 to 16" (PhD diss., University of Chicago, 1958).

teach "morality." Kohlberg oversaw some school-based programs but is said
to have mused that administrators typically wanted him to teach morality in
what he perceived were often unjust and arbitrary environments. He is said
to have quipped that through these moral education programs, he found that
"you can't teach justice in an unjust environment." It will be constructive to
touch briefly on some aspects of church culture that create a good environment for true CSF to take place. I am suggesting ways to reduce the negative
impact of the hidden curriculum on CSF. The limited space devoted to these
aspects should not be taken as a measure of their importance. The 450-page
manual for my car devotes one page to filling the fuel tank, but without fuel,
the car does not work. Without a safe and constructive climate, there is no
possibility of consistent, long-term CSF.

Safety

The church must be a safe environment. To promote this, clear guidelines
designed to exclude sexual, physical, and spiritual abuse and manipulation
must be in place. There should be effective monitoring, training, and accountability. No church can legitimately claim to be so healthy and spiritually
grounded that it does not need to be vigilant in this area. Sexual abuse in the
church is the ultimate spiritual deformation event, and its effects spread far
and wide.

Welcome

The implicit messages that welcome and exclude people are a powerful dimension of the hidden curriculum. The church in the United States has had a
particularly tragic connection with racism and racial exclusion. Jesus modeled
inclusion and welcoming, though never at the cost of speaking truth, and we
do well to strive to follow Jesus on this point and create welcoming churches.

Integrity

The leadership of the church must show itself to be honest and to live by
the principles it espouses. A lack of integrity will affect the spiritual climate
even if the hypocrisy is not revealed; as Jesus said, "Students are not greater
than their teacher. But the student who is fully trained will become like the
teacher" (Luke 6:40 NLT). Money should be spent as promised. People should
be prayed for in private. Conflict should be dealt with appropriately. Leaders
must be held accountable no matter how essential they are to the ministry. We
must be careful not to avoid confronting inappropriate behavior from pastors

and leaders because they are deemed too essential to confront or because we believe the fruit of their ministry far outweighs their deficits.

Adversity

As a rule, adversity will play an outsized role in most of our formation. In the stripping away that comes in adversity, we learn to see what counts and find that when all is said and done, God and his love are more real than anything else. If individuals are to grow through the experience of adversity, there must be a climate of worship, use of the Psalms, teaching, and prayer support to help them walk well through their various trials. Versions of the prosperity gospel implicitly deny the value of adversity and propose strategies for denying or escaping the trials of life. That can undercut CSF.

Word Saturation

A friend tells of showing up to preach at an evangelical church and realizing, to his embarrassment, that he had left his Bible at home. A helpful staff person began a search for a Bible he could use. My friend finally entered the pulpit with the only Bible they could locate—a brightly illustrated children's Bible. Scriptures provide a countercultural road map to how we are to live; they provide us with a new set of images to guide our loves and lives, and they are a means of grace as we meditate on them and take them to heart. Formation is to be shaped by the Word and uses the Word as a means of formation.

Teachability

To help create an environment in which CSF will flourish, the whole church must be oriented toward teachability. This means that people are spiritually curious, eager to grow and learn, and willing to learn from anyone. There is a respect for the teaching offices of the church as well as a recognition that we should be open to learning from anyone with a life message formed in faithfulness to God. The cancer survivor, the faithful single mom, the compassionate nurse, and the skillful kindergarten teacher who have all acquired life lessons and practical wisdom should be listened to with a spirit of teachability.

When CSF is viewed as a value-added dimension of church life and these elements of safety and welcome are not in place, then deep transformative CSF will not take place. Jesus introduced the construct of hypocrisy to ethical discourse. He railed against a religious system that he saw as shiny and bright on the outside but rotten on the inside. CSF cannot take place in performance-driven churches that so often lack these essential prerequisites.

If your church is not safe, welcoming, and permeated by a teachable spirit, then spiritual formation will not occur.

Step 2: Make Christ the Explicit Curriculum

"Putting on Christ" . . . is not one among many jobs a Christian has to do; and it is not a sort of special exercise for the top class. It is the whole of Christianity. Christianity offers nothing else at all.

C. S. Lewis[4]

To summarize, then, it appears that Christian holiness is a number of things together. . . . It is a matter of Spirit-led law-keeping, a walk, or course of life, in the Spirit that displays the fruit of the Spirit (Christlikeness of attitude and disposition). It is a matter of seeking to imitate Jesus's way of behaving, through depending on Jesus for deliverance from carnal self-absorption and for discernment of spiritual needs and possibilities.

J. I. Packer[5]

Jesus never expected us simply to turn the other cheek, go the second mile, bless those who persecute us, give unto them that ask, and so forth. . . . Instead, Jesus did invite people to follow him into that sort of life from which behavior such as loving one's enemies will seem like the only sensible and happy thing to do. For a person living that life, the hard thing to do would be to hate the enemy, to turn the supplicant away, or to curse the curser. . . . True Christlikeness, true companionship with Christ, comes at the point where it is hard not to respond as he would.

Dallas Willard[6]

At the end of Matthew's Gospel, Jesus gives a final charge to his disciples in what we know as the Great Commission. He calls his people to the tasks of outreach, discipleship, and education/formation. He tells his followers that one of the necessary elements in their formation is to "teach these new disciples to obey all the commands I have given you" (28:20 NLT). The heart of spiritual formation is to teach and train people to follow the wisdom and instructions of Christ through the enabling power of his grace made available

4. *Mere Christianity* (New York: Macmillan, 1960), 166.
5. *Rediscovering Holiness: Know the Fullness of Life with God* (Grand Rapids: Baker Books, 2009), 30.
6. *The Spirit of the Disciplines: Understanding How God Changes Lives* (San Francisco: HarperOne, 1988), 7–8.

to us by the Holy Spirit. In fact, "imitation of Christ is both a fundamental means and the glorious end of Christian formation."[7] When we speak of imitation in formation, it is, as Dallas Willard has taught us, more akin to serving an apprenticeship with Jesus than to merely mimicking selected actions of his.[8] Willard famously quipped about the Great Omission from the Great Commission and the resulting sense that discipleship is optional for Christians.

We need to emphasize that the Great Omission from the Great Commission is not obedience to Christ but discipleship, apprenticeship, to him. Through discipleship, obedience will take care of itself, and we will also escape the snares of judgmentalism and legalism, whether directed toward ourselves or toward others.[9]

CSF and the Commands of Christ

Holiness is not a condition into which we drift.

John Stott[10]

We must present the commands of Christ as part of a "package deal," our apprenticeship to Jesus. They are not mere laws or principles to follow; Jesus invites us to take on his easy yoke: "Take my yoke upon you. Let me teach you, because I am humble and gentle at heart, and you will find rest for your souls. For my yoke is easy to bear, and the burden I give you is light" (Matt. 11:29–30 NLT). Many of Jesus's commands are, in essence, Christian spiritual disciplines, such as blessing our enemies, practicing solitude, examining our conscience, fasting, receiving the sacraments with faith, and practicing biblical meditation. These commands are two-sided in that they address both "inner" and "outer" change. There is a straightforward behavioral command that shapes our habits, and there is an indispensable "inner" aspect as well. These commands of Jesus are intended for his followers, who, through their new birth and Spirit-infilling, have had the loves of their hearts changed and are beginning to want to deepen the experience of their union with Christ by following his commands.

7. Robert P. Meye, "The Imitation of Christ: Means and End of Spiritual Formation," in *The Christian Educator's Handbook on Spiritual Formation*, ed. Kenneth O. Gangel and James C. Wilhoit (Grand Rapids: Baker, 1994), 199.

8. Dallas Willard, *The Divine Conspiracy: Rediscovering Our Hidden Life in God* (San Francisco: HarperSanFrancisco, 1998), 282–83.

9. Dallas Willard, *The Great Omission: Reclaiming Jesus's Essential Teachings on Discipleship* (San Francisco: HarperOne, 2006), xiv.

10. *God's New Society: The Message of Ephesians* (Downers Grove, IL: InterVarsity, 1979), 193.

When we begin to practice Jesus's commands, we should immediately see that we are in over our heads. So we call out in prayer and recognize our need for help from others in the church. Years ago, I confessed to a friend the struggle I was having developing the habit of being prayerful throughout the day. He matter-of-factly asked me, "Are you praying about this? Don't you think your ever-present Teacher and Lord, who mastered this while on earth, wouldn't love to guide you?" There are both sides at work, the command to pray always (Luke 18:1, 7; 1 Thess. 5:17) and the enablement of this by Jesus's guidance and the empowerment of the Holy Spirit. I had to admit to my friend that I hadn't thought of turning to Jesus for guidance, and I learned that through the community.

When we understand the two-sided nature of Jesus's commands, we no longer view them as heavy burdens but see them as invitations to a more sensible way of living. Often we pull apart the commands of Jesus from the enabling patterns—the spiritual disciplines—that allow us to do what we could never do through willpower alone. One can find countless lists of Jesus's commands, and most of these are simply things to do that seem quite hard and burdensome. However, the disciplines are concrete ways to get the gospel more deeply into our hearts. As we draw our strength through our union with Christ, we daily remind ourselves, "I am accepted." We return to the Word to hear God's perspective. We repent of all that draws us away from running "with perseverance the race that is set before us, looking to Jesus" (Heb. 12:1–2). Ultimately, the imitation of Christ is accomplished by the Holy Spirit, who produces the virtues of Christ known as the fruit of the Spirit (Gal. 5:22–30). "The Spirit provides new ability by working to 'clone' believers into the image of Jesus in true righteousness and holiness (Gal. 5:22; Eph. 4:7–24; Col. 3:1–7)."[11]

When I was in college, I experienced teaching that turned the commands of Christ into soul-killing laws. A friend of mine who walked away from the faith during this time told me, in effect, that his parents made him feel plenty guilty, and he didn't need a boatload more from Jesus. But Jesus does not just say, "You're sick"; he also offers the only genuinely efficacious treatment, since he is the Great Physician of our souls (Matt. 9:12). We follow a doctor's advice because we are convinced that it will bring about positive results, and we follow Jesus's advice because we are confident that he is the smartest man who ever lived and that his words bring life. Therefore, his way of living is not a burden but the way of joy and satisfaction.

---

11. Jason B. Hood, *Imitating God in Christ: Recapturing a Biblical Pattern* (Downers Grove, IL: IVP Academic, 2013), 130–31.

A command given without the means for fulfilling it is just a burden. But Jesus has given us commands and the means (grace given through a pattern of living and a regenerated heart with new affections) that will change us. The changes enable us to obey his commands more and more and also conform to the deepest longings of our hearts. Christ provides access *into* a relationship with him, transforms us *through* that relationship, and then affects a still greater union *in* that relationship. Many evangelicals speak of the fruit of the Spirit, but almost as a mere wish, an aspiration that fruit may somehow appear. This fruit is the product of the Spirit, which comes as we press into the reality of our union with Christ by ordering our lives to walk in his way.

In Acts, *the Way* appears frequently as a term for the church and Christianity (Acts 9:2; 19:9, 23; 22:4; 24:14, 22). This speaks of the early Christians' understanding that following Jesus meant adopting not just a set of beliefs but a way of life. The phrase *the Way* picks up on imagery common in the Old Testament, in which walking is paired with the image of a road or path to illustrate the choices people should make and the ones they should avoid. The blessed person avoids taking "the path that sinners tread" (Ps. 1:1), and wise persons "do not walk in the way of evildoers" (Prov. 4:14). Paul's primary metaphor for the Christian life is that of walking in the way of Christ. He told the Corinthians that he had sent them Timothy so that by his character and ministry there, "he will remind you of my way of life in Christ Jesus," and this way of life is "what I teach everywhere in every church" (1 Cor. 4:17 NIV).[12] The array of verses below illustrates the emphasis on walking in the way of Christ in Paul's thought.

> We exhorted each one of you and encouraged you and charged you to walk in a manner worthy of God. (1 Thess. 2:12)
>
> You received from us how you ought to walk and to please God, just as you are doing, that you do so more and more. (4:1)
>
> . . . that you may walk properly before outsiders. (4:12)
>
> Keep away from any brother who is walking in idleness. (2 Thess. 3:6)
>
> For we hear that some among you walk in idleness. (3:11)
>
> As God has called each, in this way let him walk. (1 Cor. 7:17 NASB)
>
> . . . not walking in trickery. (2 Cor. 4:2 NASB)
>
> For we walk by faith, not by sight. (5:7)

12. Leland Ryken, James C. Wilhoit, and Tremper Longman III, *Dictionary of Biblical Imagery* (Downers Grove, IL: IVP Academic, 1998), 922–23.

For though we walk in the flesh, we are not waging war according to the flesh. (10:3)

And as for all who walk by this rule, peace and mercy be upon them, and upon the Israel of God. (Gal. 6:16)

We were buried therefore with him by baptism into death, in order that, just as Christ was raised from the dead by the glory of the Father, we too might walk in newness of life. (Rom. 6:4)

. . . who walk not according to the flesh but according to the Spirit. (8:4)

Let us walk properly as in the daytime. (13:13)

You are no longer walking in love. (14:15)

For we are his workmanship, created in Christ Jesus for good works, which God prepared beforehand, that we should walk in them. (Eph. 2:10)

Walk in a manner worthy of the calling to which you have been called. (4:1)

And walk in love. (5:2)

Keep your eyes on those who walk according to the example you have in us. (Phil. 3:17)

Walk in a manner worthy of the Lord. (Col. 1:10)

Therefore, as you received Christ Jesus the Lord, so walk in him. (2:6)

Walk in wisdom toward outsiders. (4:5)[13]

We need to realize that Jesus is setting forth a way of life for living in God's kingdom. If we want to live under the reign of popular culture, these commands most assuredly will seem odd and irksome. Homer Simpson summed up this outlook when speaking of his religion: "You know, the one with all the well-meaning rules that don't work in real life."[14] But it is the path of life and health that leads to flourishing.

Understanding Jesus's Growth through the Disciplines

Concrete, specific acts filled Jesus's devotional life. The devotional acts of Jesus were rich and diverse, consisting of private acts (solitude, prayer retreats), small group practices (pilgrimage, fellowship, teaching, sacraments, worship), and large group meetings (teaching, synagogue worship, healing).

13. All the quotations, unless noted, are from the ESV. Many contemporary translations tend toward abstraction in their treatment of the verses above; for example, the NIV uses *walk* in only two of them. This list was suggested in E. J. Tinsley, *The Imitation of God in Christ: An Essay on the Biblical Basis of Christian Spirituality* (Philadelphia: Westminster, 1960), 134–35.

14. Quoted in Mark I. Pinsky, *The Gospel according to the Simpsons: The Spiritual Life of the World's Most Animated Family* (Louisville: Westminster John Knox, 2001), 22.

He did not merely keep an abstract communion with God. Instead, he carried out his communion through tangible acts of piety and intimacy, which included constantly listening to and speaking to the Father. Jesus broke with Jewish tradition and prayed to God as Father on all but one occasion: the agonized cry of abandonment on the cross (Mark 15:34). He demonstrated that we must see religion not as magic or ritual but as a relationship. Just as human relationships are marked by well-developed patterns of interaction, so also our relating to God should be characterized by rich, diverse, consistent patterns.

In the four Gospels, Jesus is pictured as living a life marked by devotional practices; well over one hundred devotional acts of Jesus are recorded.[15] Some were done in private, others with his disciples, and still others in public settings. While these acts are in the background in many stories, the Gospels indeed show Jesus as a person deeply concerned with developing his spiritual life through intentional, often tangible, acts of devotion.

We can infer from his use of Scripture that Jesus was a man of meditation and study. He had a deep functional knowledge of Scripture that came from memorizing and meditating on it. The following passages from Luke provide direct evidence of Jesus's prayer life and his practices of solitude and fasting:

> He was praying in a certain place, and after he had finished, one of his disciples said to him, "Lord, teach us to pray, as John taught his disciples." (11:1)
>
> He would withdraw to deserted places and pray. (5:16)
>
> In the wilderness . . . for forty days he was tempted by the devil. He ate nothing at all during those days, and when they were over, he was famished. . . . Then Jesus, filled with the power of the Spirit, returned to Galilee, and a report about him spread through all the surrounding country. (4:1–2, 14)

Jesus adopted a lifestyle of personal and corporate communion with his Father.

Many Christians believe that Jesus's patterns of devotion flowed out of his divine nature—in other words, the divine part of him naturally sought out

---

15. I have computed the number of Jesus's devotional acts in the Gospels as 129; though this was carefully ascertained, one must be cautious about using this number too freely. This is a simple counting of "devotional acts" (a partial list includes prayer, fasting, solitude, service done in secret, anointing, meditation, Scripture memorization); some acts occurring in more than one Gospel may be counted twice. Also, in arriving at this number, the primary discipline highlighted in the text was counted, and thus secondary disciplines may be underrepresented.

God and the human part just came along for the ride. So here are some crucial questions: Did Jesus's lifestyle of devotion result in his holiness and spiritual power? Or were those merely the fruit of his unique divine-human nature?

If we take Jesus's humanity seriously, we are compelled to say that his acts of devotion contributed to the presence of the spiritual power, love, and insight that marked his ministry. It is vital that we affirm that Jesus's spiritual practices were not mere window dressing but had an effect on him and his world. Hebrews makes this point with exceptional clarity: "In the days of his flesh, Jesus offered up prayers and supplications, with loud cries and tears, to the one who was able to save him from death, and he was heard because of his reverent submission. Although he was a Son, he learned obedience through what he suffered" (5:7–8). Jesus's prayers were heard because of his submission, and he was able to submit because he had developed that discipline through acts of humility and devotion. "Ontologically, Jesus' relationship with God the Father is, of course, absolutely unique, but experientially we are invited into the same intimacy with Father God that he knew while here in the flesh. We are encouraged to crawl into the Father's lap and receive his love and comfort and healing and strength."[16]

We can learn about Jesus's spiritual development through personal disciplines and corporate formation from the story of Samuel. This story provides a striking picture of God's sovereign care and the process of spiritual formation. The story begins with a childless wife who pours out her heart to God and is given a child; she takes this special child to the tabernacle as a toddler and gives him for the Lord's service. The tabernacle turns out to be as nurturing as a street-gang hideout, but the Lord literally calls Samuel to himself. Amid hypocrisy and crass religious charlatanism, the boy grows into a righteous man. Scripture succinctly summarizes his development during this time: "Now the boy Samuel continued to grow both in stature and in favor with the LORD and with the people" (1 Sam. 2:26).

Samuel serves as a foil for the priest's two sons, Hophni and Phinehas, who are the very embodiment of narcissism. They steal from religious pilgrims, seduce women who come to the tabernacle, fail to carry out the religious duties for which they are paid, and treat the Lord with public contempt. Samuel, on the other hand, is open to the Lord and lives in this degrading place "in the presence of the LORD" (1 Sam. 2:21). The account gives every impression that the Lord has graciously reached out to Samuel and that Samuel has actively sought the Lord's favor. We leave the story marveling at what the Lord

16. Richard J. Foster, *Prayer: Finding the Heart's True Home* (San Francisco: HarperSanFrancisco, 1992), 135.

has done in calling, nurturing, and protecting the boy, and at the quality of Samuel's response.

The words written of Samuel, that he "continued to grow in stature and favor with the LORD and with people" (1 Sam. 2:26 NIV), are echoed in Luke's report that Jesus "grew in wisdom and stature, and in favor with God and men" (Luke 2:52 NIV). In this passage, Luke has just described Jesus's appearance in the temple at age twelve, when he amazed the teachers with his insight and then returned home with his parents and lived in obedience to them. At this point, Luke has pulled back the veil covering these hidden early years to tell us of the remarkable youth of Jesus and demonstrate that his growth as the Messiah took time and discipline. Eugene Peterson captures this developmental note quite well when he renders the verse this way: "And Jesus matured, growing up in both body and spirit, blessed by both God and people" (2:52 Message).

When we take seriously the two natures (divine and human) found in the incarnation, this verse makes perfect sense. Jesus lives a life of thoroughgoing love and service that is entirely in tune with the wishes of the Father, not merely because the divine has taken over the human but because, through discipline, the human has grown in wisdom and grace. We must not make this verse carry too much weight, yet it does echo the language of 1 Samuel 2:26, Proverbs 3:4, and Luke 1:80, which assume human development. Jesus serves as a model because, while vastly different from us, his moral and spiritual life developed through processes that are available to all. A robust view of the incarnation should have no difficulty with affirming the absolute uniqueness of Jesus and that his spiritual and moral growth came through the ordinary means of grace.

To test our commitment to the reality of his spiritual formation, it is worth considering two questions: Was Jesus ready even as a twelve-year-old to obey the Father and go to the cross, brought there by love for the world? And was he prepared for this at the beginning of his public ministry at age thirty?[17]

In asking these questions, I am not questioning his divinity or mission; I am asking about how he was spiritually formed to carry out his work. I would say that Jesus went to the cross when he was ready to go to the cross. He followed the Father's plan for his formation, and so he came to the point where the Father knew that he was strengthened sufficiently through trials, ongoing attention to the Spirit, and his life of devotion that he was able to engage in

17. These questions were suggested by similar questions posed in Bruce A. Ware, *The Man Christ Jesus: Theological Reflections on the Humanity of Christ* (Wheaton: Crossway, 2012), 66–67.

the spiritual battle found in the cross. Jesus was able to bear our sins out of love because by then he had learned deeply and truly that "the Son of Man came to seek and to save the lost" (Luke 19:10 NIV).

The crucial points are that Jesus grew through means that are available to us and that he has given those means to us as the ordinary way of growing up into the fullness of his love and grace. In saying this we do not denigrate his unique divine nature, nor do we presume that we can live with the same power and love as Christ. But we can truly become Christians—that is, little Christs. Orthodox writers have articulated well the radical nature of human transformation through our union with Christ. "The incarnation equally is a doctrine of sharing or participation. Christ shares to the full in what we are, and so he makes it possible for us to share in what he is, in his divine life and glory. He became what we are, so to make us what he is."[18]

What Does "Imitation" Mean for CSF?

Personal sanctification is an intensely corporate and churchly act; being built up in Christ is being built up in the Church.

E. L. Mascall[19]

When we suggest that the way to spiritual transformation lies in following Jesus, some no doubt will say this is impossible to do. They may state that we know too little about his private life to be able to copy it. Others will point out that in history we can find persons who claimed, with what seems to be complete sincerity, that they were following Jesus when all the while their lives fell short of Jesus's ethical teachings. Still others will point out that all attempts to follow Jesus are necessarily conditioned by our time and place and thus are so provincial that it would be unwise to speak of actually following him. In other words, a future generation may judge any attempt to follow Jesus as quite naive and blind to the actual realities of our social situation. And many insist that any emphasis on imitating Christ is probably a sincere, but misguided, attempt at some form of earning merit.

Despite this skepticism, we must attend to the New Testament call to pattern our lives after Jesus and recognize that our perception of his example and our faithfulness in following it will be limited. The difficulty of following him for the right reasons and in the right way is not an argument against the

18. Kallistos Ware, *The Orthodox Way*, rev. ed. (Crestwood, NY: St. Vladimir's Seminary Press, 1995), 74.
19. *Christ, the Christian and the Church: A Study of the Incarnation and Its Consequences* (London: Longmans, Green, 1963), 205.

wisdom of this path. Of course, we will do it badly because of sin within us and the blindness brought about by the age in which we live. The fact that we will inevitably follow Jesus in a way that history may judge as provincial does not remove from us the obligation to pattern our lives after his. With due humility, we can pattern our lives closely enough to draw on the strength of our union with Jesus and receive transforming grace, grow in holiness, and be a witness to the transforming power of God's grace.

The imitation of Christ addresses some of the most fundamental struggles we face as humans. What does it mean to follow Jesus? It is the thrust of this book, as E. L. Mascall suggested two generations ago, that "personal sanctification is an intensely corporate and churchly act; being built up in Christ is being built up in the Church."[20] Mascall astutely identifies the greatest misconception about imitating Christ in recent years, and that is a focus on the fruit and not the roots. We need to give our attention to imitating Jesus's pattern of formation and allow our formation to express itself in fruit that reflects Jesus's values.

Two of the great dangers in setting out to imitate Jesus are these: (1) We might fail to see it as a privilege and a joy. Remember the joy you felt in imitating a loved parent or a mentor? Such should be our feeling in setting out to "do as Jesus did." (2) We might fail to realize that through imitation, rightly done, we are refashioned in profound ways by the Holy Spirit.

Imitating Jesus's practices of spiritual growth will include the classical spiritual disciplines but must take us far beyond them as well. It is most healthy for us to speak of discipleship as the way of imitating Christ. Discipleship places our imitation in a rich theological context.

Some writers resist the use of "imitation of Christ" language because they think that it has often led to a human-centered view of sanctification. Faithful imitation respects the tension between the reality that the Holy Spirit ultimately brings about our imitation through conforming us to Christ's likeness and the fact that we must work hard and carefully at imitating Christ by adopting his lifestyle and patterns of life.[21]

---

20. Mascall, *Christ, the Christian and the Church*, 205.

21. E. J. Tinsley proposes a solution. He wants to hold together the sense of active imitation with the idea that God is actively conforming us to Christ's image. He sees maintaining this tension as vital to a robust understanding of imitation. "In a fully developed theology of the Christian life as imitation of Christ both the terms *conformitas* and *imitatio* would need to be used. The imitative life of the Christian involves both God's activity, through the Spirit, in conforming man to his image in Christ (*conformitas*), and man's forming of his moral and spiritual attention on the exemplar, Christ (*imitatio*)." E. J. Tinsley, "Some Principles for Reconstructing a Doctrine of the Imitation of Christ," *Scottish Journal of Theology* 25, no. 1 (1972): 47.

Goals within a Curriculum for Christlikeness

To correctly form a curriculum for Christlikeness, we must have a very clear and simple perception of the primary goals it must achieve, as well as what is to be avoided.

Two objectives in particular that are often taken as *primary* goals must not be left in that position. They can be reintroduced later in proper subordination to the true ones. These are *external conformity* to the wording of Jesus' teachings about actions in specific contexts and *profession of perfectly correct doctrine*. Historically these are the very things that have obsessed the church visible—currently the latter far more than the former.

We need wait no longer. The results are in. They do not provide a course of personal growth and development that routinely produces people who "hear and do." They either crush the human mind and soul and separate people from Jesus, or they produce hide-bound legalists and theological experts with "lips close to God and hearts far away from him" (Isa. 29:13). The world hardly needs more of these.

Much the same can be said of the strategies—rarely taken as primary objectives, to be sure, but much used—of encouraging faithfulness to the activities of the church or other outwardly religious routines and various "spiritualities," or the seeking out of special states of mind or ecstatic experiences. These are good things. But let it be said once and for all that, like outward conformity and doctrinally perfect profession, they are not to be taken as major objectives in an adequate curriculum for Christlikeness.[a]

a. Willard, *Divine Conspiracy*, 320.

When we reflect on the things Jesus has laid out for us to do, some of us may regard them as commands. I prefer to speak of Jesus *inviting* us to do certain things. I choose this word not simply to soften the language but rather to highlight that Jesus is inviting us to a certain way of living. He is not content to simply order us to do such and such; he wants *us* far more than he wants our actions. He wants all of us.

The compilation of Jesus's invitations you will find below may seem long, since they touch on all areas of life. Jesus intends that the disciplines work together and impact all of life. Practicing Christian disciplines puts me in a place of wanting them and engaging in them. When I have accepted the invitation to the place of prayer, worship, study, acts of compassion, integrity, and keeping commitments, I am more open to the work of the Holy Spirit, more able to draw strength from my union with Christ, and more open to change. Therefore, the practices contained in these invitations put me in a place that can impact and change the loves and core attitudes of my heart. They are a spiritual thoroughfare to God's grace and power and, thereby, a way to expand my love, obedience, and repentance, clarifying my beliefs and deepening my trust in God.

We do well to see the invitations of Jesus in the context of the two great commands he gave: to love God and to love neighbor. The focus on loving God and neighbor is the spiritual North Star we follow in seeking to understand Jesus's teaching. The invitations of Jesus that follow the two great commands come as applications of the call to the twofold love of God and neighbor. At the heart of the "Love God" invitation, we must not merely hear "try harder and harder." Marguerite Shuster has cautioned that "exactly insofar as we get captured by the mystique of imitating Christ and neglect the unglamorous tasks of trusting him and obeying him in the most ordinary moments of our everyday lives, we have forgotten who he is and who we are."[22] We need to hear "Love the loveable Father," "Love the Lover of our soul," and "Receive his embrace." Out of that safe place, as secure spiritual children, we seek to live out these invitations—not to earn love and affection but to grow in the likeness of the one we admire and want to be like.

> CSF seeks to foster a joyful apprenticeship in which we learn to live out the great invitations of Jesus, especially those concerning the life of prayer and love as we realize that being built up in Christ is being built up in the church.

The Great Invitations of Christ

The Christian stands, not under the dictatorship of a legalistic "You ought," but in the magnetic field of Christian freedom, under the empowering of the "You may."

Helmut Thielicke[23]

The invitations of Christ contain words that convict us and expose our self-centered and self-protective strategies of self-improvement (e.g., "forgive your enemies") and words that point us to the grace that enables us to do what we could never have done on our own (e.g., the call to pray for our enemies,

---

22. Marguerite Shuster, "The Use and Misuse of the Idea of the Imitation of Christ," *Ex Auditu* 14 (1998): 79.

23. Quoted in Dallas Willard, *The Spirit of the Disciplines: Understanding How God Changes Lives* (San Francisco: HarperOne, 1988), 265.

which in turn enables us to forgive and love them). A number of years ago while reading Scripture, I was struck by my need to forgive someone. It was a spiritual turning point for me; for the first time in my life, I saw the command of Christ—"Forgive!"—and my inability and unwillingness to carry it out. My perception of the magnitude of the wrong done (now, in retrospect, I am amazed at how small the injury was) and the person's lack of remorse made it seem impossible for me to extend forgiveness. In that place of brokenness, where I could see and feel my inability to do what I should do, I did what I could do: I committed myself to pray for the person and the situation. That dedicated prayer led, over a period of time, to my ability to release the person from my anger and thirst for revenge—to experience the freedom of forgiveness.

First, *Jesus invites us to love and obey God*: "He said to him, 'You shall love the Lord your God with all your heart, and with all your soul, and with all your mind.' This is the greatest and first commandment" (Matt. 22:37–38). Second, *Jesus invites us to love one another*: "'You shall love your neighbor as yourself.' On these two commandments hang all the law and the prophets" (22:39–40). He also says this earlier, in Matthew 7:12: "In everything do to others as you would have them do to you; for this is the law and the prophets." In the Gospel of John, Jesus says, "I give you a new commandment, that you love one another. Just as I have loved you, you also should love one another. By this everyone will know that you are my disciples, if you have love for one another" (13:34–35).

The great tradition of CSF sees these two commands as central to the mission of Christian formation. These can become vague platitudes, and that is why we need to be constantly aware of the specific invitations to living in the kingdom that Jesus gives. Jesus's instruction in Matthew 28:20 is not merely that we are to teach people *about* everything Jesus commanded but that we are to "instruct them in the practice of all I have commanded you" (Message). The Message version "in the practice of" nicely captures the nuance here of the word often rendered "to obey."

The takeaway from this admonition should not be to slavishly seek out a comprehensive list of what Jesus commanded and then teach those as practices but to realize that our instruction must be so constituted that people are learning how to practice what Jesus asks us to do. This means that learners must be in workshops and spiritual apprenticeship experiences as well as being instructed. How does one find what Jesus "commanded"? By reading and searching the Scriptures. Jesus's call to obedience is not limited just to his literal commands but includes the moral and ethical teaching of all the Scriptures, such as the Ten Commandments. Our curriculum for Christlikeness must include specific training on how to set aside worry, how to avoid looking with lust on another, how to set one's mind on the things above, and so on.

I have made the tongue-in-cheek assertation that the current evangelical fascination with expository preaching has distracted us from the task of CSF. I make this claim because a fixation on preaching can lead to viewing Christians as passive recipients—people who just need to absorb "truth"—and so the most pertinent factor in a person's spiritual development is the quality of preaching they are exposed to. This point of view denigrates the need to train learners in a hands-on way to do what Jesus commanded.

In his final charge to his followers, Jesus told them, "Go out and train everyone you meet, far and near, in this way of life, marking them by baptism in the threefold name: Father, Son, and Holy Spirit. Then instruct them in the practice of all I have commanded you. I'll be with you as you do this, day after day after day, right up to the end of the age" (Matt. 28:19–20 Message). To instruct them well, we need to have a clear grasp of Jesus's invitations. The table below is a starting point for thinking about this, but I want to emphasize that we should not be on a quest to identify all Jesus's commands. This list is intended as a help for discerning what the people in a particular community need to learn to do at a particular moment to follow Jesus more closely.

Jesus's Invitations to a Life of Flourishing

Abide in Jesus.	"Abide in me as I abide in you. Just as the branch cannot bear fruit by itself unless it abides in the vine, neither can you unless you abide in me." (John 15:4)
Abide in the Scriptures.	"Then Jesus said to the Jews who had believed in him, 'If you continue in my word, you are truly my disciples; and you will know the truth, and the truth will make you free.'" (John 8:31–32)
Act out of love, not worry.	"For God has not given us a spirit of fear and timidity, but of power, love, and self-discipline." (2 Tim. 1:7 NLT)
Avoid hypocrisy.	"But the wisdom from above is first pure, then peaceable, gentle, willing to yield, full of mercy and good fruits, without a trace of partiality or hypocrisy." (James 3:17)
Baptize new disciples.	"Go therefore and make disciples of all nations, baptizing them in the name of the Father and of the Son and of the Holy Spirit." (Matt. 28:19)
Be born again.	"Jesus answered him, 'Very truly, I tell you, no one can see the kingdom of God without being born from above.'" (John 3:3)
Be grateful.	"Rejoice always, pray without ceasing, give thanks in all circumstances; for this is the will of God in Christ Jesus for you." (1 Thess. 5:16–18)

Believe in Jesus.	"Do not let your hearts be troubled. Believe in God, believe also in me." (John 14:1)
Beware of false prophets.	"Thus says the LORD of hosts: 'Do not listen to the words of the prophets who prophesy to you; they are deluding you. They speak visions of their own minds, not from the mouth of the LORD.'" (Jer. 23:16)
Do not commit adultery.	"You shall not commit adultery." (Exod. 20:14)
Get away to pray.	"But Jesus often withdrew to the wilderness for prayer." (Luke 5:16 NLT) "Then Jesus said, 'Let's go off by ourselves to a quiet place and rest awhile.'" (Mark 6:31 NLT)
Give generously.	"The point is this: the one who sows sparingly will also reap sparingly, and the one who sows bountifully will also reap bountifully. Each of you must give as you have made up your mind, not reluctantly or under compulsion, for God loves a cheerful giver." (2 Cor. 9:6–7)
Keep the Ten Commandments: worship no other gods, have no idols, don't misuse God's name, observe the Sabbath, honor your parents, don't kill, don't commit adultery, don't steal, don't lie, don't covet.	Exod. 20:2–17; Deut. 5:6–21
Learn deeply that we are one in Jesus.	"For in Christ Jesus you are all children of God through faith. As many of you as were baptized into Christ have clothed yourselves with Christ. There is no longer Jew or Greek, there is no longer slave or free, there is no longer male and female; for all of you are one in Christ Jesus." (Gal. 3:26–28)
Listen to God's voice.	"Listen for GOD's voice in everything you do, everywhere you go; he's the one who will keep you on track. Don't assume that you know it all. Run to GOD! Run from evil!" (Prov. 3:6–7 Message)
Love your enemies, pray for them, and bless them.	"But I say to you, Love your enemies and pray for those who persecute you." (Matt. 5:44)
Shape your praying by the pattern of the Lord's Prayer.	"He was praying in a certain place, and after he had finished, one of his disciples said to him, 'Lord, teach us to pray, as John taught his disciples.' He said to them, 'When you pray, say: Father, hallowed be your name . . .'" (Luke 11:1–2)
Shine like stars.	". . . so that you may be blameless and innocent, children of God without blemish in the midst of a crooked and perverse generation, in which you shine like stars in the world." (Phil. 2:15)
Show hospitality and welcome the stranger.	"When God's people are in need, be ready to help them. Always be eager to practice hospitality." (Rom. 12:13 NLT) "When a foreigner resides among you in your land, do not mistreat them. The foreigner residing among you must be treated as your native-born. Love them as yourself, for you were foreigners in Egypt. I am the LORD your God." (Lev. 19:33–34 NIV)

Speak the truth.	"So then, putting away falsehood, let all of us speak the truth to our neighbors, for we are members of one another." (Eph. 4:25)
Take, eat, and drink at his table.	"So Jesus said to them, 'Very truly, I tell you, unless you eat the flesh of the Son of Man and drink his blood, you have no life in you. Those who eat my flesh and drink my blood have eternal life, and I will raise them up on the last day.'" (John 6:53–54)
Teach others.	"The purpose of my instruction is that all believers would be filled with love that comes from a pure heart, a clear conscience, and genuine faith." (1 Tim. 1:5 NLT)

Spiritual practices are essential to CSF, but we must never reduce CSF to teaching spiritual practices. Jesus did not mature only by what he practiced; he also was shaped by what he believed, by the friends he associated with, and by his ongoing conversation with the Father in partnership with the Spirit. We begin with an emphasis on teaching practices because they are essential, and they are absent from the curriculum of formation in most evangelical churches. Spiritual disciplines may be talked about and advocated, but being trained in them is often the null curriculum for evangelical CSF. We implicitly say, "These are nice but not essential, and they will automatically come to you when you have been taught or preached to sufficiently about them."

Step 3: Develop a Rich and Comprehensive Explicit Curriculum for Christlikeness

The fruit of a life in Christ is a life like Christ.

Andrew Murray[24]

Where to begin in developing a curriculum for Christlikeness? We must work diligently to establish a clear road map (explicit curriculum) for our CSF endeavors, and we must seek to lessen the adverse effects of our hidden curriculum. I talk with many people who have left the faith, and most of them tell me it was over issues that are part of the hidden curriculum (hypocrisy, abuse of power, lack of financial integrity) rather than explicit teachings of the church. And we need to discern and repent of our null curriculum, those essential things we have omitted (e.g., living out our union with Christ, spiritual disciplines, the role of race in our society and church).

24. *Like Christ: Thoughts on the Blessed Life of Conformity to the Son of God* (London: James Nisbet, 1896), 11.

Woven through the rest of the book, you will find a curriculum for teaching believers to follow Jesus's call to become his disciples. The curriculum is a lifelong course of study designed to promote spiritual transformation. Its crucial elements include the teaching of core Christian knowledge, service-learning opportunities, training in key spiritual practices, and the continual re-presentation of essential spiritual truths (such as forgiveness, handling conflict, stewardship of time and money, authority in spiritual conflict). Coupled with these there should be opportunities for individuals to be coached through specific applications of the gospel to personal issues. The curriculum, then, is not so much a linear sequence (though it must have some linearity to it) as a spiral, in which topics are re-presented and re-appropriated.

A curriculum must provide concrete guidance for our educational and formational work. In the following table, I have identified four spiritual commitments, designated as the four pillars of formation; these serve as the framework for cultivating the practice of Jesus's great invitations. They are *receiving*, *remembering*, *responding*, and *relating*. These four basic commitments summarize the dimensions I find at work in churches and communities of faith where true spiritual formation has taken place. The *receiving* dimension highlights our need to focus on Jesus and be open to his grace for spiritual formation. Christian spirituality's concern that we learn from Christ and receive God's enabling grace separates it from the cultural assumption that any spirituality will do as long as we follow it sincerely. *Remembering* describes the process of learning to remember, deep in our hearts, who we are—and, more important, whose we are. The next dimension, *responding*,

Four Dimensions of Community Formation

Dimension	Description	Community Practices
Receiving	The cultivation of spiritual openness and continual repentance	Confession, worship, sacraments, prayer
Remembering	Transformational teaching leading to a deep awareness of our being part of God's community and his beloved children	Teaching, preaching, evangelism, meditation, spiritual guidance, small groups
Responding	Formation occurring for and through service	Discernment, honoring relational commitment, setting aside prejudices, ministries of compassion
Relating	Formation taking place in and through community	Hospitality, handling conflict well, honoring relationships, Sabbath observance, attending to the pace of life

reminds us that the enterprise of formational changes of character and action does not exist for our private ends but to enable us to serve others and the world through love. Finally, *relating* affirms that spiritual formation takes place best in and through community.

The deep longing for Christlikeness is a longing for God himself and is the primary motivator for profound spiritual transformation. Seeking Christlikeness is a lifelong endeavor that requires both personal and corporate commitments.

Step 4: Reclaim the Biblical Images for CSF

In a rich and complex undertaking, we employ metaphors and images to capture the complexities and nuances of CSF. Authors writing about formation have used images like "children are wet cement" and the "discovery of our true self." Our metaphors for CSF (e.g., spiritual journey, soul care, growing in grace, shaped by the Word, abiding in the vine) shape our practices and programs. Few factors will have a more significant impact on the nature of a church's formation program than the images it uses to talk about it. An older friend of mine recalls driving into town from the family farm one winter day with his father on the snow- and ice-covered road and spotting a hand-lettered sign reading, "Choose your rut carefully, you'll be in it for 12 miles." Choose your images for CSF with care. They will shape the church's formation. A church that sees the primary task of formation as "eat this book" will have a very different set of practices than one that uses the image of an "inward journey" as its controlling metaphor.

In this section, I will suggest three images for those who carry out formation and then three families of images that can supply vibrant and biblically based images to guide our formation programs. Popular spirituality literature offers metaphors like "the inner quest," "soul tending," or "finding your true self," and while these have evocative power, they are not tethered firmly to the rich biblical imagery of formation. Let me underscore my conviction: if you are not intentional about the images you employ to cast the vision for your CSF approach, these images will be set for you by our culture, popular authors, and formation gurus of various stripes.

Images for Formation Leaders

Shepherd-Teachers

Sheep are the most frequently mentioned animals in the Bible, and the figure of the shepherd is quite prominent as well. The prominence of this image comes from the reality of the Bible's agrarian setting and "the qualities of sheep and shepherds that made them particularly apt sources of metaphor for spiritual realities."[25] Raising sheep in the biblical world was very different from what I experienced as a boy on our farm in Oregon with its fenced fields and reliably green pastures. In the ancient Near East, a flock's well-being depended on the shepherd's care and protection. The person seeking to guide and cultivate CSF has a similar task: they must provide pastoral care and also guard people against misguided strategies and beliefs. This care and guarding will most often be carried out through the activity of teaching because in church programs, people will most likely encounter intentional CSF through educationally based spiritual formation.

Servants

In helping people grow in their discipleship of Jesus, it is tempting to give them what we think they need. The notion of ministry as "meeting needs" became a mantra in late-twentieth-century Christian education. However, we are to serve those we have been entrusted with and not just give them what they say they need or thrust our favorite book, curriculum, or topic at them. C. S. Lewis showed his exasperation with this self-focused pastoral leadership when he wrote, "I wish they'd remember that the charge to Peter was Feed my sheep; not Try experiments on my rats."[26] The servant metaphor stresses the humility of the leaders and reminds us that we are servants of God, who is the actual agent of change. Paul makes this plain in writing to the Corinthians, "Who do you think Paul is, anyway? Or Apollos, for that matter? Servants, both of us—servants who waited on you as you gradually learned to entrust your lives to our mutual Master. We each carried out our servant assignment. I planted the seed, Apollos watered the plants, but God made you grow" (1 Cor. 3:5–6 Message). In CSF, we seek to nurture faith in God and the development of virtues and always ask how to truly serve our learners, not just please them. Merely giving them our hot take of the moment will not meet "their needs."

Doctors (Soul Physicians)

Human brokenness needs to be healed, and the soul needs to be put in order for spiritual restoration to occur. When Jeremiah grieves over Jerusalem and the fate of his people, he describes their plight with medical imagery: "Is there no balm in Gilead? Is there no physician there? Why then is there

25. Ryken, Wilhoit, and Longman, *Dictionary of Biblical Imagery*, 782.
26. C. S. Lewis, *Letters to Malcolm: Chiefly on Prayer* (New York: Harcourt, Brace & World, 1963), 5.

no healing for the wound of my people?" (Jer. 8:22 NIV). There is no healing because there is no repentance. In the Pastoral Epistles, Paul uses the image of health and healing to describe the effects of teaching. False teaching can be like gangrene, which "will spread" and destroy the body (2 Tim. 2:17).

In contrast, Paul desires that Christians be "sound in the faith" (Titus 1:13; 2:2), and the word he uses conveys the sense "that they may be healthy in the faith."[27] And this is promoted by being taught and holding on to healthy doctrine (1 Tim. 1:10; 6:3; 2 Tim. 1:13). In 1 Timothy, Paul warns against people whose teaching is spiritually unhealthy: "Some people may contradict our teaching, but these are the healthy words of the Lord Jesus Christ. These teachings promote a godly life" (6:3 author's trans.). In the early church, there was a strong emphasis on God as the Divine Physician in part because there was not the sharp disjunction between "body" and "soul" that is found in contemporary Western thought but also because they wanted to emphasize that the deep personal and societal restoration that comes through the gospel is no less dramatic than recovery from a disease or plague. Luke Dysinger describes how firmly established this image became: "By the end of the fourth century there existed a well-established tradition of illustrating Christian spiritual practices through analogies based on the theory and vocabulary of classical medicine."[28]

Images for the Process of Spiritual Formation

The influential twentieth-century philosopher-educator John Dewey complained that educators were constantly guilty of either-or thinking.[29] Instead of recognizing the need for both experience and educational content in schools, these writers tended to emphasize one at the expense of the other. We could count the same as true for writers about the Christian life. In the next three sections, we will look at three sets of images for the spiritual life: nurture (agriculture, gardening, human growth, intimacy), training (race, battle, struggle), and death and resurrection (dying with Christ, being born again). To capture the complexities and nuances of CSF, the biblical writers employed these images, and we would do well to honor their emphasis.

Images of Nurture

Jesus and John the Baptist challenge their hearers to produce good "fruit" (Matt. 21:43) and "fruit" originating in true repentance (3:8). Jesus speaks

27. William D. Mounce, *Pastoral Epistles* (Grand Rapids: Zondervan, 2000), 400.
28. Luke Dysinger, OSB, *Psalmody and Prayer in the Writings of Evagrius Ponticus*, Oxford Theological Monographs (Oxford: Oxford University Press, 2005), 104.
29. John Dewey, *Experience and Education* (New York: Simon & Schuster, 1997), 17.

metaphorically about fruit to make a point about how one can judge a person's character: "A good tree produces good fruit, and a bad tree produces bad fruit. A good tree can't produce bad fruit, and a bad tree can't produce good fruit. . . . Yes, just as you can identify a tree by its fruit, so you can identify people by their actions" (7:17–18, 20 NLT). In his parable of the sower and the seed, Jesus illustrates how the condition of our hearts affects our response to the gospel. When he explains the meaning of the parable to his followers, he tells them, "The seeds that fell on the good soil represent honest, good-hearted people who hear God's message, cling to it, and patiently produce a huge harvest" (Luke 8:15 NLT). The image of Jesus as the true vine (John 15) vividly communicates that we need to stay spiritually connected to Christ. (Incidentally, we often misread this image as being just about "me abiding in Jesus," when the actual image and language have a strong community focus: when the branches are connected to the vine, a marvelous crop of grapes is produced.) The concreteness of agriculture makes the more abstract subject of CSF easier to understand.

The biblical writers also used agricultural imagery to capture part of the interplay between human and divine in formation. For example, when Paul describes the work he and Apollos do and then writes of "God, who makes things grow" (1 Cor. 3:7 Message), it is clear that God is the actual cause of all the spiritual growth. Yet in saying this, Paul does not diminish the importance of human participation. Agriculture requires sustained, systematic work performed at the right time and carried out with experience-based expertise, but all human efforts are subject to weather, pests, disease, and war. Agriculture illuminates the beautiful symmetry between God and his people that is at play in the process of CSF. Therefore, we go about our formation work doing what we can and being prayerfully receptive, especially about those areas outside our direct influence.

"You happen to be God's field in which we are working" (1 Cor. 3:9 Message). The field is the primary location of the work of farming. To flourish, a field must be cultivated, planted, tended, watered, protected, and harvested, and the farmer will be more focused on the total crop than on one individual plant. The illustration is a communal or population-based image. In many of the New Testament agricultural images, the focus is on the big picture, on how abundant the harvest is, and not just on the output of a single plant. Nevertheless, in CFS there must be a both-and emphasis on the individual and the group.

Images of Training and Struggle

Paul uses imagery drawn from the Hellenic games to illustrate the need for training and discipline in the Christian life: "Do you not know that in a race the runners all compete, but only one receives the prize? Run in such a way that you may win it. Athletes exercise self-control in all things; they do it to receive a perishable wreath, but we an imperishable one. So I do not run aimlessly, nor do I box as though beating the air; but I punish my body and enslave it, so that after proclaiming to others I myself should not be disqualified" (1 Cor. 9:24–27).

The emphasis of this race image is a call for Corinthian believers to adopt the singular focus of a trained athlete who follows Christ. In Philippians 3:13–14, Paul compares an athlete's efforts to straining to pursue Christ well. "The image of 'straining forward, . . . press on toward the goal' evokes the picture of the racer who looks neither to the left nor to the right to check the progress of the competition or be swayed by any diversion."[30] In the Pastoral Epistles, the imagery is developed further: the importance of rigorous training (1 Tim. 4:7–8), endurance (4:8), following the rules so that one is not disqualified (2 Tim. 2:5), and winning an imperishable crown (1 Cor. 9:25). The emphasis in this set of images is on the need for training, discipline, and rigor.

Satan was soundly defeated at the cross as Jesus "disarmed the powers and authorities, . . . triumphing over them by the cross" (Col. 2:15 NIV), and yet biblical writers recognize that Satan is still active and a significant cause of distress for Christians. He is busy in his constant work of accusation (Rev. 12:10) and "prowls around like a roaring lion, looking for someone to devour" (1 Pet. 5:8 NLT). We now live between the time of the cross and the final victory. The church is called to wage battle "against the rulers, against the authorities, against the cosmic powers of this present darkness, against the spiritual forces of evil in the heavenly places" (Eph. 6:12). This struggle against the dark spiritual forces is both a corporate responsibility and a personal one for every Christian.

Some Christians are concerned that when battle imagery is applied to sanctification, it often emphasizes struggle and risk such that a life of grace-dependency is diminished. Not many writers are as adroit as John Bunyan in *The Holy War* in capturing the reality of this spiritual struggle without minimizing the place of grace in the midst of it. The armor-of-God imagery from Ephesians is full of battle, struggle, alertness to Satan's craftiness, and God-given grace/power. We are told from the outset of this passage that we are to "be strong in the Lord and in the strength of his power" (Eph. 6:10), and the description "whole armor of God" (6:11) reminds us that the armor is of God's design. God gives battle armor to those he has called, but apparently it could just sit and gather dust. Ephesians, therefore, admonishes us to

30. Ryken, Wilhoit, and Longman, *Dictionary of Biblical Imagery*, 693.

"take up the whole armor of God" (6:13). The armor is defensive, and only one offensive weapon is mentioned: Scripture, here described as "the sword of the Spirit" (6:17).

At an individual level, the battlefield is the human heart. In Proverbs, we are admonished, "Guard your heart, for it determines the course of your life" (4:23 NLT). The heart/soul is the center of our being; in it our growth is solidi-fied. We are warned not to give a "foothold to the devil" (Eph. 4:27 TLB) and instructed to wage war against "the devil's strongholds" (2 Cor. 10:4 TLB). The picture here is of a territorial battle that is being keenly contested. The battle will turn as we or the enemy secure footholds and establish strongholds. Again, our temptation may be to see the struggle merely in individual terms, but Jesus declares that the "gates of hell shall not prevail against" the church (Matt. 16:18 KJV), the corporate might of the body of Christ.

Images of Death and Resurrection

The pattern of death and rebirth is an archetypal paradigm present through-out the pages of the Bible. The pattern shows itself in the flood (Gen. 6–9), as God destroys the entire world, except for Noah's family and selected animals, and then brings forth life on the earth out of the barrenness of the destruction. Genesis poignantly summarizes the image: "After the flood, Noah began to cultivate the ground, and he planted a vineyard" (9:20 NLT). In the exodus, the people of Israel experience a rebirth: after four hundred years of slavery in Egypt, they escape from the deathlike grip of bondage and move out to worship and serve God. The pattern is immediately repeated in the death zone of the wilderness, followed by the birthlike entry into life in the promised land. This imagery "from death to rebirth underlies most of the OT, preoc-cupied as it is with lament giving way to praise, servitude to freedom, exile to return."[31]

In the New Testament, the central death-rebirth image is that of Jesus's death on the cross and subsequent resurrection. The victory over death secured by the resurrection event is the basis of the Christian's claim to new life. Jesus described the Christian's regeneration as a person being born again (John 3:1–8). When we trust Christ for salvation, God makes us alive. "Even when we were dead through our trespasses, [God] made us alive together with Christ" (Eph. 2:5). The central Christian initiation ceremony of baptism symbolizes death and rebirth. Paul says that believers are "buried" with Christ: "Therefore we have been buried with him by baptism into death, so that, just as Christ

---

31. Ryken, Wilhoit, and Longman, *Dictionary of Biblical Imagery*, 697.

was raised from the dead by the glory of the Father, so we too might walk in newness of life" (Rom. 6:4).

Imagery of death and resurrection is missing from much of the contemporary CSF literature. The absence of these radical and supernatural components can reduce CSF to little more than religious self-help. This is unfortunate because these images can remind us that actual formation is, first and foremost, the work of our forming God. Jesus's death and resurrection make our true formation possible and provide the grace we need to experience true spiritual change.

These three image families—nurture, training, and death and resurrection—capture many of the essential elements of CSF. Though in our personal devotional lives we may find that certain images resonate more deeply with us, it is important in our teaching ministry that we provide a balanced treatment of these images. Other people may be at a point where a cluster of images that are not our favorites may help to illuminate the path they need to travel. In addition, the "whole counsel of Scripture" uses these multiple images in a way that safeguards us from promoting an imbalanced approach to the spiritual life. An effective way to evaluate a community's Christian formation practices is to review the comprehensive set of formation images found in Scripture and compare those to the images used in the community's worship, teaching, and discipleship.

Six False Models of Spiritual Formation

> To correctly form a curriculum for Christlikeness, we must have a very clear and simple perception of the primary goals it must achieve, as well as what is to be avoided.
>
> Dallas Willard[32]

Before we look in detail at this book's curriculum for following Jesus, it will be helpful to identify some myths about spiritual growth that often derail the most sincere attempts at spiritual formation.[33] Often these are the result of emphasizing one truth at the expense of others. True spiritual formation, the curriculum for Christlikeness, will always be a rich, grace-filled, multidimensional proposition.

32. *Divine Conspiracy*, 320.
33. In this section, I am indebted to Henry Cloud and John Townsend, *Twelve "Christian" Beliefs That Can Drive You Crazy: Relief from False Assumptions* (Grand Rapids: Zondervan, 1995).

Biblical Images for Spiritual Formation

Nurture. The image-rich phrases below emphasize the gradual but certain changes that Christian nurture can bring about. The dominant thread of these metaphors is the growth seen in plants and animals that are well cared for. Also included in this group are images of the interior. In an age obsessed with beauty and impression management, the spiritual life invites us to cultivate and attend first to our interiors.

Potter and clay: "Yet, O LORD, you are our Father; we are the clay, and you are our potter; we are all the work of your hand" (Isa. 64:8).

Apprentice and disciple: "An apprentice doesn't lecture the master. The point is to be careful who you follow as your teacher" (Luke 6:40 Message).

Vine and branches: "I am the vine, you are the branches. Those who abide in me and I in them bear much fruit, because apart from me you can do nothing" (John 15:5).

Hunger and thirst: "Blessed are those who hunger and thirst for righteousness, for they will be filled" (Matt. 5:6).

Famine/drought: "The time is surely coming, says the Lord GOD, when I will send a famine on the land; not a famine of bread, or a thirst for water, but of hearing the words of the LORD" (Amos 8:11).

Growth: "I planted, Apollos watered, but God gave the growth. So neither the one who plants nor the one who waters is anything, but only God who gives the growth" (1 Cor. 3:6–7).

Human growth: "Like newborn infants, long for the pure, spiritual milk, so that by it you may grow into salvation—if indeed you have tasted that the Lord is good" (1 Pet. 2:2–3).

The Quick-Fix Model

I have talked with many people who have the idea that God's primary way, and desired way, of working in our lives is through a quick spiritual fix. They believe that if they are really in the place of growth, God will simply "zap" them. This is a pernicious teaching because it undercuts the long-term obedience that so often is the path of spiritual growth. One of the common metaphors for the Christian life in Scripture, and in the work of spiritual writers throughout the centuries, is a long journey. Implicit in the stories of the spiritual heroes of the Bible (think of Abraham, Jacob, David, and Peter) is a

Plants: "Blessed are those who trust in the LORD, whose trust is the LORD. They shall be like a tree planted by water, sending out its roots by the stream. It shall not fear when heat comes, and its leaves shall stay green; in the year of drought it is not anxious, and it does not cease to bear fruit" (Jer. 17:7–8).

Heart/soul: "Keep your heart with all vigilance, for from it flow the springs of life" (Prov. 4:23).

Training and struggle. The following images capture the call to personal responsibility, action, and discipleship.

Journey: "You will do well to send them on in a manner worthy of God; for they began their journey for the sake of Christ" (3 John 6–7). Early Christians were known as followers of "the Way" (Acts 9:2).

Coming home: "At that time I will bring you home, at the time when I gather you; for I will make you renowned and praised among all the peoples of the earth, when I restore your fortunes before your eyes, says the LORD" (Zeph. 3:20).

Brokenness: "He heals the brokenhearted, and binds up their wounds" (Ps. 147:3).

Athletics: "Athletes exercise self-control in all things; they do it to receive a perishable wreath, but we an imperishable one" (1 Cor. 9:25).

Putting on and taking off: "Let us then lay aside the works of darkness and put on the armor of light" (Rom. 13:12). "As God's chosen ones, holy and beloved, clothe yourselves with compassion, kindness, humility, meekness, and patience" (Col. 3:12).

Battle and struggle: "Put on the whole armor of God, so that you may be able to stand against the wiles of the devil. For our struggle is not against enemies of blood and flesh, but against the rulers, against

spiritual development in growth and wholeness that takes place over a lifetime. Moses was in formation for eighty years before he led Israel out of Egypt.

The Facts-Only Model

This model leads people to believe that the most significant variable in determining whether a person grows or not is their intake of spiritual truth. I have heard this model explicitly taught from the pulpit, but more often people simply pick it up as they observe that the ministries in their church that are intended to support change are all centered on teaching. Christians *must* feast the authorities, against the cosmic powers of this present darkness, against the spiritual forces of evil" (Eph. 6:11–12).

The race: "Let us run with perseverance the race that is set before us" (Heb. 12:1).

Death and resurrection. The following images, foundational to Christian formation, are those of rescue, love, redemption, and justification. While these words have come down to us as theological terms, they are rooted in concrete images like freeing a slave or being declared not guilty in a courtroom. At the heart of these images is the initiative of God, who, because of his love, has freed us from what enslaved us.

Redemption: "You were bought with a price; do not become slaves of human masters" (1 Cor. 7:23).

Passover: "Clean out the old yeast so that you may be a new batch, as you really are unleavened. For our paschal lamb, Christ, has been sacrificed" (1 Cor. 5:7).

Cross: "For the message about the cross is foolishness to those who are perishing, but to us who are being saved it is the power of God" (1 Cor. 1:18).

Disease and healing: "He himself bore our sins in his body on the cross, so that, free from sins, we might live for righteousness; by his wounds you have been healed" (1 Pet. 2:24).

Exile: "They confessed that they were strangers and foreigners on the earth. . . . But as it is, they desire a better country, that is, a heavenly one. Therefore God is not ashamed to be called their God; indeed, he has prepared a city for them" (Heb. 11:13, 16).

Open door: "I know your deeds. See, I have placed before you an open door that no one can shut" (Rev. 3:8 NIV).

upon truth, and yet that is only one discipline in an array of activities that Christians need to participate in to grow in the likeness of Christ. The metaphor of feasting on truth connotes dining at a banquet with others, following rules of etiquette, eating what is served when it is served, and attending to interests of fellow banqueters, not gorging oneself alone and for one's own comfort.

We must integrate the intake of spiritual truth into all relationships; learned truth must impact one's relationships with both God and people. As Christians study Scripture, they will find multiple instructions to practice truth with one another in relationships. Scripture instructs us:

Submit to one another. (Eph. 5:21 NIV)

Be kind to one another, tenderhearted, forgiving one another. (4:32)

Bear with one another and, if anyone has a complaint against another, forgive each other. (Col. 3:13)

Be devoted to one another in love. Honor one another above yourselves. (Rom. 12:10 NIV)

Be completely humble and gentle; be patient, bearing with one another in love. (Eph. 4:2 NIV)

Love one another. (John 13:34)

Welcome one another. (Rom. 15:7)

Agree with one another. (1 Cor. 1:10 NIV)

Teach and admonish one another in all wisdom. (Col. 3:16)

Encourage one another and build each other up. (1 Thess. 5:11 NIV)

Understanding information and knowledge as being directly tied to experiences within relationships is what Carol Lakey Hess calls "a retrieval of Aristotle's concept of practical wisdom and its relationship to practice." Hess declares that "knowing is active, practical, and experiential if it is true knowing."[34]

The Emotional Model

This model tells us that we are changed most profoundly when we have deep emotional or spiritual experiences. I have personally seen the power and emotionality of true revival. We will certainly find that true spiritual growth will touch our emotions deeply.

However, the emotional model goes so far as to suggest that change primarily comes when our emotions are deeply stirred. This is incomplete; to effect whole formation, the turning of repentance involves the emotions and the intellect, the heart and the mind—the whole person. Another limitation of this model is that it emphasizes positive, feel-good emotions. Indeed, some Christians equate growth with an emotional state that is always positive and are overwhelmed when they find themselves experiencing, as the psalmists did, the darker emotions of loss, grief, and despair over sin. Others assume that it is profitable to be motivated by guilt or an obligating list of "shoulds." Nevertheless, suffering and pain are the needed catalysts for the brokenheartedness that open us to leave behind our self-made idols and seek God and his grace.

---

34. Carol Lakey Hess, "Educating in the Spirit" (PhD diss., Princeton Theological Seminary, 1990), 221.

The Conference Model

Conferences and special spiritual assemblies can have a powerful effect on a spiritual life. There is a certain validation that we experience when we seek out teaching, share the experience with hundreds or thousands of other people, and hear some of their testimonies as we eat meals together and talk with speakers. However, mountaintop experiences at conferences or similar events might hide two potential problems. First, when they focus on the future, they might reinforce a perspective that what has been part of one's past is not critical or does not need to be redeemed. Second, individuals may be motivated to make resolutions that they are not mature enough to keep over the long term. Conferences are times of renewal or special training, but we must not see them as indispensable spiritual filling stations that become our primary source of nurture and guidance on the journey.

The Insight Model

Recognizing our patterns of sin and our patterns of self-protection is so important in the spiritual life. However, insight and introspection are, again, one aspect of spiritual growth, and we should never regard them as the essence of our spiritual lives. When we give insight too much prominence, it often ends up supporting a diseased introspection that actually impedes our spiritual lives rather than contributing to them. An outcome of a diseased introspection might include a preoccupation with our choices and their consequences. Then a person becomes focused on behavior choices and the law rather than on God's grace and his provision.

The Faith Model

In some circles it is popular to say that all spiritual growth stems from surrender to God. Certainly, submission and growth in faith are important aspects of our ongoing relationship with God. However, through practicing a variety of spiritual disciplines, we often come to see areas where we need to surrender, issues we might never recognize if we simply focus exclusively on pondering areas where we lack faith. This model often is overly confident about our ability, while sitting in a protracted worship service, to identify the parts of our lives where we lack faith and trust. Additionally, when we have correctly identified areas where we lack faith, surrender does not mean that God does all the work; we have to do our part as well. Surrendering to God and working on our relationship with him in no way decrease our need to cultivate healthy human relationships. Surrender is vital, but it is usually a by-product of living faithfully before God and seeking to carry out his great invitations. In the process of seeking to follow Christ, we become more aware of the things we must give up.

These six models seem so attractive because they fit right into our consumer view of religion. They appeal to those who think their growth is dependent simply on consuming the "right thing." The deep longing for Christlikeness is a longing for God himself and the primary motivator for deep spiritual transformation. Seeking Christlikeness is a lifelong endeavor that requires personal and corporate commitment to both active and passive stances. To explore a curriculum of Christlikeness in a more detailed fashion, the four dimensions of *receiving*, *remembering*, *responding*, and *relating* will be developed carefully in the chapters that follow.

Developing a Curriculum for Christlikeness: A Summary

Step 1: Discern how to strengthen your church as a safe and welcoming community in which a teachable spirit is present. First, have the courage to recognize that "your system is perfectly designed to produce the results you are getting."[35] The hidden and null curriculums are contributing to spiritual deformation in your church. Instead of blaming learners for their lack of commitment, leaders of CSF efforts should think hard about why they are not getting the results they expected from long-term exposure to gospel-centered teaching. Second, bathe the entire development of your CSF curriculum in prayer.

Step 2: Make Jesus and his teachings utterly attractive. Structure your curriculum so that it moves from just "telling about" to actually teaching the practices that marked Jesus's life. Build the curriculum around active community engagement "so that being built up in Christ is being built up in the Church."[36]

Step 3: Develop a rich and comprehensive explicit curriculum for Christlikeness. The process of CSF is ongoing and must be rich and multidimensional, for even those mature in Christ face the deformative pressure of the world, the flesh, and the devil. I suggest four categories to use as a gauge for measuring its breadth: *receiving*, *remembering*, *responding*, and *relating*.

Step 4: Reclaim the biblical images for CSF. Our culture is awash in images of inner change and spirituality that will not guide one toward Jesus. Employ the rich array of figurative language used in the Bible to describe the deep

35. Willard, *Divine Conspiracy*, 308.
36. Mascall, *Christ, the Christian and the Church*, 205.

transformation of CSF. The foundational metaphors that should shape those leading in CSF are shepherd-teachers, servants, and doctors (soul physicians).

For Further Reading

De Sales, Francis. *Introduction to the Devout Life.* Vintage Spiritual Classics. New York: Vintage Books, 2002. A detailed late-sixteenth-century classic text on spiritual well-being for the ordinary life.

Foster, Richard J. *Celebration of Discipline: The Path to Spiritual Growth.* 3rd ed. San Francisco: HarperSanFrancisco, 1998. A contemporary spiritual classic that provides an excellent introduction to the spiritual disciplines.

Hood, Jason. *Imitating God in Christ: Recapturing a Biblical Pattern.* Downers Grove, IL: IVP Academic, 2013. A clear statement of why imitation is an important construct in discipleship.

Issler, Klaus. *Living into the Life of Jesus: The Formation of Christian Character.* Downers Grove, IL: IVP Books, 2012. An exploration of spiritual formation into the character of Christ.

Law, William. *A Serious Call to a Devout and Holy Life: The Spirit of Love.* Edited by P. G. Stanwood. Classics of Western Spirituality. New York: Paulist Press, 1978. A call by a man of great piety and social concerns to live entirely by the will of God.

Pennington, Jonathan. *The Sermon on the Mount and Human Flourishing: A Theological Commentary.* Grand Rapids: Baker Academic, 2017. A book that shows how the Sermon on the Mount is intended to lead us to a life of flourishing through the cultivation of gospel virtues.

Sande, Ken. *The Peacemaker: A Biblical Guide to Resolving Personal Conflict.* 3rd ed. Grand Rapids: Baker Books, 2004. A biblically grounded treatment of how to handle conflict in a Christ-honoring way.

Smith, James K. A. *Desiring the Kingdom: Worship, Worldview, and Cultural Formation.* Grand Rapids: Baker Academic, 2009. The first volume of a trilogy in which Christian education is conceived as counter-formation to the secular liturgies of our age.

Thomas à Kempis. *The Imitation of Christ.* Edited and translated by William Creasy. Notre Dame, IN: Ave Maria, 2004. An immensely popular book on imitating Christ that is filled with remarkable wisdom about the human spirit.

Tinsley, E. J. *The Imitation of God in Christ: An Essay on the Biblical Basis of Christian Spirituality.* Philadelphia: Westminster, 1960. A gem from an earlier generation that argues for the importance of the ideal of imitating Christ in Christian spirituality.

Willard, Dallas. *The Divine Conspiracy: Rediscovering Our Hidden Life in God.* San Francisco: HarperSanFrancisco, 1998. An emphasis on learning from Jesus, with a dense and comprehensive treatment of life in the kingdom of God. The author writes, "The really good news for Christians is that Jesus is now taking students in the master class of life."

————. *The Spirit of the Disciplines: Understanding How God Changes Lives*. New York: HarperOne, 1988. A remarkable exploration of how the spiritual disciplines work in our spiritual transformation.

THREE

Receiving

Formation of the Heart
by Grace for the Broken and Thirsty

We live from our hearts.

Dallas Willard[1]

Most of us are blessed by experiences in which the love of God is made real for us. Our problem is that we are not paying attention, and therefore miss the blessing of discovering the intimate presence of God in our everyday lives. Without receiving love, we cannot love others, no matter how hard we try.

Howard L. Rice[2]

Attending to our restlessness, of course, can be hard work, for it assumes continuous growth and change.

John H. Westerhoff III[3]

1. *Renovation of the Heart: Putting on the Character of Christ* (Colorado Springs: Nav-Press, 2002), 13.
2. *Reformed Spirituality: An Introduction for Believers* (Louisville: Westminster John Knox, 1991), 42, 166.
3. *Spiritual Life: The Foundation for Preaching and Teaching* (Louisville: Westminster John Knox, 1994), 36.

What are we to receive? We are to imbibe the healing, vitalizing, sustaining, and strengthening grace of God that we need for supporting and growing our spiritual lives and healing our souls.

How do we do this? We learn in community to feast on God's grace, by learning to listen and be open before God, and by having a vision for the changed life and recognizing our deep brokenness.

What stance does this require? Openness/brokenness: a disciplined "showing up" to meet God and a commitment to the indirect path of spiritual training.

When I was a boy in Oregon, I passed by a greenhouse on my way to the swimming pool. In the late spring, I can remember seeing the windows cleaned and glistening in this greenhouse, filled with bright annuals. Shortly after school was out, the greenhouse was whitewashed. Blocking out the direct light kept the greenhouse cooler on hot days, which was necessary for some of the more tender plants that replaced the sun-loving annuals. A few years ago, as I stood in a freshly whitewashed greenhouse, I was given a glimpse of the spiritual life. I saw myself as a sun-loving plant placed in the limited light of the greenhouse. There was indeed enough light to survive, but not enough to blossom or flourish. I thought of my life in a church and Christian college, where the ambiance provides enough light to allow one's spiritual life to survive, but more light is needed to flourish. Then I imagined the whitewashing lime on one pane being wiped away. I received direct morning light. Then another pane was cleared overhead, and I received the sunlight at noon. I was allowed to see that my spiritual life was surviving on the light streaming in through just a few windows and that God had given me a multitude of windows: personal Bible reading, meditation, listening prayer, intercessory prayer, praying the Scriptures, the sacraments, fellowship, accountability, service, study, Bible memorization, worship, mentoring, solitude, fasting, and many more. How much more light was available to me? It could come streaming from many angles!

A sense of humble receptiveness on the part of the Christian community is so essential to true spiritual formation. A receptive stance requires corporate and individual humility and spiritual openness. We must promote appropriate humility and brokenness on the part of God's people so that we will be receptive to the Spirit's work of formation and reformation in our lives. I refer to this desired brokenness as *optimistic brokenness*. I use the qualifier *optimistic* because we should not be content simply to give the message of how hard life is and to catalog our moral failures. Still, all of this must have the purpose of making us more reliant on God by admitting God's claim on our lives and receiving the hope and healing he has to offer.

Creating a Culture of Openness

To experience true and deep spiritual formation, we must be willing to open our hearts to the work of the Spirit. The call for spiritual vulnerability is a perennial theme in CSF. From the early desert writers, we hear Abba Poemen say, "Do not give your heart to that which does not satisfy your heart."[4] It is all too easy to give our hearts over to a shiny object that turns out to be a mere distraction and not at all what we say is most important. In the Reformation era, John Calvin observed the importance of opening one's heart to the Scriptures: "It now remains to pour into the heart itself what the mind has absorbed. For the Word of God is not received by faith if it flits about in the top of the brain, but when it takes root in the depth of the heart."[5] And the contemporary spiritual formation systematizer Adrian Van Kaam sees the importance of heart change: "The heart attuned to the heart of Christ is like a finely calibrated radio receiver. . . . In humility and gratitude, we open the doors of our hearts to Father, Son, and Holy Spirit. Only when we live in this chamber of intimacy can we go forth as healing hearts in a wounded world."[6] In this chapter, we will explore what churches can do to help foster a stance of being receptive to God's work in our hearts.

Three perspectives must be embedded in our corporate life maps to foster spiritual receiving:

- A deep sense of our sin (both personal and corporate) and knowing what the cross says about our sin
- An awareness of the reality of our yearnings and how the embrace of God helps us live with them
- A deep-seated conviction that all growth comes from grace through our union with Christ

Personal Brokenness

A genuine spiritual openness has, at its core, personal brokenness that results in humility and a tender openness to God's work in us. As a small child, I witnessed the adventures of my family with a passive-aggressive mule we named Speedy Mule. Mistreatment by its previous owner had reduced

---

4. Quoted in Benedicta Ward, *The Sayings of the Desert Fathers: The Alphabetical Collection* (Kalamazoo, MI: Cistercian Publications, 1975), 178.

5. John Calvin, *Institutes of the Christian Religion*, ed. John McNeill, trans. Ford Lewis Battles (Philadelphia: Westminster, 1960), 1:583.

6. Adrian Van Kaam and Susan Muto, *Formation Theology*, vol. 3, *Formation of the Christian Heart* (Pittsburgh: Epiphany Association, 2006), 16.

this animal to a passive and pathetic life. He was a "broken" animal, and his brokenness had left him skittish and wary of everyone. That is not the type of brokenness I am speaking of. Real brokenness at the heart level does not result in "bitterness, cynicism, or low self-esteem"[7] but rather in a realistic assessment of our abilities, an acknowledgment of our utter dependence on God, a deep sense of how easily we can be deceived about our motives, and a glimmer of awareness of how our sinning comes from our unwillingness to face our deep unsatisfied thirsts.

In the story of the prodigal son (Luke 15:11–32), Jesus pictures two young men who have made choices that have kept them, at first, from experiencing their father's embrace. I find myself returning to this story again and again. As a child, I learned this as a redemption story of the waiting father who welcomes back his estranged son. I knew it in a primarily sentimentalized version, with no hint of the cross, but I came to delight in the picture of God welcoming the rebellious sinner back. I could identify with the rebellion of the younger son and with his desire to return when he hit rock bottom.

Some time ago, I found myself reading the story from the perspective of the older son. For years he had been just a stage prop for me. He was not a full-fledged character but merely a foil to show off the father's great love. But then I strangely began to wonder, *Could I be the elder brother? Could I be that overly socialized, highly compliant one, envious of the sins of others?* Yes! Like the older brother, I thought God was lucky to have me on his team. I was compliant and deserving of fair treatment—just like the Pharisees for whom the story was first told. What was most shocking was to find that the eldest son, in his pride, also missed the father's embrace. Henri Nouwen writes about his realization that he too was an eldest son:

> For my entire life I had been quite responsible, traditional, and homebound. . . . I suddenly saw myself in a completely new way. I saw my jealousy, my anger, my touchiness, doggedness and sullenness, and most of all, my stubborn self-righteousness. I saw how much of a complainer I was and how much of my thinking and feeling was ridden with resentments. For a time it became impossible to see how I could ever have thought of myself as the younger son. . . . I had been working very hard on my father's farm, but had never fully tasted the joy of being at home.[8]

7. Alan Nelson, *Broken in the Right Place: How God Tames the Soul* (Nashville: Nelson, 1994), 7.
8. Henri J. M. Nouwen, *The Return of the Prodigal Son: A Meditation on Fathers, Brothers, and Sons* (New York: Doubleday, 1992), 21–22.

We desperately need to see that intimacy with God and the transformation it brings can easily be blocked by the bitterness and pride the older son exemplifies. That rebellion keeps us away from God is a truism; that pride in our own compliance and competence could keep us away is shocking. Sadly, the story of the prodigal ends without resolution. The older son resists and misses the embrace. I fear, at times, that so many false spiritualities simply turn younger sons into older brothers, "who expect their goodness to pay off, and if it doesn't, there is confusion and rage."[9]

To be broken means that we recognize we are personally powerless to manage our lives in a way that will bring the kind of life we most deeply long for. Brokenness also involves acknowledging that we face problems we cannot overcome by willpower alone. It is the experience of many Bible heroes: Abraham, Moses, Hannah, David, and Paul.

The Bible most commonly employs brokenness as an image for people overwhelmed by troubles that change them. Old Testament writers typically express this by saying that the "heart" or "spirit" is "broken." That metaphorical language represents feelings of anguish and despair and a loss of hope or of a sense of well-being. In the Bible, as in life, brokenness comes in two forms. The outcome of the experience of brokenness is what differentiates them. Some people leave the experience wounded, despairing, and not fully functional. Others leave it humbled and changed, and even more effective. Paul captures the difference when he writes to the Corinthians, "Now I rejoice, not that you were grieved, but that your grief led to repentance; for you were grieved in the way God intended so that you might not suffer loss in anything through us. For godly brokenness produces a repentance leading to salvation, without regret, but the sorrow of the world produces death" (2 Cor. 7:9–10 author's trans.).

In the Bible, genuinely broken people turn to God for help. Confessions of brokenness regularly occur in the immediate context of petitions for God's rescue or confessions of faith in God (Ps. 34:17–18). Openness to God awakens his compassion and moves him to bind up the brokenhearted (Isa. 61:1). In Psalm 147:2–3, the psalmist employs the language of healing the brokenhearted to celebrate God's saving actions toward the postexilic community in their struggle against political opposition and economic adversity.

At the outset of his public ministry, Jesus quotes Isaiah 61:1 to explain his mission (Luke 4:18–19). Subsequently, he displays great concern for binding up the brokenhearted in his focus on the spiritually "sick" (Matt. 9:12; Mark 2:17; Luke 5:31), his frequent calls for repentance (Matt. 4:17; Mark 1:15; Luke

9. Timothy Keller, *The Prodigal God* (New York: Dutton, 2008), 52.

13:3), his gentle dealings with sinful people (Luke 7:36–50; 19:1–10), and his parables of acceptance for the repentant (15:11–32; 18:9–14).

Every Christian is a broken person. To enter the kingdom, we acknowledge that the inner peace we yearn for can never come by our efforts but only as we admit our powerlessness to conquer our self-centeredness and then turn over the rule of our lives to Christ. We need to live the Christian life as broken people. The grace of God—the grace we need for healing, for the freedom to be good, and for the profound joy we long for—only flows downhill. It is available to the humble: "God opposes the proud, but gives grace to the humble" (1 Pet. 5:5).

Humility and Teachableness

CSF requires that we cultivate openness to God. We should be intellectually open like the Bereans, who "were more open-minded than those in Thessalonica, and they listened eagerly to Paul's message" (Acts 17:11 NLT). We should pray for openness to Scripture as the psalmist did: "Open my eyes to see the wonderful truths in your instructions" (Ps. 119:18 NLT); eyes opened, we would come to treasure and obey it. John Calvin saw teachableness as an intellectual virtue that should mark churches, and this chiefly manifested itself when the Scriptures were approached with a noble mind and a teachable spirit. He puts it succinctly: "For our wisdom ought to be nothing else than to embrace with humble teachableness, and at least without finding fault, whatever is taught in Sacred Scripture."[10]

We must seek to discern God's voice and the reality of Christ's indwelling us amid everyday events so we can hear his call to us. Think of Elisha's servant, who missed seeing God's provision until "Elisha prayed, 'O LORD, open his eyes and let him see!' The LORD opened the young man's eyes, and when he looked up, he saw that the hillside around Elisha was filled with horses and chariots of fire" (2 Kings 6:17 NLT). It is so easy for us to go about our days and miss what God is seeking to communicate: "You have seen many things, but pay no attention; your ears are open, but you do not listen" (Isa. 42:20 NIV). A humble openness to listen and be taught is the rich, fertile soil God delights to use to grow his good fruit.

As a speaker in various churches, I confess how precious an open and teachable spirit is to a teacher. Its presence is almost palpable—it affects the teaching space and generates a bond of trust between teacher and student. When learners clearly are receptive, that calls forth the teacher's best effort,

---

10. Calvin, *Institutes*, 1:237.

deep respect, and a holy caution, lest this trust be violated. A listening, receptive spirit is not a spiritual luxury. Jesus asserts that hearing his voice is essential to being a true disciple: "My sheep hear my voice. I know them, and they follow me" (John 10:27). A stance of openness must be cultivated to hear God's Word. The refusal or inability to hear spiritually is one of the most stinging indictments given by God: "This is what the LORD says: 'Stand by the ways and see and ask for the ancient paths, where the good way is, and walk in it; then you will find rest for your souls.' But they said, 'We will not walk in it.' And I set watchmen over you, saying, 'Listen to the sound of the trumpet!' But they said, 'We will not listen'" (Jer. 6:16–17 NASB).

There is a great need for wise and godly persuasion in our church education and formation programs. All of us are closed on some issues and must be persuaded if we are to move to a better position. Consider the negative effects of racism, which Christians must recognize as a false gospel that offers a sense of righteousness through perceived superiority. Many of us who have grown and repented in this area did so because persuasive messages confronted our sinful blindness.

When I speak of persuasion, I am endorsing the subtle and subversive teaching of Jesus and the prophets. For them, persuasion was not just cranking up the volume and intensity of the message—it was the skilled and artful confrontation of their audiences' errant ways and beliefs. Through drama, parables, and questions, these teachers actively sought to affect their hearers while always realizing that it is God who changes hearts—we inform and invite.

Openheartedness

Related to the teachable spirit is the condition of openheartedness. Paul reminds the Corinthians that he has shown them openheartedness in his ministry and urges them to "widen your hearts also" (2 Cor. 6:13 ESV). He prays that the Ephesians will experience having "eyes of [the] heart" opened so that they can perceive their spiritual reality of now having a "glorious inheritance" (Eph. 1:18 NIV). His prayer is that "the lights will go on inside people so that they know God and understand the benefit of the gospel."[11] This plea by Paul has a different emphasis than the teachability we have just mentioned. Openheartedness, vulnerability before God, and the ability to perceive the reality of our union with Christ are individual and corporate experiences. They are

---

11. Klyne Snodgrass, *Ephesians*, NIV Application Commentary (Grand Rapids: Zondervan, 1996), 74.

supported by the community's teachable spirit and are outworkings of our Spirit-birthed openness to the reality of who we are in Christ—and who we are in the body of Christ.

Adrian Van Kaam has written the most comprehensive theory of spiritual formation. In his work, he integrates the rich CSF tradition found in what he terms "the masters of spiritual formation" with the insights of contemporary psychology. His theory could be called *cardio-centric* because of the emphasis he places on the heart in formation. He writes extensively about the importance of keeping the heart appropriately open to the Lord. He makes the case that "awe, wonder, and marvel" are dispositions essential to cultivating a receptive heart. Van Kaam's keystone virtue of humility supports these dispositions. In a series of maxims on guarding one's heart, we catch the prominence of humility in his thought: "Express gratefulness to God on the spot for every good that comes your way. Take credit for nothing. The disposition of humility dampens the devastating flare-ups of your pride-form. Only God's love counts."[12] We are to clothe ourselves with "compassion, kindness, humility, meekness, and patience" (Col. 3:12), for these virtues foster the presence of "the peace of Christ ruling in our hearts" (3:15 adapted). Teachability, spiritual curiosity, and humility help form the "good soil" (Mark 4:8) so that "in simple humility, let our gardener, God, landscape you with the Word, making a salvation-garden of your life" (James 1:21 Message).

A recurring emphasis in this volume is that we would do well to avoid pitting "head knowledge" against "heart knowledge." That dichotomy is foreign to Scripture. As Gary Newton helpfully observes, "In order to understand the dynamics of heart-deep teaching, we must affirm the value of both objective, propositional truth and the experiential way we come to know truth."[13] The knowledge that is valued in Scripture is a stable knowledge that one acts on, as is clear in James 1:22: "But be doers of the word, and not merely hearers who deceive themselves." This is beautifully expressed in the depiction of the two followers with the resurrected Lord on the road to Emmaus: "They said to each other, 'Were not our hearts burning within us while he was talking to us on the road, while he was opening the scriptures to us?'" (Luke 24:32). Jesus's clear and evocative teaching, in which "he interpreted to them the things about himself in all the scriptures" (24:27), together with their faith, their commitment to following him, and their teachable spirit led to

---

12. Van Kaam and Muto, *Formation Theology*, 3:136.
13. Gary C. Newton, *Heart-Deep Teaching: Engaging Students for Transformed Lives* (Nashville: B&H Academic, 2012), 12.

The Importance of Heart Affections

A person who has a knowledge of doctrine and theology only—without religious affection—has never engaged in true religion. Nothing is more apparent than this: our religion takes root within us only as deep as our affections attract it. There are thousands who hear the Word of God, who hear great and exceedingly important truths about themselves and their lives, and yet all they hear has no effect upon them, makes no change in the way they live.

The reason is this: they are not affected with what they hear. There are many who hear about the power, the holiness, and the wisdom of God; about Christ and the great things that he has done for them and his gracious invitation to them; and yet they remain exactly as they are in life and in practice.

I am bold in saying this, but I believe that no one is ever changed, either by doctrine, by hearing the Word, or by the preaching or teaching of another, unless the affections are moved by these things. No one ever seeks salvation, no one ever cries for wisdom, no one ever wrestles with God, no one ever kneels in prayer or flees from sin, with a heart that remains unaffected. In a word, there is never any great achievement by the things of religion without a heart deeply affected by those things.[a]

a. Jonathan Edwards, as excerpted and modernized in Richard J. Foster and James Bryan Smith, *Devotional Classics: Selected Readings for Individuals and Groups* (San Francisco: HarperOne, 2005), 20–21. The original statement can be found in Jonathan Edwards, *Religious Affections* (New Haven: Yale University Press, 1960), 101–3.

a deep heart learning or, as Willard calls it, "*experiential involvement* with what is known," by which he means that we experience "actual engagement with it."[14]

In Scripture, the heart is the seat of the mind, will, and emotions. It is the control center of the whole life. The heart contains our motives; it is the engine that drives us. It is equivalent to character, core personality, or motivational structures.[15] In the heart reside the answers to the questions "What have you set your hopes on?" and "What gives you meaning?" In an Augustinian view, the heart's loves direct our lives. We can think of the heart as containing the "operating system" of our lives.

14. Willard, *Renovation of the Heart*, 51.
15. See Tremper Longman, *Proverbs* (Grand Rapids: Baker Academic, 2006), 153–54; Bruce K. Waltke, *The Book of Proverbs: Chapters 1–15* (Grand Rapids: Eerdmans, 2004), 91–92; Timothy Keller, "Preaching to the Heart without Being Pietistic" (lecture, Ockenga Lectures on Preaching at Gordon-Conwell Theological Seminary, South Hamilton, MA, 2006).

Community Practices to Foster Teachableness and Openheartedness

The invitation to be a people of love contains an invitation to receive. The love we are to share is not the love of well-intentioned willpower but a grace-saturated love infused by God. This compassion is "poured into our hearts through the Holy Spirit" (Rom. 5:5) and produces the tender, long-suffering love Christ invites us to share. Disciplines that engender a soft and submissive heart toward God are clear responses to the core invitation to love and obey God.

Worship and Confession

To worship is to be fully occupied with the attributes of God—the majesty, beauty, and goodness of his person, powers, and perfections.

Kenneth Boa[16]

Worship is the first and most fundamental act of a congregation, an act that separates it from all other human groups. . . . Every part of the public worship of God goes counter to the prevailing culture.

C. Ellis Nelson[17]

Worship plays a crucial role in shaping Christians' formative vision. Formation can come only when worship is truly centered on God and not done merely as a means toward the end of formation. One significant obstacle to growth that many people experience is their limited or distorted view of God. It is in truly creative and engaging worship that we not only confess what is true about God but also experience God and learn firsthand of his character. Jesus observed the capacity of children to be wholehearted in faith and wonder. His maxim "Whoever does not receive the kingdom of God as a little child will never enter it" (Luke 18:17) is rooted in the observation that awe, wonder, trust, and faith seem easy and natural for children. The "sophistication" of adulthood stunts our formation when it diminishes our capacity to marvel and stand in awe before God, his Word, and creation. Actual spiritual formation can be conducted only in an atmosphere permeated by mystery, wonder, awe, reverence, and beauty.

Worship is the primary corporate spiritual discipline of the church. The discipline aspect of "worship" is to make our collective activity worship.

16. *Conformed to His Image: Biblical and Practical Approaches to Spiritual Formation* (Grand Rapids: Zondervan, 2001), 86.
17. *How Faith Matures* (Louisville: Westminster John Knox, 1989), 175.

Worship is not always easy: it involves deep intimacy, openhearted reverence, and awe. On a personal level, we may encounter barriers and distractions that keep us away from a worship service or distract us while we are there. On a corporate level, leading people into sincere worship—"worship in spirit and truth" (John 4:24)—is not automatic. It is unwise to assume that simply gathering people together results in worship. We need to both instruct and offer a thoughtful call to worship God with sincerity in our whole beings.

Worship cultivates a receptive attitude and opens us to receive God's grace. Confession in worship acknowledges our errors and our participation in corporate sins. Receiving and extending forgiveness can re-establish in us our lived sense of our standing as forgiven before God. Preaching and sharing in the sacraments plow the soil of our souls and plant seeds for future harvests. Sometimes all these facets of spiritual agriculture occur during the same time of worship. One of the basic formational gestures of worship is a call for us to look up and out to God rather than down and in at our problems and our solutions or around at what others are doing and how they regard us. The simple gesture of the posture of looking up and out to God can become a sign of cultivated receptivity. We have the pattern of Jesus's posture in the high priestly prayer of John 17:1, when "he looked up to heaven and said . . ." He did not close his eyes and bow his head; he raised his eyes in expected intimacy with the Father. This is not to say that other postures are wrong or inappropriate but rather that our posture can contribute to the expression of our souls. In the ministry of the Word and sacraments, we learn to open ourselves and receive from God. We hear the truth of God proclaimed and receive the grace-filled words. We are built up as we receive the sacrament of communion and strengthened as we trust in Christ's work on our behalf.

The Greek word for confession is *homolegeō*, and it means "to say the same thing." When we speak of confessing our faith or confessing sins, we are acknowledging that, to the degree possible, both we and God are saying the same thing. To confess our sins means that we stop calling our actions "a necessary evil" or saying "I had no other choice" or "Everyone else is doing it." Instead, we acknowledge—as God already has—that they are sins, and they are wrong. Confession is a potent spiritual action, and through it we open ourselves to the process of growth and spiritual repair at deep levels. Lauren Winner shares candidly of her experiences with confession during her struggle with chastity:

> The rite of confession is, to my mind, the most mysterious and inexplicable of the Christian disciplines. In fact, many Christians do not observe a formal order of confession at all. I have never really understood intellectually what happens

at confession; rather, I have taken on faith that in the confessional God's grace is uniquely present, regardless of my ability to articulate why or how. So it is fitting that in that moment full of grace I made a real beginning of chastity, because it is only God's grace—and not my intellectual apprehension of the whys and wherefores of Christian sexual ethics—that has tutored me in chastity.[18]

Repentance follows confession, for it speaks not only of us acknowledging our sin but also of a commitment to respond to grace and act differently in the future.

Several years ago, I talked with a friend who told me that he was spiritually stuck. Part of his problem was wondering where to go next spiritually since he had "taken care of the big sins in my life." I do not know if my friend simply didn't understand or if this was a symptom of his church. But here was a man who, after several decades in the church, had not learned to make repentance and confession a true part of his life. We must always recognize that, while we hold forth a vision of deep and substantial change, our task is the spiritual formation of broken and imperfect people; therefore, one of our primary treatment options is that of humble confession and repentance.

> Worship filled with prayer and praise and opportunities for confession, repentance, receiving the sacraments, hearing and giving testimonies of God's activity, and learning/challenge is the most important context of community formation.

Finally, in terms of worship, we need to make sure that the message of God's amazing love is continually and creatively taught. Revelation 12 tells us that Satan's full-time occupation is that of accusing Christians. Our adversary is lurking not so much to tempt us into new sins as to defeat us through our doubting of God's love and goodness, which then takes us to the narcissism and self-soothing behavior often adopted as a strategy to placate our self-loathing that is exacerbated by Satan's accusations. Woven into our teaching on God's love must be the reality of God's grace. In simple terms, we need to remember that God's grace has two aspects, pardon and power; we must present both and teach people how to avail themselves of both.

Providing a Vision for Transformation

The conviction that change and growth are possible and worth the effort is essential to spiritual formation. Vision—moral and spiritual vision, more

18. Lauren F. Winner, *Real Sex: The Naked Truth about Chastity* (Grand Rapids: Brazos, 2005), 14.

than merely a vision that moves us emotionally—is part of what provides the hope that transformation is a real possibility. This idea of vision is reflected in Paul's urging that we should have "a view of things" that would cause us to press forward spiritually (Phil. 3:12–15 NIV). Vision is what a friend of mine found when he went to his first AA meeting, where he found "hope, the possibility of sobriety." It is what a former student found when, through teaching, prayer, and therapy, she realized that she could step free from her family's generational patterns of anger and abuse. She found "a picture of another way of living," and that picture has guided her life. With the same perspective, Ray Anderson has written that "spiritual healing begins with the recovery of hope."[19]

Willard's suggestion that Vision-Intention-Means is a basic pattern of human goal achievement provides a helpful way of thinking about vision. Vision is the mental picture of what life could look like when the desired changes are made. Intention is the desire for the vision to be actualized and the decision to pursue it. And means are the activities, methods, and life patterns we put in place to achieve the vision/goal. Willard provides an illustration of how learning a language requires all three of these to be present:

> Consider the case of those who wish to speak a language they do not presently know, say French or Arabic or Japanese. In order to carry through with this simple case of (partial) personal transformation, they must have some idea of what it would be like to speak the language in question—of what their lives would then be like—and why this would be a desirable or valuable thing for them. They also need to have some idea of what must be done to learn to speak the language and why the price in time, energy, and money that must be expended constitutes a bargain, considering what they get in return. In the ideal case, all of this would be clearly before them and they would be gripped by the desirability of it. Now, this is the vision that goes into the particular project of learning the language. Unless one has it—or, better, it has them—the language will pretty surely not be learned.[20]

When I was a new Christian, a mentor encouraged me to read spiritual biographies. I read a few and found the genre somewhat disappointing, but I did notice that these books provided me with a vision for a spiritually transformed life. A starting point for CSF comes through providing a vision that makes spiritual transformation desirable.

19. Ray Anderson, *Self-Care: A Theology of Personal Empowerment and Spiritual Healing* (Wheaton: Victor Books, 1995), 236.
20. Willard, *Renovation of the Heart*, 83.

James Prochaska and colleagues have extensively studied behavior change and a person's readiness to implement new, healthier behavior. Prochaska has documented how the nature of a person's desire to change shifts during the process of actual behavior change. Much of his work has focused on smoking cessation. He shows that a person may begin with an intention to simply quit smoking but that to maintain abstinence, their intention must shift to a more comprehensive desire for a healthy lifestyle.[21] In CSF, discipleship needs to move from eliminating self-defeating patterns to embracing a call to love and holiness. Our intention deepens and is strengthened by success, our vision of spiritual flourishing becomes richer, and we learn through experience that these practices work.

In a pluralistic society like ours, there are competing visions—visions that would lead toward hedonism, toward seeking fulfillment through work, toward environmental consciousness, and toward creating a family-centered life. Then there are grand visions: in the words attributed to the overseer of Chicago's elaborate 1893 Columbian Exposition, "Make no little plans; they have no magic to stir men's blood and probably themselves will not be realized. Make big plans; aim high in hope and work."[22] The vision I am speaking of is not simply grand: a vision for CSF has the power to remind us that hope and healing are possible through Jesus. It offers encouraging words that, in Christ, we no longer are enslaved to doing merely what we "want to do." It also shows a realistic process that we can follow to become apprentices of Jesus.

Vision is the wild card of spiritual formation. There are churches that one would expect to be rather marginal in terms of formation because they are, say, large and impersonal or have relatively poor educational programs or little to no soul care—yet they consistently produce dedicated followers of Christ. One reason for this is vision. The ability to cast a vision of change and discipleship is a powerful means of grace. I know of many people whose spiritual lives have been forever transformed through a vision-communicating speaker who was able to call them to a different way of life by giving them a

21. James O. Prochaska and Janice M. Prochaska, *Changing to Thrive: Using the Stages of Change to Overcome the Top Threats to Your Health and Happiness* (Center City, MN: Hazelden, 2016), 33–63. For an influential Orthodox presentation of Christian living with a strong emphasis on intention, see Theophan the Recluse, *The Path to Salvation: A Manual of Spiritual Transformation* (Forestville, CA: St. Herman of Alaska Brotherhood, 1996).

22. This maxim is often quoted in Chicago and attributed to Daniel Burnham, the overseer of the 1893 World's Columbian Exposition and co-creator of the famous Plan of Chicago. While this quotation captures his style of strategic leadership, the quotation comes from a paraphrase by his business partner of a speech he gave in London. See Patrick Reardon, "Burnham Quote: Well, It May Be," *Chicago Tribune*, January 1, 1992.

moral/spiritual vision. And yet vision alone is not the key to church health. Jim Wilder wisely observes, "We kill the church when we make Christianity about fulfilling a vision. When a church, staff, program, or outreach is forced to service a vision, striving is about to begin. Joy and peace levels fall—casualties of striving to fulfill visions."[23]

A transforming vision serves as a map and a source of empowerment as individuals come to see that they can live differently. One person likened receiving this vision to Christ calling Lazarus from the grave. This person had been trapped in anger and lust, so much so that he could not maintain any long-term relationships. Then, he said, a speaker "called me out of my tomb. Realizing I could change was half the battle, but I still had to get the grave clothes off." One simple way to cast a vision is through the use of testimonies like this one in which people tell their stories, often by being interviewed, of God's grace and the joy they found in more fully following Christ.

Modeling Brokenness

In emotionally healthy churches, people live and lead out of brokenness and vulnerability. . . . It is leading out of failure and pain, questions and struggles—a serving that lets go.

Peter Scazzero[24]

Communities marked by a constructive and pervasive sense of brokenness all have leaders who are open about their own brokenness. Some have seen the bottom through their own experiences; these people have known the betrayal of a spouse, their own indiscretions, or struggles with drugs and alcohol and have come to trust Christ more deeply as a result. Other congregations are headed by people whose stories are less dramatic but who, through deep empathy for others and a heightened sense of their sinfulness and failure to love well, nevertheless own the brokenness of humanity and their own need for healing.

A subtle myth pervading much of ministry holds that we minister most effectively when we are at "the top of our game." I remember a speaker who urged young seminarians to be secure in their faith because they are to stand on the dock and throw out the lifesaving ring to those who are drowning. There is a degree of wisdom in the picture, but it gives the idea

---

23. Jim Wilder, *Renovated: God, Dallas Willard and the Church That Transforms* (Colorado Springs: NavPress, 2020), 171.
24. *The Emotionally Healthy Church* (Grand Rapids: Zondervan, 2003), 110.

that we minister out of our competence to those who are spiritually incompetent. The metamessage we send out is this: "Once I was messed up just like you, and now since I've gotten my life squared away, wouldn't you like to become like me?" Over time, that puts intense pressure on the minister to keep looking good so that people will want to be like the minister. And we miss the joy and power of ministering out of our weakness: "Therefore I am content with weaknesses, . . . for whenever I am weak, then I am strong" (2 Cor. 12:10).

We need to put far more emphasis on the fact that we are all in this together. We all suffer from the same deadly disease of sin, and we are all in the same treatment facility. While there is progress, and while there is hope, there are also relapses, and there is an ongoing struggle. Leaders in teaching, preaching, and pastoral ministry need to be open about the reality of struggle. If they want to create a climate that supports authentic recognition of our brokenness, they must be aware of brokenness in their own lives. However, they must be careful not to fall into the type of narcissistic brokenness in which a leader's public "confession" ends up making their struggle, rather than God and his grace, the central message.

Providing Places for Broken People

One of the clearest ways we minister to people who have aches and hurts in their lives is by putting in place programs, services, and people to help them with the struggles of life. All Christians struggle with sin and brokenness. When we see our problems named clearly, we are more likely to recognize that we need to seek help rather than simply try to look good. Often such support is provided by offering specialized ministries with trained leaders, such as AA meetings or grief groups.

In actuality, Scripture addresses all human problems. However, it takes a deeply thoughtful approach to Scripture to make the deep life connections that open us to healing. An illustration of this comes from teaching Galatians. When I was in college, I led a Bible study based on Galatians. My approach was to expose the spiritual stupidity of the Galatian Christians and warn my group members to avoid the spiritual legalism seen in their reliance on circumcision. As I led the study, I made it clear that the problem facing the Galatians was not "my issue." However, I have since come to realize that Galatians demonstrates that all of us rely on false gospels to help bolster our fragile sense of righteousness. Whoever teaches that letter wisely will help those they teach to see how we all, by nature, are legalists who distrust God's grace and seek to justify ourselves. Such wise and well-studied pastoral teaching can do wonders in opening a Christian's eyes to the pervasive problem of Christian self-reliance. Likewise, the Psalms explore the human experience, and when well taught, they help us become aware of the depth of our sin and our neediness. We can learn to lay our experiences alongside those of the psalmists, who saw themselves as broken and yet recognized that they were broken before a God of immense love and grace.

The Bible contains many stories of dysfunctional heroes because its purpose is to show us our exceptional God, a God of love and grace and power who works through people who have limitations—just like we do. These stories help us develop a vocabulary to identify and describe the reality of brokenness in our own lives. Admitting to brokenness is not to doubt the healing and restoring grace of God. Rather, the brokenness needs to call us to dynamic discipleship, which grows through faith beyond the mere acknowledgment that brokenness is all that we can expect from life.

Discernment

Devout conversation on spiritual matters greatly helps our progress, particularly where people of like mind and spirit are bound to each other in God.

Thomas à Kempis[25]

We all face decisions throughout life and find ourselves asking about God's will in a given situation. One of the tasks of spiritual leaders in the church is to meet with people and, through prayer and scriptural counsel, to offer wisdom and godly perspective on situations they face. As an elder and spiritual director, I often have done this when a crisis has emerged, when people are facing issues that have boxed them in. In such cases, discipleship looks very costly, and the community can help us discern the best path in a realm of hard choices. Churches should seek to build into their culture encouragement to turn to others for discernment in times of decision making so that people can receive wisdom from the body of Christ.

> The fertile field for formation is a community genuinely aware of the depth of their sin and the reality of their spiritual thirst. True formation requires that the community deeply understands that they cannot cure the sickness of their souls through willpower alone.

25. *The Imitation of Christ*, ed. and trans. William Creasy (Notre Dame, IN: Ave Maria, 2004), 38.

Criteria for Discernment

The history of the church is littered with the stories of people who claimed guidance from the Spirit when the prejudices of self-deception reigned instead. From the earliest days of Judaism and Christianity, awareness of this danger has prompted faithful people to articulate criteria by which to judge the authenticity of claims regarding the Spirit.

- *Fidelity to Scripture and tradition.* At the top of any list of criteria, we can find the test of fidelity to the essential vision of the sacred writings and teachings that constitute the faith tradition. Applying this guideline is more complex than simply citing biblical passages, however. It requires us to know Scripture as a whole and to continue searching it with the guidance of the Spirit.
- *Fruit of the Spirit.* Another indication of the authenticity of spiritual discernment is the degree to which the outcomes nurture the fruit of the Spirit in a person or community (Gal. 5:22-23). We usually give priority to the virtue of love.
- *Inner authority and peace.* One indication of the work of the Spirit is a deep sense of peace and calm certainty about the prompting of the Spirit. Such inner authority is distinct from dogmatism because it is humble, serene, and open to correction.
- *Communal harmony.* The Spirit works toward reconciliation and harmony among people. The presence of this harmony is an indication of the Spirit's presence (John 17:23; Acts 4:32; 1 Cor. 3:1-3; Eph. 4:3). Again, however, there is no easy rule. Sometimes the Spirit's prophetic work is divisive rather than unitive, at least for a time, as

To recap the discussion earlier in this chapter of how to foster spiritual openness, it requires that people perceive the church to be a safe place. As a first step, we seek to remove all forms of spiritual and physical abuse and to diminish the grip of racial prejudice. A further step is to ground people in a clear process of discernment. With discernment comes a sense of spiritual safety, as people through practice "have their senses trained to distinguish between good and evil" (Heb. 5:14 NASB). With the security that comes from discernment, we are more able to open our hearts to God.

The Christian community is uniquely qualified to offer discernment for its members. A perennial problem in seeking the best route forward is that when it leads us to protest injustice. Also, there are forms of super-ficial placidness that entail a "tyranny of the majority," violating true harmony.

- *Enhancement rather than extinction of life.* The Spirit is a Spirit of life and wholeness and health. Experiences and promptings of the Spirit should contribute to wholeness, personal empowerment, heightened selfhood, and positive relationships. Insights that disempower, diminish creativity, fragment persons, or contribute to relational dysfunction are suspect.

- *Integrity in the process of discernment.* A final indication that an experi-ence or prompting is of the Spirit is the degree to which the person or community has engaged in a discernment process with integrity. To be sure, the Spirit blows where it will, and even the most diligent dis-cernment does not yield any guarantee of the Spirit's presence. Never-theless, a person's or a community's action is more suspect to the extent that it ignores or violates dimensions of the practice of discernment. When a group or individual has refused to consider various alternatives, failed to heed advice, avoided issues of faith, and suppressed deep emo-tions, then their decision is suspect.

None of these criteria is absolute; each of them is open to distortion and exception. In the end, spiritual discernment depends on faith. We do our best within the forms we have, but we ever depend on the mysterious emergence of the Spirit, who resonates and persuades and, always, comes as a gift.[a]

a. Adapted from Frank Rogers Jr., "Discernment," in *Practicing Our Faith: A Way of Life for a Searching People*, ed. Dorothy C. Bass, 2nd ed. (Hoboken, NJ: Wiley & Sons, 2010), 114–16. Reprinted with permission of Wiley & Sons, Inc.

people do not see the big picture. Church leaders can help those seeking guidance to remember the core teachings of Scripture that are relevant to the situation and can help guard against having fear or peer pressure dominate the decision-making process.

Helping People Live Well with their Homesickness

It was the Unicorn who summed up what everyone was feeling. He stamped his right fore-hoof on the ground and then cried: "I have come home at last! This is my real country! I belong here. This is the land I have been looking for all my life, though I never knew it till now. The reason why we loved old Narnia is that it sometimes looked a little like this. Bree-hee-hee! Come further up, come further in."

C. S. Lewis[26]

There have been times when I think we do not desire heaven but more often I find myself wondering whether, in our heart of hearts, we have ever desired anything else.

C. S. Lewis[27]

You stir man to take pleasure in praising you, because you have made us for yourself, and our heart is restless until it rests in you.

Augustine of Hippo[28]

If we are centered in ourselves, we experience the strangeness and restlessness of the homeless spirit that yearns for God. Even if we are centered in God, we groan at the brokenness of creation and yearn for redemption. That is why we see everywhere the use of the metaphors of pilgrimage and sojourn to describe human life.

Carol Lakey Hess[29]

We are born homesick—longing for a land and a way of life we have never directly experienced but which we know is somewhere, or at least ought to exist. We live in a lifelong culture shock. God designed us to live in a perfect environment—free of disease, with affirming, open, and caring relationships, meaningful work, and an ideal face-to-face relationship with God. But as a result of sin, we live in a less than perfect world, and we find ourselves aliens, never entirely at home. We are somewhat like a piece of highly sophisticated electronic equipment designed to operate in a temperature- and humidity-controlled environment because its use in anything other than that proper atmosphere means it is subject to ongoing maintenance problems. We are searching for that perfect environment that will free us from our maintenance issues. We are like émigrés who have settled in a new land and raised a family but still yearn to return to the homeland forever closed to them. The apostle Paul describes this unsettledness forcefully when he says that it is as if all of us have been "groaning in labor pains" (Rom. 8:22).

26. *The Last Battle* (New York: Collier Books, 1970), 162.
27. *The Problem of Pain* (New York: Macmillan, 1962), 145.
28. *Confessions*, trans. Henry Chadwick (New York: Oxford University Press, 1991), 3.
29. "Educating in the Spirit" (PhD diss., Princeton Theological Seminary, 1990), 214–15.

Exiled from Eden

God designed humankind to live in the garden of Eden. This garden is the Bible's picture of how God intended people to live. The Bible describes Eden with evocative language. It images God's provision in the rivers that water the land, the lush vegetation, the animals, the garden's beauty, and the companionship of another human being. It is also called "the garden of God" (Ezek. 31:8–9), and we are told that God walked in the garden and communed with Adam and Eve (Gen. 3:8). While there was work to do in the garden, it was not toilsome. Life in the garden was not one of unchanging ease but a time of creativity and work that used all of one's strength and imagination, and all this took place in an unspoiled land marked by beauty and true companionship. Beauty, symmetry, and simplicity marked life in the garden.

All this was lost after the fall. When sin entered the garden, the human experience changed forever. Upon eating the forbidden fruit, Adam's and Eve's "eyes were opened, and they suddenly felt shame at their nakedness" (Gen. 3:7 NLT) and were fearful when they heard God walking in the garden (3:8). "The impulse to cover themselves and to hide from God embodies the essential change that has occurred, encompassing shame, self-consciousness, and the experience of loss and the awareness of separation from God."[30]

Part of our yearning for Eden is the desire for a whole and open relationship in which we are fully known and understood. When things are set right at the end of this age, we will stand before God and, for the first time, be fully known by someone and yet not afraid because "perfect love expels all fear" (1 John 4:18 NLT). When another person learns something about our deepest thoughts and fears, they hold a certain power over us. We are very careful about whom we open up to, for fear that we might be rejected when our true selves are revealed. So imagine standing before God, being fully known and yet feeling more completely loved than ever before. When Eden is restored, when we go home to heaven, the children of God will experience the reality of being fully known and having no fear. Only then will we have a deep sense of finally being home and fully understood. This sense of being deeply known is conveyed in an image from the book of Revelation. Jesus encourages those who remain faithful in Smyrna by telling them, "I will give to each one a white stone, and on the stone will be engraved a new name that no one knows except the one who receives it" (Rev. 2:17 NLT). George MacDonald used this verse as a basis for a meditation

---

30. Leland Ryken, James C. Wilhoit, and Tremper Longman, *Dictionary of Biblical Imagery* (Downers Grove, IL: IVP Academic, 1998), 263.

The Cry of the Soul

Emotions are the language of the soul. They tell us if we are moving toward God or away from him. Emotions are like messengers from the front lines of the battle zone. Our tendency is to kill the messenger.

Our emotional struggles reflect far more than our battle with people and events; they reveal our deepest questions about God. Anger asks: Is God just, or will he let the wicked win? Will God protect me? Fear asks: Can I trust God to protect me from harm? Jealousy asks: Is God good, or will he leave me empty and bless others? Despair asks: Will God leave me isolated and alone? Contempt asks: Does God love me, or will he turn away in disgust? Shame asks: Does God love me, or will he hate me if he sees me as I really am?

God's mysterious method of persuasion is the path of pain. Affliction opens the heart to a change in direction. Doubt, confusion, even radical struggle are required before we are inclined to surrender to his goodness. Surrender is not possible without a fight. Although we should not glorify the struggle, it is apparently provoked by God and is therefore part of the process of transformation.[a]

a. Adapted from Dan B. Allender and Tremper Longman III, *The Cry of the Soul: How Our Emotions Reveal Our Deepest Questions about God* (Colorado Springs: NavPress, 1994). Used by permission.

in which he pondered the wonder of being known by God and having that deep knowledge coalesced into a worthy name. "The true name is one which expresses the character, the nature, the being, the *meaning* of the person who bears it. It is the man's own symbol—his soul's picture, in a word—the sign which belongs to him and to no one else. Who can give a man this, his own name? God alone. For no one but God sees what the man is, or even, seeing what he is, could express in a name-word the sum and harmony of what he sees."[31]

An essential discovery in the spiritual life is the recognition that life, this side of Eden, is difficult, that it never measures up to our expectations, and that our attempts to fix this disquiet simply do not work. Until we come to this recognition, we will live under the illusion that our restlessness is situational. Our natural inclination is to blame our spiritual ennui on the stresses and deprivation of the moment. It takes courage and grace to see it for what

31. George MacDonald, *Unspoken Sermons: First Series* (London: Longmans, Green, 1897), 106.

it is: a chronic ache at the core of our being. If we do not see the longing as a given, we will tend to treat it with the if-only cure. This strategy assumes that our spiritual restlessness can be satisfied by a change of circumstances: "If only I had a new job." "If only I had her as a friend." "If only I found the right church." The list of if-onlys is limitless, and, sadly, many Christians have lists as long as those of their secular neighbors, but their lists are "spiritual."

We Are Thirsty and Broken

Brokenness eliminates the need for a self-preserving agenda.

Julie A. Gorman[32]

Brokenness forces us to find a source of love outside ourselves. That source is God.

Jerry Sittser[33]

A biblical image for the restless homesickness of Eden is thirst: a persistent, life-directing soul thirst. The Bible sees humans as thirsty people who will do almost anything to satiate this need. Everyone is thirsty for God, but not all learn to declare, "My soul thirsts for you; my whole body longs for you in this parched and weary land where there is no water" (Ps. 63:1 NLT). The story told over and over in the Bible is of those who seek to satiate their thirst in their own way (through power, idolatry, pleasure, money). Yet for those who take their thirst to God, Jesus gave a promise: "Blessed are those who hunger and thirst for righteousness, for they will be filled" (Matt. 5:6). The Bible openly acknowledges thirst and unsettledness and invites everyone: "Come, all you who are thirsty, come to the waters; and you who have no money, come, buy and eat! Come, buy wine and milk without money and without cost. Why spend money on what is not bread, and your labor on what does not satisfy? Listen, listen to me, and eat what is good, and your soul will delight in the richest of fare" (Isa. 55:1–2 NIV).

God invites the thirsty: "Come, all you who are thirsty, come to the waters." The language of the invitation is lovely. In a single verse, God invites us four times to "come." The invitation is not given to a select few but is extended to "all" who thirst, and that is everyone. It is a remarkable invitation; it acknowledges our need and yet preserves our dignity. We are invited to come

32. *Community That Is Christian*, 2nd ed. (Grand Rapids: Baker Books, 2002), 198.
33. *A Grace Disguised: How the Soul Grows through Loss* (Grand Rapids: Zondervan, 2004), 185.

and buy. It is an image of the marketplace, where goods are procured not by groveling or begging but by the exchange of money. But here is the irony: we are invited to "buy wine and milk without money and without cost." God acknowledges our thirst and invites us to come to a market where we can receive the water, milk, wine, and bread we need, and yet the money of exchange is not our own but a currency of his grace. Isaiah 55:2 addresses the foolishness of denying our thirst or trying to satisfy it ourselves. Isaiah simply asks why people waste their money on food that does not satisfy them. The implied answer is "For no good reason."

The prophet Jeremiah used a compelling image drawn from everyday life in ancient Israel to make a similar point. A major challenge of living in the land of Israel is the struggle for good sources of water. In Jeremiah's day, water was available from several sources: streams, wells, and cisterns. Streams were commonly referred to as "living water" because of their movement and good quality; people considered them the best water source a village could have because they were easy to draw from and were fresh. Wells were difficult to dig, and it required a great deal of labor to shore up the walls and maintain the equipment for getting the water out. Drawing from a well involved lowering a bucket and bringing the water up. Though well water was of varying quality, people considered it to be far better than water from cisterns.

Cisterns were plastered holding tanks for rainwater and were the least desirable source of community water. The ancient equivalent of a rain barrel was easy to construct and could supplement a household's water needs, but cisterns had real limitations. They could crack, and the water could become stale and contaminated. With these sources of water in mind, consider Jeremiah's indictment: "For my people have done two evil things: They have abandoned me—the fountain of living water. And they have dug for themselves cracked cisterns that can hold no water at all!" (Jer. 2:13 NLT).

That is how God understands our failure to take our thirst to him. We are like a village that says, "Let's not use the stream for a source of water, but let's go out and dig cisterns in the sand (does sand hold water?) and rely on them instead." This would never happen. However, to enter the marketplace of grace and to buy the bread, water, wine, and milk without cost, we need to acknowledge that we cannot provide these necessities on our own. We must admit that we often operate out of the conviction that we know how to meet our needs far better than God does. We must continually remind ourselves that obedience to God's plan may cost us convenience but never joy. Obedience amounts to accepting the gracious invitation of God to a more sensible way of living—the path of joy, the path of sanity.

Quenching Our Thirsts through Idolatry

Do you want to be made well?

> Jesus (John 5:6)

What do you want me to do for you?

> Jesus (Matt. 20:32)

Whenever we wanted comfort, confidence, consolation, or celebration, we turned to a substitute for God. Substitutes for God are actually idols.

> Victor Mihailoff[34]

The Scriptures consistently expose people as both thirsty and foolish. We long for the satisfaction we were built to enjoy, but we all move away from God to find it.

> Larry Crabb[35]

Our thirsts and our shortsighted strategies to relieve them reveal what Pascal saw as the great tension of the human condition: our grandeur as bearers of the divine image and our misery as sinners who inhabit a world racked by sin.[36] We are people with an eternal destiny who were designed to rule with God, and hence our longings reflect the majesty of the *imago Dei* and the genetically remembered joys of Eden. Yet in our foolishness we adopt self-defeating strategies for quenching our thirsts. New Testament writers count lusts—inordinate desires for things rooted in the world and not God—as major impediments to our lives with God. When Peter urges Christians "to abstain from fleshly lusts, which wage war against the soul" (1 Pet. 2:11 NASB), he is writing not about our homesickness but about those "original longings" that have become, through practice, so strongly linked to wrong objects. Classically, these deformed yearnings are referred to as our *passions*. Since we think we need the objects of our lusts (material goods, certain experiences, pleasant escapes) for life to be full, we may use whatever resources we can to get them, and hence, idolatry comes into play.

---

34. *Breaking the Chains of Addiction: How to Use Ancient Eastern Orthodox Spirituality to Free Our Minds and Bodies from All Addictions* (Salisbury, MA: Regina Orthodox Press, n.d.), 17.

35. "Longing for Eden and Sinning on the Way to Heaven," in *Christian Educator's Handbook on Spiritual Formation*, ed. Kenneth Gangel and James Wilhoit (Grand Rapids: Baker, 1997), 95.

36. John R. Cole, *Pascal: The Man and His Two Loves* (New York: New York University Press, 1995), 153.

Our soul-thirst is powerful, and it makes all of us idolaters. To be sure, not many of our contemporaries bow before actual pagan altars. Nevertheless, the Bible sees idolatry as a universal problem. To be alive is to be an idolater. One of the most basic questions in spiritual formation must be "What am I doing about my idols?" not "Do I have any idols?" This is not just a rhetorical overstatement. Consider Paul's appeals to early Christians: "Therefore treat the parts of your earthly body as dead to sexual immorality, impurity, passion, evil desire, and greed, which amounts to idolatry" (Col. 3:5 NASB). "For a greedy person is an idolater, worshiping the things of this world" (Eph. 5:5 NLT). The Bible makes it clear that our communities have a unique ability to keep us away from idolatry or to promote idolatry.

I have found that telling people of their idolatry, naming it clearly, is often welcome news to broken people. When I listen to the stories of distress by those caught in patterns of sinning, they often seem so perplexed by what could have brought them to the place of sin they now routinely experience. Many want to attribute it simply to "being weak and sinful" or to "patterns learned in childhood." I have come to realize that when we allow people to blame their sinning simply on "being weak and sinful," we can create spiritual victims rather than disciples. The word we need to hear is that all sin flows out of breaking the first two commandments, to have no other gods and to have no idol (Exod. 20:3–5). Why do I lie? At the level of my soul, it is because I think that something other than God is a quicker way to the happiness I crave. Why do I constantly defend myself and protect my reputation? I do this because I am insecure in my belief that God is for me, and I find a sterling reputation to be an idol I can lean on.

Christians often are unwilling to admit the allure of sin. I remember sitting with a young woman who was tormented by shame and guilt over her sexual adventures and relational dishonesty. She kept wondering aloud why she fell into these defeating patterns, which "are so dumb." She was shocked when I suggested that "sex works." It provided her a quick and tangible, gratifying interlude and gave a short-term answer to her longing for intimacy and being needed. We can begin to get some leverage in dealing with sin when we see that we do it for "positive reasons." We sin because our longings are so strong that at the operational level—not at the verbal level, where we confess "Jesus is Lord"—we feel that something in addition to Jesus is necessary for our happiness and well-being. We will never find the full freedom promised in the gospel if all we want from Jesus is relief.

Feeding on Ashes

Little children, keep yourselves from idols.

1 John 5:21

Man's nature, so to speak, is a perpetual **factory** of idols.

John Calvin[37]

Part of the amazing power of idols in our lives comes from their creation of a whole way of looking at the world. This is especially true in the context of community. We come to believe, at the level of our souls, that a certain new car, a certain new job, or our current flirtation will bring the happiness we need and deserve, happiness that God will probably fail to give us. All religions come with what sociologist Peter Berger calls a "plausibility structure,"[38] an overall explanation for how the world operates that is so pervasive it is almost invisible to us. When we exhort someone to "stop daydreaming and get realistic," we reveal that our plausibility structure has no room for their approach: it just does not make sense to us. What is particularly pernicious about idolatry is that it creates delusional structures that blind us to the fact that we are pursuing idols of our own—for example, career advancement above everything else. Look at how Isaiah describes the delusional effect of actual idolatry in speaking to a people mired in idolatry. The prophet describes idols: "Their eyes are closed, and they cannot see" (Isa. 44:18 NLT). He is aware of the power of the idol's plausibility structure when he asserts, "The person who made the idol never stops to reflect" (44:19 NLT). His summary of the idolater's condition is quite graphic: "The poor, deluded fool feeds on ashes" (44:20 NLT). Idolaters feed on ashes even though they think they are getting the best that is available. Yet God offers, "I would feed you with the finest of the wheat, and with honey from the rock I would satisfy you" (Ps. 81:16 NASB).

> The wood-carver measures a block of wood
>   and draws a pattern on it.
> He works with chisel and plane
>   and carves it into a human figure.
> He gives it human beauty
>   and puts it in a little shrine.

37. Calvin, *Institutes of the Christian Religion*, ed. John McNeill, trans. Ford Lewis Battles (Philadelphia: Westminster, 1960), 1:108.

38. Peter L. Berger, *The Sacred Canopy: Elements of a Sociological Theory of Religion* (Garden City, NY: Doubleday, 1967), 45, 46.

He cuts down cedars;
    he selects the cypress and the oak;
he plants the pine in the forest
    to be nourished by the rain.
Then he uses part of the wood to make a fire.
    With it he warms himself and bakes his bread.
Then—yes, it's true—he takes the rest of it
    and makes himself a god to worship!
He makes an idol
    and bows down in front of it!
He burns part of the tree to roast his meat
    and to keep himself warm.
    He says, "Ah, that fire feels good."
Then he takes what's left
    and makes his god: a carved idol!
He falls down in front of it,
    worshiping and praying to it.
"Rescue me!" he says.
    "You are my god!"

Such stupidity and ignorance!
    Their eyes are closed, and they cannot see.
    Their minds are shut, and they cannot think.
The person who made the idol never stops to reflect,
    "Why, it's just a block of wood!
I burned half of it for heat
    and used it to bake my bread and roast my meat.
How can the rest of it be a god?
    Should I bow down to worship a piece of wood?"
The poor, deluded fool feeds on ashes.
    He trusts something that can't help him at all.
Yet he cannot bring himself to ask,
    "Is this idol that I'm holding in my hand a lie?"

                Isaiah 44:13–20 NLT

Ashes are a biblical image for destruction and wastedness. Ashes are the result of battle and devastation, as seen in Jeremiah's picture of a "whole valley of the dead bodies and the ashes" (Jer. 31:40). The references to the destruction of Sodom and Gomorrah picture them as turned "to ashes" (2 Pet. 2:6 NIV). Ashes symbolize things that are weak, fleeting, and empty, as in "Your maxims are proverbs of ashes" (Job 13:12).[39] Feeding on idols symbol-

---

39. Ryken, Wilhoit, and Longman, *Dictionary of Biblical Imagery*, 50.

izes our settling for what is worthless or far less than what the Father has for us. The above passage from Isaiah 44 shows that when we settle for idols, our discernment becomes dulled, and we miss what should be obvious.

Spiritual formation must continually return to the truths of sin, cross, redemption, grace, and true holiness because the prevailing plausibility structures of our culture push us in the direction of idolatry and false gospels. American religion has a deep moralistic flavor, which gives us the impression that we can earn God's favor by doing good. Sociologist Christian Smith has identified the core religious outlook in the United States as Moralistic Therapeutic Deism; its core tenet, Smith says, is that "God wants people to be good, nice, and fair to each other."[40]

> Our soul-thirst is powerful, and it makes all of us idolaters. The Bible sees idolatry as a universal problem. Communities have a unique way of embodying a corporate pride that blinds us to forms of idolatry. Also, faith communities can challenge idolatrous practices like racism in ways an isolated Christian seldom will.

James Smith writes of God's love: "We did not earn it, we cannot lose it."[41] The message of God's love must be proclaimed over and over. Many Christians find themselves in Smith's position: "For years I related to God as if he sat in a swivel chair. When I did something bad, God would turn his back to me until I made amends when he would swivel back and accept me again. I kept God constantly on the move." We must reject the false dichotomy that would have us choose either proclaiming God's love or "getting serious about discipleship."

Acting as though what the Bible says of God's transforming love is true requires stepping out in faith. Sadly, few formation programs are done in faith and by faith. We often do them in the flesh, thinking we can orchestrate spiritual growth through our means. We are fundamentally fearful of trusting God for spiritual growth in the lives of those we minister to, as witnessed by our lack of emphasis on prayer for their growth compared with our striving after it.

Why Brokenness Is at the Heart of Community Formation

Understanding our pervasive brokenness is at the heart of true community formation. Unless we make brokenness a major focus, we will not catch the truth that "the church is not a museum for saints, but a hospital for sinners." A basic premise in medical care is that you will be honest in describing your

40. Christian Smith with Melinda Lundquist Denton, *Soul Searching: The Religious and Spiritual Lives of American Teenagers* (New York: Oxford University Press, 2005), 162.

41. James Bryan Smith, *Embracing the Love of God: The Path and Promise of Christian Life* (San Francisco: HarperSanFrancisco, 1995), 21.

symptoms to the examining physician; a basic tenet in spiritual care is that honesty before God precedes healing. However, a basic premise of American folk wisdom is "If it ain't broke, don't fix it."

Unless people see that they have a deep spiritual need that cannot be satisfied by simply trying harder, they will have little interest in spiritual formation. A culture of pretending and simply trying to look good short-circuits true formation, and that is the default discipleship map of many evangelical churches. To create a climate of formation, we must make clear to people how to use their brokenness—their contrition over self-protective strategies, over the brokenness of their hearts, over the pain of letting themselves down—and the deep longings of their souls so eloquently cataloged in the psalms to drive them to God in and through his community.

Unfortunately, the more time we spend around churches, the less we tend to see ourselves as sinners and the more we see ourselves as "people who are getting it together." The gospel promises profound transformation for those who follow Christ. However, there will always be places of sin and rebellion in our lives. I now am less inclined to think of charting our sanctification as it

Godly Sorrow: The Compunction That Brings Deep Change

Godly Sorrow	Worldly Sorrow
Broken/humbled/softened	Wounded/hardened/cynical
Synonyms: contrite, humble, softened, stripped of (some negative characteristic), broken in the right place	Synonyms: devastated, immobilized, crushed, hardened, nonfunctional, broken in the wrong place
Truly broken persons approach life with a humble spirit born from encountering the tragic with wisdom, appropriate acceptance, and deep reliance on God.	Wounded persons have a primary self-understanding of being wounded and hurt, with a hardening and bitter spirit marked by making excuses, defending themselves, and blaming others.
The godly response to a painful experience is trust that God supports and provides the strength needed.	The worldly response to a painful experience often is to escape the pain or to blame others for it.
The amount of pain experienced through brokenness depends on (1) the nature of the brokenness (jealousy, pride, greed, lustful thoughts, etc.), (2) how deeply it has become a part of one's life, and (3) how responsive one is to the discipline.	The spiritually hardened have adopted elaborate self-protective measures. The experience of "good pain," which teaches us about God and ourselves, is often missed.
The truly broken feast on truth and are aware of their limitations.	The wounded often dwell on darkness through worry, diseased introspection, self-hatred, and blaming others.

is often pictured (see fig. 5). While this kind of "straight-line thinking" does help us grasp the process of our sanctification, it does not take into account the dynamic nature of our relationship with God. Where does the dark night of the soul fit on this linear path? What about times of brokenness when we see new areas of sin in our lives?

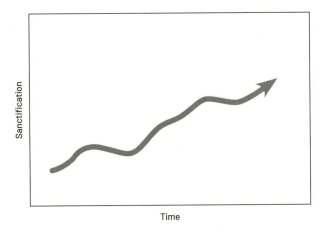

Figure 5. Progress in sanctification

Sin or Sickness

For many Christians, being a sinner is little more than a demographic fact—like height, sex, race, or hair color. When sin is described as a disease or malady rather than as a theological abstraction, people are more likely to understand. In a number of his writings, the psychologist J. Harold Ellens goes to some length to show the debilitating effects of sin:

> The metaphor of sickness contributes a dynamically constructive dimension to the notion of sin. It sets human disorder in the context of grace. It also holds up the seriousness of that disorder in a manner that cannot readily be rationalized into superficial notions of legalistic transgressions. Moreover, the metaphor of sickness invites a realistic remedy, a formula of cooperation with God who embraces us unconditionally. It moves toward the notion of redemptive growth and healing as a divinely ordered process for our lives in Christ. It frees us to see our redemptive possibilities as we mature through instruction and guidance, and grow from the pain of acknowledging the inevitable consequences of our orphaned condition and sinful behavior.
>
> A superficial concept of sin is too optimistic about the human condition and too pessimistic about the redeeming intent and function of God's grace.

God intends not merely judgment and forgiveness but the healing of our generic disease and craziness. He invites us to grow, not merely to shape up. The biblical concept of sickness can help us to appropriate these truths, making our concept of human sin and our understanding of God's grace more profoundly adequate to the healing of human failure.[42]

Ellens also suggests that when we view salvation solely in legal terms, we often miss the deeply healing and restorative dimensions of salvation. He contrasts two ways that people often think of salvation. One is judicial—and right, as far as it goes. The other is more holistic and sees the end of salvation not just as "taking the punishment" but as spiritual restoration and wholeness.

The Depth of Our Sin

Many unexpected events contribute to our growth in joyful obedience. So do our developed thought patterns. For example, insights into our depravity combined with a growing awareness of our capacity for wrongdoing can produce a proper view of sin. When we see the depth, persistence, and hideousness of our sin, we may develop sharp concerns about whether real transformation is possible. But seeing our sin for what it is need not lead to despair; it can lead to spiritual liberation. When we perceive the actual depth of our sin instead of merely being embarrassed over individual sins, we are prompted to seek the grace that can heal. On the other hand, when we respond to our sin problem by telling ourselves "I'm all right" or "I'm doing better; it's been a long time since I . . . " or "What can I expect? I'm so messed up," that is a sign that we are not open to significant transformation. It is our sin in a broad sense, not just our individual sins, that must be dealt with. Within us is a contradictory cauldron of self-destructive, egocentric, self-protective, sensual, control-seeking lusts that breed the sins we hate. It is right to attack sin from the outside by ceasing our destructive behaviors, but it is far more essential to work from the inside out (what Paul called our flesh [Gal. 5]) to reduce the pull that sin has on our lives. Paul observed that outward-oriented rules could result in prideful "will worship" (Col. 2:23 KJV).

When we regret our sins of omission (good things left undone) as keenly as our sins of commission (bad things done), we have begun to understand sin. And when we, like Daniel in his great prayer (Dan. 9), acknowledge that we have participated in the sins of our nation and grieve over these wrongs, we open one of the windows to real inner transformation. Furthermore, it is

42. Adapted from J. Harold Ellens, "Sin and Sickness: The Nature of Human Failure," in *Counseling and the Human Predicament: A Study of Sin, Guilt, and Forgiveness*, ed. LeRoy Aden and David G. Benner (Grand Rapids: Baker, 1989), 74–75.

often through our dealings with those we perceive as unlovely that we catch a glimpse of the sin that pulls us into self-centered and hurtful acts.

Our view of sin has immense implications for spiritual formation. Our view of sin can exist at a variety of levels: there will be a community understanding reflected in the worship and preaching of the church, a personal theological position (i.e., what you would say if asked about sin), and the personal lived reality (i.e., how you act and feel about the sin in your own life and the world). Place yourself on the continuum in figure 6 by indicating how you view sin. The left side of the continuum represents a view that emphasizes observable "bad things." If you tend to think about sin in your life in terms of lists of bad things you do or have done, you fall more on the left side of the continuum. The right end of the continuum emphasizes sin as an outflow of a bent will and sin-sick heart. For example, if you are as repulsed by the awareness that you are the kind of person who would seek to get ahead by lying as you are by the actual lie you told, you fall more on the right side of the continuum.

View of Sin

External (sins)   Internal orientation (sin)

Figure 6. Sins-sin continuum

The Depth of Our Yearnings

But there are many kinds of idols, and the most dangerous ones are not those we fashion with our hands, but those we unconsciously carry with us in our heads.

André Louf[43]

Indeed, if we consider the unblushing promises of reward and the staggering nature of the rewards promised in the Gospels, it would seem that Our Lord finds our desires not too strong, but too weak. We are half-hearted creatures, fooling about with drink and sex and ambition when infinite joy is offered us, like an ignorant child who wants to go on making mud pies in a slum because he cannot imagine what is meant by the offer of a holiday at the sea. We are far too easily pleased.

C. S. Lewis[44]

Our view of our yearnings also affects our spiritual lives. Do we, as a people, sense our longings as deep thirsts that only God can begin to satisfy? Or do we

43. *Tuning In to Grace: The Quest for God*, trans. John Vriend (Kalamazoo, MI: Cistercian Publications, 1992), 16.
44. *Weight of Glory* (New York: Macmillan, 1980), 3–4.

think these desires for completeness should have disappeared from the Christian or that we can satisfy them by our efforts? Now take a moment to place yourself on the continuum in figure 7. The left side describes the sense that spiritual longings persist, even for the maturing Christian—perhaps a longing for a world of justice, a desire to make a meaningful contribution, or a passion for intimacy and companionship. The position denoted by the right side sees our thirsts as being fully met or able to be met in the right circumstances. This perspective is quite optimistic about grace overcoming our inner disquiet. Here, the yearnings that persist are seen to be the result of compromised discipleship.

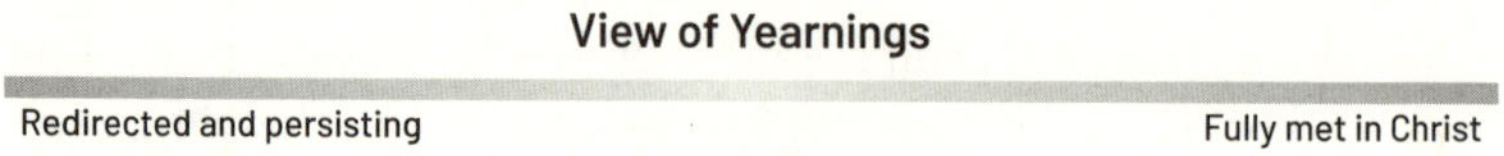

View of Yearnings

Redirected and persisting   Fully met in Christ

Figure 7. Yearnings continuum

We can combine figures 6 and 7 to form a 2 × 2 matrix (fig. 8). There are four basic ways to combine responses to questions about sin and yearnings. The matrix helps us visualize how our view of sin and our view of yearnings affect our basic approach to discipleship. Communities of faith set their foundations through their teaching and faith mentoring. It is a great gift when a community helps a believer live from a position of brokenness—but *optimistic* brokenness.

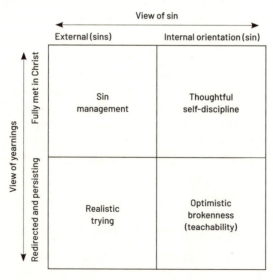

Figure 8. Sin and yearnings matrix

Sin Management

Here there is a focus on external sin and a perception that yearnings are met. Often a person in this category will be quick to tell you what they have done wrong. The focus is on sins of commission (sins of action) rather than sins of omission (sins of not doing). There is a strong tendency to believe that one can overcome these sins by just trying harder to stop doing them. There is also an embarrassment about the aches of the heart, a sense that they really should not be there. These aches seem to be evidence that a person is not living as faithfully as they should. This quadrant represents spiritual life that is marked by striving and denial. The Pharisees were adept sin managers, highly skilled in denying glaring omissions and heaping rules on the backs of others in a strategy of painstaking prevention of sins. This pervasive focus on sin management in evangelicalism was a prominent theme in Willard's analysis of the church's lack of commitment to spiritual formation. As he sums it up, "History has brought us to the point where the Christian message is thought to be essentially concerned only with how to deal with sin: with wrongdoing or wrong-being and its effects. Life, our actual existence, is not included in what is now presented as the heart of the Christian message, or it is included only marginally. That is where we find ourselves today."[45]

Thoughtful Self-Discipline

In this quadrant, sin is seen as heart orientation, but yearnings are unacknowledged. People in this category have come to see the inherent nature of their sin and are not optimistic about just willing it away. They recognize the need to change from the inside out. Often their sense of brokenness focuses more on their sin than on their yearnings. From their experience of aches and disappointments they see a need to take their sin seriously and know they have a problem they cannot fix on their own. They remain optimistic that on this side of heaven, their yearnings will vanish when their discipleship increases and the pervasive hold sin had on them decreases. There is a tendency in this orientation to build discipleship programs around "accountability," which is an important feature of Christian community life, but accountability alone does not lead to inner transformation. And as a friend observed, accountability tends to emphasize what can be observed and counted. We do well to remember the words of the Fox to the Little Prince: "Here's my secret. It is very simple: we see well only with the heart. The essential is invisible to the eyes."[46]

45. Dallas Willard, *The Divine Conspiracy: Rediscovering Our Hidden Life in God* (San Francisco: HarperSanFrancisco, 1998), 41.
46. Antoine de Saint-Exupéry, *The Little Prince* (n.p.: Classica Libris, 2019), chap. 21, Kindle Loc. 504.

Realistic Trying

This quadrant sums up the experience of people who focus on external sin and have a deep sense that their yearnings persist. At some level, their dreams have been shattered. They have come face to face with disappointments in life, and they realize that these are not anomalies but that life is hard—potentially filled with joy, but hard. A friend who was living at this place had the mantra "Life is hard, then you die; God is good." At the same time, the depth of these people's sin has not fully struck them. In this quadrant, there is an overwhelming sense, as marked by the "great disappointment," of a moment when they see that they are climbing a ladder that leans against the wrong wall. Many spiritual writers tell of the "great disappointment" (terminology varies) that often occurs in adulthood when persons come to see the tragic reality of brokenness in a new way. This often involves some level of awareness that our favorite projects are not all that we thought they were or that a relationship cannot bear all that we are demanding of it. Our response to this great disappointment can go two ways: it may be a blessed brokenness in which we turn to God, or we may turn toward cynicism and self-protectiveness. Here we sense the presence of the tragic more than the presence of an idolatrous heart bent away from God. Cynicism often marks people in this quadrant.

Optimistic Brokenness

The one who is here sees sin as a bent-heart condition and recognizes that thirsts persist. We are born homesick with restless hearts, and we live our lives as desire-ers, but the power of these desires is changed for those of us in Christ who now see our desires as evidence of our brokenness. This is the quadrant that is most open to true spiritual formation—marked by a teachable spirit. The fields have been plowed and prepared in the hearts of these Christians. There is a willingness to see sin as a grievous problem that we cannot simply will away and to recognize that on this side of heaven, where the tragic is present in life, we will always feel ill at ease. This orientation is labeled *optimistic brokenness* because of the deep optimism about the power of grace to set things right. In biblical language, optimistic brokenness is *hope*. We can trace much of the spiritual success in the Psalms to this view. Psalm 51 offers a compelling model of painful self-disclosure before God combined with relief and optimism that rise even as pride and self-protection diminish.

Optimism about our formation is the fruit of good doctrine. We Christians believe in a triune God who is the object of worship: Father, worthy of praise, delivering judgment and salvation with sovereign, loving wisdom; Son, visible exemplar of divine excellence, Savior of the world; Spirit, in whom we delight, Source of life abundant. We Christians believe in a good creation that was twisted by the fall and is being restored through Christ; our understanding of salvation is bookended by the positive. Christians have a reason for gratitude and hope. What this means concerning CSF is that as communities or as individuals, we gauge our expectations not by our own experiences of conflict or failure, not by a myopic focus on sin, Satan, or society but by the truth of Scripture. The truth is that we can change, as men and women have testified throughout Christian history.

Yet humans are fickle, and that hinders truth-based optimism. Psychologists have documented what has come to be termed the *negativity bias*: a conviction that in life, "bad is stronger than good."[47] We have probably all experienced a day that was ruined by a single negative event. As one writer aptly puts it, the brain seems designed to be "Velcro for bad experiences but Teflon for good ones."[48] Human beings are seemingly on the prowl for potentially threatening data more than for soothing data.[49] Natural selection would seem to have favored the hunter-gatherers who were more wary and skittish. And the negative data we find sticks with us more than the positive. This helps explain why people have found that part of the power of a gratitude journal comes from the daily reminders of the positive. Christians can mistakenly spiritualize this negativity basis, believing that their self-criticism and their brooding on past mistakes indicate they are taking their sin and brokenness seriously. Yes, our sinfulness is real, and "the heart is deceitful above all things" (Jer. 17:9 NIV), but we have reason to be optimistic because of our union with Christ and the work of grace that is working in us. Despite our negativity bias, we Christians must live with optimism because "he who began a good work in you will carry it on to completion until the day of Christ Jesus" (Phil. 1:6 NIV).

A generation ago, researchers described routinely quitting in the face of failure as "learned helplessness."[50] In their initial studies with animals, these researchers noted that when animals were exposed repeatedly to what seemed like a random and inescapable noxious stimulant, they soon learned not to bother to try to escape—even when a clear escape route was present. Depression, poor health choices, and a lack of resiliency are associated with learned

47. Roy F. Baumeister, Ellen Bratslavsky, Catrin Finkenauer, and Kathleen D. Vohs, "Bad Is Stronger Than Good," *Review of General Psychology* 5, no. 4 (2001): 323–70.

48. Rick Hanson, *Hardwiring Happiness: The New Brain Science of Contentment, Calm, and Confidence* (New York: Crown, 2013), 2.

49. John Gottman and Nan Silver, *Why Marriages Succeed or Fail: What You Can Learn from the Breakthrough Research to Make Your Marriage Last* (New York: Simon & Schuster, 1994).

50. Steven Maier and Martin Seligman, "Learned Helplessness at Fifty: Insights from Neuroscience," *Psychological Review* 123, no. 4 (July 2016): 349–67.

helplessness in humans. Similarly, through spiritual setbacks, inadequate discipleship, and exposure to an implicit theology of sin management (that the Christian life largely consists of managing and minimizing sin), one can fall into learned spiritual helplessness—when in fact the Spirit of Christ invites us into so much more.

Negativity bias and learned helplessness are not conducive to CSF. Perhaps 90 percent of our mental activity is essentially automatic, and some of this is the constant background of noisy negative ruminations.[51] Distracting thoughts, worries, and self-focused daydreams draw us away from the call to "walk by faith, not by sight" (2 Cor. 5:7 ESV). The desert writers remind us that it is not only the content of these thoughts that is the problem but also the way they can distract us from the life of prayer and virtue: like burrs, they attach themselves to other thoughts and quickly form a train of negative thinking.[52] Thus our approach to CSF must affirm—and reaffirm again and again—the hope in Christ that sees us through to ever-greater conformity with Christ. It is not enough simply to engage in the practice of spiritual disciplines. The practice must be accompanied by gratitude, hope, humility, curiosity, and wisdom, or it may become drudgery. Furthermore, in the journey of discipleship we are bound to lose our way or fall along the path sooner or later. We should respond to these hardships not by giving up the vision or lowering our expectations but rather by throwing off whatever may hinder our return to the race—which we should run with perseverance, fixing our eyes on Jesus, "the author and finisher of our faith" (Heb. 12:2 KJV). Willard places great emphasis on the need for a vision to guide people in their CSF: "The vision and the solid intention to obey Christ will naturally lead to seeking out and applying the means to the end."[53]

The upcoming sections will explore the nature of our yearnings and our brokenness. It is helpful to think of formation having two sides. One side is the formative work of teaching the Word, administering the sacraments,

---

51. Susan Nolen-Hoeksema, *Women Who Think Too Much: How to Break Free of Overthinking and Reclaim Your Life* (New York: Holt, 2003); Mark Williams and Danny Penman, *Mindfulness: An Eight-Week Plan for Finding Peace in a Frantic World* (Emmaus, PA: Rodale Books, 2011), 1–31. Negative self-attacking is explored from a Christian ministry perspective in Leanne Payne, *Restoring the Christian Soul: Overcoming Barriers to Completion in Christ through Healing Prayer* (Grand Rapids: Baker, 1996), 19–24.

52. Evagrius, *Talking Back: A Monastic Handbook for Combating Demons*, trans. David Brakke (Collegeville, MN: Liturgical Press, 2009), 26–30; Mary Margaret Funk, *Thoughts Matter: Discovering the Spiritual Journey* (Collegeville, MN: Liturgical Press, 2012), 7–8; Gabriel Bunge, *Despondency: The Spiritual Teaching of Evagrius Ponticus on Acedia* (Yonkers, NY: St. Vladimir's Seminary Press, 2012), 56–57.

53. Willard, *Renovation of the Heart*, 89. See also Richard J. Foster, *Celebration of Discipline: The Path to Spiritual Growth*, 3rd ed. (San Francisco: HarperSanFrancisco, 1998), 8.

and using the gifts of the people of God in grace-saturated ministries. The other side is fostering a receptive spirit on the part of God's people. Without a receptive spirit, born through brokenness, there is no openness to grace and typically little interest in true formation.

One confusing message that many people receive about brokenness is the sense that broken persons are welcomed at the front door of the church, but once you have entered, brokenness is no longer acceptable. The problem is that even if we escape the life that was increasing our spiritual disarray and we allow the body of Christ to enfold us, we still bring our memories, wounds, and baggage with us. The message that broken people need to hear is that we all struggle with issues from our pasts and that our characters are in formation. Jesus claimed that he came for the sick, not the healthy (Luke 5:31). With such a physician to help us, who would want to pretend to be well? The question of discipleship is not "Are you struggling?" but "What are you doing with these struggles?" "Where is God in the midst of these struggles?" "What plans are you making to grow into a more whole life in the face of these struggles?" We need to emphasize that the existence of struggle does not make us ineligible to be disciples.

Feeding on God's Grace

> We must be on our guard not to try to build up again what grace has broken down.
>
> André Louf[54]

> Grace is God's free gift, with repentance the way to access it.
>
> Philip Yancey[55]

> We must stop using the fact that we cannot *earn* grace (whether for justification or for sanctification) as an excuse for not energetically seeking to *receive* grace.
>
> Dallas Willard[56]

CSF requires that we actively and continually receive from God. We need to be extraordinary consumers of his grace; we need to receive his words of

54. *Tuning In to Grace*, 10.
55. *Rumors of Another World: What on Earth Are We Missing?* (Grand Rapids: Zondervan, 2003), 149.
56. "Spiritual Formation in Christ: A Perspective on What It Is and How It Might Be Done," *Journal of Psychology and Theology* 28, no. 4 (2000): 257.

love and correction, his forgiveness, his affirmation, his life, and the list goes on. Without receiving from God, there is no true formation.

Some years ago, I was reading Ole Hallesby's classic *Prayer*, which gave me a powerful image of what grace is for the Christian. Hallesby wrote his book in his native Norway during the early twentieth century, and it is steeped in a warm piety that shows his firsthand experience of prayer. He wrote it from the perspective of a caring pastor who knew his congregants well. To help readers understand prayer, Hallesby suggests a parallel with the early twentieth-century treatment for tuberculosis, before the arrival of modern miracle drugs.

Let us think of patients who are ill with tuberculosis. "The physician puts them out in the sunlight and fresh air, both in summer and in winter. There they lie until a cure is gradually effected by the rays of the sun. . . . The treatment is most successful if the patients lie very quietly and are passive, exerting neither their intellects nor their wills. It is the sun which effects the cure. All the patients need to do is to be in the sun." Prayer, Hallesby suggests, is just as simple:

> We are all saturated with the pernicious virus of sin; every one of us is a tubercular patient doomed to die! But "the sun of righteousness with healing in its wings has arisen" [Mal. 4:2]. All that is required of us, if we desire to be healed both for time and for eternity, is to let the Son of righteousness reach us, and then to abide in the sunlight of His righteousness.
>
> To pray is nothing more involved than to lie in the sunshine of His grace, to expose our distress of body and soul to those healing rays which can in a wonderful way counteract and render ineffective the bacteria of sin.[57]

Shortly after I read and pondered these words, my second daughter was born, and I was privileged to be given a vivid picture of sun-born healing. When we brought her home, she was jaundiced. This is a fairly common condition in newborn infants, the most observable symptom being a yellowing of the skin and the whites of the eyes brought about by too much bilirubin in the newborn's red blood cells because the tiny liver is not yet functioning at full capacity. Light helps break down the bilirubin into waste products that the kidneys can eliminate, and in severe cases, carefully controlled phototherapy under special lights is used. Our daughter had mild jaundice, so the doctor told us to use sunlight. We brought her home, placed her on a blanket spread out in front of a window, and let the sunlight effect the cure. In just a diaper, she lay on a blanket, and as she slept, the sunlight helped break down the toxins that her tiny liver was not able to process.

57. Ole Hallesby, *Prayer* (Minneapolis: Augsburg, 1994), 16–17.

What a picture of sun-born healing! Our daughter was completely passive before the cure. She was completely passive in the sunlight. We carried her there and moved her as the sunlight shifted and the day passed; the cure did not depend on her but on her being kept in the light. At the time, I juxtaposed the image of our dear one, sleeping essentially naked in the sun, with the image of a neighbor's child. A year and a half earlier while out for a walk, we had stopped to talk with parents who were out strolling with their firstborn daughter. It was a sunny but cool March day, and our neighbor's child was in a baby bunting with just a wee bit of her face showing and lying in a stroller covered by a canopy. Her parents explained that her physician had told them that she had jaundice and should be out in the sun! As I thought of her out-doors, but not in the sunlight, and looked at our newborn lying in the sun, I thought of my own life before God. I remembered Richard Foster's words: "How often we fashion cloaks of evasion—beam-proof shelters—in order to elude our Eternal Lover. But when we pray, God slowly and graciously reveals to us our evasive actions and sets us free from them."[58]

I stand in need of divine healing. Yet I realize that so often I come to God revealing only the tiniest patch of skin for his healing light. We need to seek cleansing and renewal. For me, the clothing that blocks the healing light of Jesus most often is my pride, seen in the form of denial. I deny that I need cleansing. I think I can take care of my problems by myself. Yet Isaiah reminds us that those who seek to heal themselves spiritually are unable to do so because they are "like the tossing sea that cannot keep still; its waters toss up mire and mud" (Isa. 57:20).

One of the tragic misunderstandings in our present religious milieu is the popular notion that grace is merely a description of God's kindness toward us. In thinking about grace, it seems that people often see it exclusively as having to do with justification, the gracious act of being declared righteous. While grace is God's free and unmerited favor, it is also his regenerating and strengthening power. There are over one hundred references to grace in the English New Testament, and fewer than 10 percent of these refer principally to justification. Grace has much to do with how we live. For too many people, grace is about how we are "saved," and work is about how we "grow." Yet the New Testament is clear that grace is God's merciful and restoring power as well. Chuck Miller led pastoral renewal retreats for years, and one of his opening exercises was to send pastors out for a time of reflection with the task of prayerfully examining a list he provided of all the New Testament references to grace. A common response from the pastors was that they had

---

58. Foster, *Celebration of Discipline*, 33.

never realized how much grace was directly relevant to our everyday lives and not just our regeneration.

The way of grace is a pathway of change. That path leads us to depths of character, integrity, joy, and true friendship with God. The truly good news of the gospel is that God wants us to be his friends and invites us to live in relationship with him. When we see the outstretched hand of God, our whole view of the spiritual life changes. Instead of seeing it as just something else to do for a God who is distant, we see it for what it is: an offer for us to spend time with the Savior, who draws near every day and in every moment. Receiving is more than avoiding the harmful; it is cultivating an openness to the spiritually helpful.

In Jesus's day, many people believed that spiritual danger came primarily from certain outward actions or events, but Jesus reminded them that we are most harmed by what comes from within. He said, "For out of the heart come evil thoughts, murder, adultery, sexual immorality, theft, false testimony, slander. These are what defile a person" (Matt. 15:19–20 NIV). We are also affected by the culture in which we live, which bombards us with subtle messages and false images that have a deadening effect on our spirits. The world seeks to "squeeze you into its own mould" (Rom. 12:2 Phillips). This slight but ever-so-effective pressure leaves our souls deformed and encrusted with the dust that blinds us to the ultimate reality of God. Remember that *grace* is also a verb, powerful and active, and not just a noun.

Community Spiritual Practices That Support Receiving

The life of the individual believer, his personal salvation, and personal Christian graces have their being, bloom, and fruitage in prayer.

E. M. Bounds[59]

Prayer is a way to express faith, a meditation about what one wants by reason of having faith.

C. Ellis Nelson[60]

Prayer is one of the most essential acts of receiving. In prayer, we have direct interaction with God and the opportunity to receive his care and grace. Naturally, we put ourselves in a posture of receiving. While we often think of prayer as primarily a personal spiritual discipline, the emphasis in the New

59. *The Complete Works of E. M. Bounds on Prayer* (Grand Rapids: Baker, 1990), 369.
60. *How Faith Matures*, 142.

Testament is on believers gathering to pray corporately (Acts 4:31; 8:15; 13:3; Eph. 6:18; James 5:14). A primary place where corporate prayer happens in the church is in our gatherings for worship. Here, through corporate prayers and times for quiet, reflective prayers, people have the opportunity to pray and see prayer modeled for them. There are many other venues in which prayer can be a corporate activity of the church. When the disciples asked Jesus to teach them to pray, the first word in his sample prayer was a corporate word—*Our Father*. Jesus invited them (and us) not only into communication with the Father but also into intimacy with the Father.

My personal prayer life has been dramatically enhanced by corporate experiences of prayer. My first sustained time of individual prayer was on a corporate prayer retreat, where we had prayed together as a group and then were given time to pray individually yet near one another. The forty-five minutes I spent alone in prayer were the longest amount of time I had ever prayed, and the experience initiated me into a pattern of extended personal times of prayer. Some of the ways churches can cultivate a receiving stance through prayer include the following:

Prayer meetings. Christians can gather spontaneously or on a planned basis to pray for the needs of the church, the world, specific missions, social concerns, or individual needs. These meetings allow Christians to be informed in their praying and to experience the solidarity that comes as people join together in prayer.

Prayer ministries. Much soul work occurs as people listen to sermons and worship God, and having a prayer team that can meet and pray with people following a service can be a valuable avenue of spiritual formation. Prayer teams can be part of an ongoing pastoral care program in a church.

Prayer retreats. Some of my most memorable times of corporate prayer occurred on half-day prayer retreats for church or a ministry. The focus of these gatherings should not be on teaching people to pray but on actually giving people an opportunity to experience solitude and prayer.

Special seasons of prayer. During times of transition or discernment in a church, the leadership may want to call the church to a season of twenty-four-hour prayer, with people coming to the church to pray through the issues at hand.

Prayer chains. Letting people know the prayer needs in a congregation begins to weave the priority of prayer into the fabric of the church. People learn that the first response to a crisis should be a call for prayer.

Prayer immersion. This involves having sessions with those who long to develop intimacy with God but have never been in a corporate setting that encouraged spontaneous prayer. Leaders can use the hymnody of the church to pray out loud and then expand on the lines of the hymns, giving folks a starting place. Martin Luther used the Lord's Prayer as a structure for long prayer times, going word by word or phrase by phrase, and speaking with God about the significance of the words in his life.

Opportunities for practicing prayer. Churches can provide simple exercises affirming God's willingness to hear people's everyday prayers as eloquent expressions of their hearts.

Benediction can be formalized at the end of a worship service and be little more than the clergy's closing remark. However, benediction is a powerful means of providing grace to other believers. It is intended to be *bene* (good) words, not merely words for closing the service. Benediction offers an important way in which Christians who are trained in spiritual disciplines and seek to live in God's grace can make it available to other people. God has entrusted his grace to us, as well as finances, talents, and creation, to steward: "Serve one another, as good stewards of God's varied grace" (1 Pet. 4:10 ESV). As stewards of his greatest resource, let us take on this stewardship with joy-filled seriousness. Teaching on the role of blessing, particularly aimed at parents, families, and leaders, is a crucial teaching in the church. It is also important to train people to place themselves in a stance to receive the true benediction that Jesus offers through the church as we gather for worship.

Intercession for the needs of others is one of the most loving things a Christian can do. The secret time in prayer is an act of charity. Indeed, one of the ways we "bear one another's burdens" (Gal. 6:2) is by specific prayer. We can encourage believers to foster genuine prayer for one another by offering simple instruction and resources on how to pray for those with various needs. Through intercessory prayer, both the one who prays and the one who is being prayed for can receive evidence of God's grace to them.

Jesus Invites Us to Repent and Draw Close to God and Jesus

Confession in the presence of a brother is the profoundest kind of humiliation. . . . Confession is discipleship. Life with Jesus Christ and his community has begun.

Dietrich Bonhoeffer[61]

61. *Life Together: The Classic Exploration of Faith in Community*, trans. John W. Doberstein (Harper & Row, 1954), 114–15.

Formation in Faith and through Faith

When I wrote *A Long Obedience* twenty years ago, I was a parish pastor writing for my parishioners, the people I knew best in the place I knew best. Two convictions under-girded my pastoral work. The first conviction was that everything in the Gospel is livable and that my pastoral task was to get it lived. It was not enough that I announce the Gospel, explain it or whip up enthusiasm for it. I want it lived—lived in detail, lived on the streets and on the job, lived in the bedrooms and kitchens, lived through cancer and divorce, lived with children and in marriage. The second conviction was that my primary pastoral work had to do with Scripture and prayer. I was neither capable nor competent to form Christ in another person, to shape a life of discipleship in man, woman or child. That is supernatural work, and I am not supernatural. Mine was the more modest work of Scripture and prayer—helping people listen to God speak to them from the Scriptures and then joining them in answering God as personally and honestly as we could in lives of prayer. This turned out to be slow work. From time to time, impatient with the slowness, I would try out ways of going about my work that promised quicker results. But after a while it always seemed to be more like meddling in these people's lives than helping them attend to God.

More often than not, I found myself getting in the way of what the Holy Spirit had been doing long before I arrived on the scene, so I would go back, feeling a bit chastised, to my proper work: Scripture and prayer; prayer and Scripture. But the *and* is misleading. Scripture and prayer are not two separate entities. My pastoral work was to fuse them into a single act: Scripture-prayer, or prayerScripture. It is this fusion of God speaking to us (Scripture) and our speaking to him (prayer) that the Holy Spirit uses to form the life of Christ in us.[a]

a. Eugene H. Peterson, *A Long Obedience in the Same Direction: Discipleship in an Instant Society* (Downers Grove, IL: InterVarsity, 2000), 201–2. Used by permission of InterVarsity Press.

Genuine repentance is brought about, ultimately, neither by the fear of consequences nor by the fear of rejection, but as a ministry of the Holy Spirit, who gives to us a deep conviction of the mercy of God.

Robert M. Norris[62]

62. Introduction to *Pursuing Holiness in the Lord*, by Jonathan Edwards, ed. T. M. Moore (Phillipsburg, NJ: P&R, 2005), 7.

The gospel is an invitation to an abundant life in the kingdom of God. The gospel is not merely the good news that begins the Christian life; it should also provide a pattern for our living. We must be gospel-centric people who recognize that "the Christian life is a process of renewing every dimension of our life—spiritual, psychological, corporate, social—by thinking, hoping, and living out the 'lines' or ramifications of the gospel."[63]

Confession should be an important part of church life. I have seen public confession made very appropriately as a result of church discipline when there was an offense grievous enough that it needed to be confessed and repented of before the body. In that moment of brokenness, Christians can gather in prayer and love in a spirit of restoration around the person who makes confession. I have also experienced, in times of revival and renewal, confessions before the body of Christ in which people told of how God was at work and what burdens were laid aside. The power of such confessions to further revival is remarkable and beautiful.

The open perspective of a receiving attitude models the life of Jesus, who lived in dependence on God: "I do as the Father has commanded me, so that the world may know that I love the Father," Jesus said (John 14:31). This stance of openness reflects humility on our part as we learn that "apart from me [Jesus] you can do nothing" (15:5). True Christianity is a charisma, a gift of the Spirit. We cannot build a community as one thinks of building a house or school. We can, however, foster a lifestyle of corporate receptivity, which is the rich, fertile soil out of which a graced community springs.

A thorough understanding of *receiving* is necessary to see *remembering*, *responding*, and *relating* in a grace-oriented manner. In our state of human brokenness and extreme need, the gospel brings grace to those who own their brokenness and seek repentance instead of building idols. Repentance includes a vision for a change brought by humbly acknowledging sin and devoting oneself to investing in a life shaped by Jesus's invitations to a life of flourishing. Jesus laid out a road map for those who could see that their idols were empty and who wanted to turn away to a different path. In the chapters that follow, we must remember the grace and vision received and then respond and relate to others with these things in mind. In receiving grace, we are enabled to remember who we are and to whom we belong, we are called to a response of service, and we find that the spiritual formation we are seeking happens best in and through the community.

63. Timothy J. Keller, "The Centrality of the Gospel," sermon on Gal. 2:6–14, Redeemer Presbyterian Church, 1359 Broadway, New York, November 2, 1997, www.redeemer2.com/re sources/papers/centrality.pdf.

The Role of Suffering

Through pain, we often develop a hunger for change.

Peter Scazzero[64]

We are often most spiritually open in times of suffering, and we especially need the body of Christ to keep us open to God and his grace. In times of suffering, we benefit significantly from the solidarity expressed by people praying for us and by the healing, restoration, and comfort made available through such prayers. When individual suffering comes, we can recognize the value of intentional solidarity already experienced in times of ease; from habit, we still sense a connection with the rest of the body of Christ. As we minister to others and as we receive the ministry of love and care by the body of Christ, we are put in a position that makes us more and more receptive. In times of war, natural disaster, and persecution, the church suffers together and witnesses to a watching world by showing the reality of Christ's love.

When I finished my initial research for this book and reviewed the tales of grace I had listened to, I was tempted to say that community spiritual formation could be boiled down to "helping people suffer well." This response would beg the question of how we can do that, which is part of the intent of this book. Pastoral care plays a vital role in helping people grow during times of loss and affliction. In recent years, many churches' resources have shifted to "enhancing the Sunday morning experience"; in that shift away from pastoral care, CSF was diminished. I have written about openheartedness and CSF; clearly, suffering and loss can be a catalyst of great spiritual openness. We need pastoral care to help people process their loss and suffering well.

We are to grow in grace: "Grow in the grace and knowledge of our Lord and Savior Jesus Christ" (2 Pet. 3:18). We are to be "rooted and grounded in love" (Eph. 3:17). We are to be "rooted and built up in him" (Col. 2:7). Peter's prayer should be ours: "May grace and peace be yours in abundance" (2 Pet. 1:2). Grace is essential to our growth, and we must cultivate a humble dependence on grace in ourselves and those to whom we minister. We may rely on the promise that "God is able to bless you abundantly, so that in all things at all times, having all that you need, you will abound in every good work" (2 Cor. 9:8 NIV). Because reliance on God's grace generated evidence in the lives of the Corinthians, Paul gratefully wrote, "I always thank my God for you because of his grace given you in Christ Jesus. For in him you have been enriched in every way—with all kinds of speech and with all knowledge—God

64. *Emotionally Healthy Church*, 74.

thus confirming our testimony about Christ among you" (1 Cor. 1:4–6 NIV). A curriculum for Christlikeness, which confirms Jesus Christ as Lord and Savior, must lead us to see our brokenness and wretchedness and teach us where and how to receive the sustaining grace that God freely offers.

For Further Reading

Allen, Diogenes. *Spiritual Theology: The Theology of Yesterday for Spiritual Help Today*. Cambridge, MA: Cowley, 1997. A comprehensive spiritual theology grounded in historical sources.

Allender, Dan B., and Tremper Longman III. *The Cry of the Soul: How Our Emotions Reveal Our Deepest Questions about God*. Colorado Springs: NavPress, 1994. A book in which the authors use the Psalms to intently study anger, fear, envy, jealousy, abandonment, despair, contempt, and shame in order to better understand the heart of a person, the heart of God, and their relationship.

Augustine. *The Confessions*. Translated by Maria Boulding. Vintage Spiritual Classics. New York: Vintage Books, 1998. The first and most influential Christian spiritual autobiography, told with an eye on the longings of the heart and a celebration of grace poured out on the repentant.

Banks, Robert J. *Paul's Idea of Community*. Rev. ed. Peabody, MA: Hendrickson, 1994. A clearly written examination of what the author sees as Paul's unique contribution to the Christian community.

Hausherr, Irénée. *Penthos: The Doctrine of Compunction in the Christian East*. Cistercian Studies Series 53. Kalamazoo, MI: Cistercian Publications, 1982. A classic study of the role of brokenness (compunction) in the Eastern church.

Muto, Susan, and Adrian Van Kaam. *Commitment: Key to Christian Maturity*. Pittsburgh: Epiphany Association, 2002. A book that explores in depth what it means to experience commitment in the threefold path of spiritual deepening: listening, liberation, and love.

Smith, James Bryan. *Embracing the Love of God: The Path and Promise of Christian Life*. San Francisco: HarperSanFrancisco, 1995. A brief yet immensely practical guide to opening oneself to the love of God.

FOUR

Remembering

Remembering What God Sings over You

After that generation died, another generation grew up who did not acknowledge the LORD or remember the mighty things he had done for Israel.

Judges 2:10 NLT

Remember that you were a slave in Egypt, and diligently observe these
statutes.

Deuteronomy 16:12

> Remember this and consider,
>   recall it to mind, you transgressors,
>   remember the former things of old;
> for I am God, and there is no other;
>   I am God, and there is no one like me.

Isaiah 46:8–9

Men more frequently require to be reminded than informed.

Samuel Johnson[1]

---

1. "The Rambler. Numb. 2. Saturday, March 24, 1749–50," in *The Works of Samuel Johnson* (London: Nichols and Son, 1816), 4:13.

> Spiritual remembering . . . involves gratefully recalling the past moments of
> epiphany or dramatic awakening in life so that we can muster the courage and
> perspective to continue seeking God and God's will.
>
> Robert Wicks[2]

> The church is always more than a school, but the church cannot be less than
> a school.
>
> Jaroslav Pelikan[3]

What are we to remember? We are to remember who we are (God's beloved
children), how we came to this place/position through Christ, whose we are
(I belong not to myself but to my faithful Savior Jesus Christ), what God
intends for our lives, where wisdom for living is found (in Scripture, "which
[is] able to give you the wisdom that leads to salvation" [2 Tim. 3:15 NASB]),
and the joyful responsibilities of life in Christ's kingdom.

How do we do this? We do this as we hear people testify to the work of
God in their lives and notice God's work in our life too. We do this as we
read and hear the stories of God's faithfulness to his people throughout the
centuries. We do this as we learn of God and his wisdom for us. We do this
as we remember our baptism and its meaning. And we do this as we learn
spiritual practices that keep our minds focused on God.

What stance does this require? It requires humility and a willingness to learn.

Where does remembering occur? Though there are particular benefits to
remembering in solitude and others to remembering in solidarity, we seek to
practice both, knowing that we are individual members of a body. Both personal history and corporate memory can inform our remembering. We reflect
alone so that we might serve by sharing our reflections with others; they, in
turn, share their reflections and inform further times of solitude.

When we speak of remembering in CSF, we have in mind more than nostalgia.
It is a call to live in light of a spiritual reality whose grip on us can fade over
time. Consider the Bible's call to remembrance:

Remember the sabbath day, and keep it holy. (Exod. 20:8)

Remember this day on which you came out of Egypt, out of the house of
   slavery. (13:3)

---

2. *Everyday Simplicity: A Practical Guide to Spiritual Growth* (Notre Dame, IN: Sorin
Books, 2000), 55.
3. *The Christian Tradition: A History of the Development of Doctrine* (Chicago: University
of Chicago Press, 1971), 1.

Remember that you were a slave in the land of Egypt, and the LORD your God brought you out from there with a mighty hand and an outstretched arm; therefore the LORD your God commanded you to keep the sabbath day. (Deut. 5:15)

Remember his covenant forever, the word that he commanded. (1 Chron. 16:15)

Remember the former things of old; for I am God, and there is no other. (Isa. 46:9)

Remember Lot's wife. (Luke 17:32)

Remember that you were at that time without Christ, . . . having no hope and without God in the world. (Eph. 2:12)

Remember Jesus Christ, raised from the dead, a descendant of David—that is my gospel. (2 Tim. 2:8)

Remembering who we are and whose we are should be an important activity in our lives. Forgetting our core identity as beloved children of God, the value of the guidance of the Bible, and the value of Christian community is a constant problem in our experience of discipleship. Eugene Peterson wryly observed, from his pastoral ministry, that "most of the people that we deal with most of the time are dominated by a sense of self, not a sense of God."[4] David learned to "keep the LORD always before [him]" (Ps. 16:8) and that constant remembering needs to be built into our lives, individual and corporate. We remember by calling to mind what has happened to us but also by learning in new and more significant ways of God's work in the world and the reality of his mission in and through his church.

One of the chief goals of Hebrew education was to make sure the people would never forget and would, therefore, always fear God and obey his commandments. In Hebrew thought, the chief spiritual malady was forgetfulness. Thus one of the chief ends of education was the remembrance of the mighty acts that God had performed on behalf of his people. We are indeed forgetful pilgrims, and we need to be reminded of the good things that God has done in our lives, in the lives of our brothers and sisters in Christ, and in salvation history. In an age in which we are bombarded with information and everything seems to be recorded, we can just as easily forget to remember. Accordingly, in our teaching, we must take time for testimony, reflection, and remembrance. We remember best when concrete examples of what God has

4. Eugene H. Peterson, *Working the Angles: The Shape of Pastoral Integrity* (Grand Rapids: Eerdmans, 1987), 11.

done are brought to mind. Stories of God's work in individual lives reveal the personal nature of the interaction between God and a person or group. They remind us that our gracious God is a person to whom we can respond and with whom we can relate.

In this chapter, I suggest two complementary ways of helping us remember: (1) guarding our hearts from thoughts and dispositions that pull us away from God and (2) grounding ourselves in the reality of the gospel and its invitation to a life of flourishing.

Remembering to Listen to God Sing over Us

> The LORD, your God, is in your midst,
> a mighty one who will save;
> he will rejoice over you with gladness;
> he will quiet you by his love;
> he will exult over you with loud singing.
>
> Zephaniah 3:17 ESV

There is a song that is being sung for you; right now, God is singing over you and wooing you. It is a song that beckons you to realize that you are the beloved. God beams with delight in you, and my earnest hope is that you can hear these words as they are sung over you. And not only hear them but also live with a deep sense that God cherishes you. This song, sung with fierce tenderness, comes with the invitation to rest in his love as the beloved.

Indeed, "the Holy One of Israel" (Isa. 1:4 NIV) "who lives in unapproachable light, whom no one has seen or can see" (1 Tim 6:16 NIV) and "who is worthy of eternal praise" (Rom. 1:25 NLT), this Holy God—"the LORD is robed in majesty and armed with strength; indeed, the world is established, firm and secure" (Ps. 93:1 NIV)—has chosen to enter into a relationship with his creation and invites us to live in friendship with him. "Now we can rejoice in our wonderful new relationship with God because our Lord Jesus Christ has made us friends of God" (Rom. 5:11 NLT). The holiness and splendor of God, which assure us that he can and will keep the relational commitments and promises he makes with us, are also coupled with a great tenderness and compassionate care. We see both the power and the tenderness of God in the exodus, when "the LORD brought us out of Egypt with a mighty hand and an outstretched arm, with great terror and with signs and wonders" (Deut. 26:8 NIV), and when he says, "I led them with cords of human kindness, with ties of love. To them I was like one who lifts a little child to the cheek, and I bent down to feed them" (Hosea 11:4 NIV).

Living with a certain sense of being the beloved changes everything. When we live as the beloved, our sense of worth is not built on fragile comparisons with others or grounded in affirmations from others. Resting and living in our belovedness give us a place to stand and allow us to be vulnerable and to open our hearts to God. God does not just sing this song from above us, as it were, but from our very hearts. Augustine writes, "God is closer to us than we are to ourselves."[5] These are comforting words because we experience so much of life as divided beings. We want one thing, yet we choose another; we yearn to be with those we love, but we become caught up in activities that pull us away. At times, we feel disconnected from our very center. That is why Augustine's reminder that "God is closer" is such a balm. Our beckoning, singing God is closer to us than we are to ourselves. This is the message of the apostle Paul, who tells us what is at the heart of his preaching: "And the secret is simply this: Christ in you! Yes, Christ in you bringing with him the hope of all glorious things to come" (Col. 1:27 Phillips). Moses knew this reality of God-at-hand. He had seen the power of God in delivering his people from slavery, and he knew of God's intimacy: "What other great nation has gods that are intimate with them the way GOD, our God, is with us, always ready to listen to us?" (Deut. 4:7 Message). Having God-at-hand is not necessarily good news; a crabby roommate is close at hand but hardly good news. But a God of compassion, grace, and love, who is for you, is close at hand, and in fact, through the reconciliation work of the cross, we are united to him.

In our day-in-and-day-out lives, we are more likely to dwell on a single negative comment than on the breathtaking beauty of the sunset we savored on our commute home. This is also true in our lives with God. This is not to suggest that our brains are full of bad data about God—there isn't any. But we are more alert to threatening data; our ears prick up to the news of a newly found cause of cancer or a threat to our job. We need to hear God's love song, but our brains are more adept at remembering threats and insults. So our work at basking in God's love is an uphill battle.

As you know, the God-close-at-hand is not the whole story, because many generations ago there was a betrayal of this love that has affected all of us, making it hard for us to hear God's tender song. We have become fearful and skittish creatures. Oh, that these words of his love might touch every corner of your being and reverberate through your soul, working their divine healing. Yet in our brokenness, we are seemingly deaf to this song—we are more attuned to those things that feed our fears.

5. Author's paraphrase of Augustine, *Confessions*, trans. Vernon Bourk, Fathers of the Church (Baltimore: Catholic University of America Press, 1953), 21:59–60.

Do you know what the most frequent command in the Bible turns out to be? What instruction, what order, is given, again and again, by God, by angels, by Jesus, by prophets and apostles? What do you think—"Be good"? "Be holy, for I am holy"? Or, negatively, "Don't sin"? "Don't be immoral"? No. The most frequent command in the Bible is: "Don't be afraid." Don't be afraid. Fear not. Don't be afraid.

The irony of this surprising command is that, though it's what we all really want to hear, we have as much difficulty, if not more, in obeying this command as any other. We all cherish fear so closely that we find we can't shed it even when we're told to do so.[6]

We live in a world with real and imagined threats, and we may smile at the perspective of Mark Twain: "I am an old man and have known a great many troubles, but most of them have never happened."[7] We do know that "man that is born of a woman is of few days and full of trouble" (Job 14:1 KJV). In this age of anxiety, we naturally seek to avoid threats and prudently become self-protective, but the stance of self-protection makes it hard to open one's heart. So we find that fear and love work against each other. As P. D. James observed, "Perfect love may cast out fear, but fear is remarkably potent in casting out love."[8] N. T. Wright concludes his comments on fear by reminding us, "Let's make no mistake about it: until you learn to live without fear, you won't find it easy to follow Jesus."[9]

We face the world either with our hearts open and a stance of love or bound in self-protection and with our hearts closed by fear. We open our hearts through surrender to God and trust in his goodness and care. As Jean-Pierre de Caussade urges us, "Tell everyone who loves God about self-abandonment. . . . He wishes only that they desire to be united with him so that he can guide, direct and befriend them."[10] We open our hearts through cultivating trust, surrender, and vulnerability to God.

We so often cannot hear the words that bring the life and healing we yearn for. Yet the invitation to listen to the song and live as the beloved is real. Jesus's central teaching was about the reality of God's loving and powerful presence among us. The message of God's availability was so welcomed by those who heard it that they simply called it "the Good News." And what good news it

6. N. T. Wright, *Following Jesus* (Grand Rapids: Eerdmans, 2009), 66.
7. Widely attributed to Mark Twain, but attribution is uncertain. It was first published in the early twentieth century as an isolated quotation.
8. P. D. James, *Time to Be in Earnest* (London: Faber & Faber, 2011), 81.
9. Wright, *Following Jesus*, 67.
10. Jean-Pierre de Caussade, *Abandonment to Divine Providence*, trans. John Beevers (Garden City, NY: Image Books, 1975), 63.

is. God not only sings but also invites us to be healed so we can hear and heed this song of tender love. A principle this suggests for CSF is that we need to encourage Christians to avoid consumption of media that heightens anxiety and fear. Christians should be informed, but we need to realize that "fear sells" and that it diminishes our tendency to trust God and love others. Also, the disposition of fear is a learned and cultivated way of viewing the world that needs to be addressed by direct instruction on how to "set your minds on things above" (Col. 3:2 NIV).

What does God sing? The chorus of our three-person God says to us, "I have called you by name and fashioned you in the depths of the earth and knitted you together in your mother's womb. You are my workmanship and were created and equipped to do good in the world. You are my treasured possession, and I have carved your name on the palms of my hands—I will never forget you or leave you. I am wooing you to come and rest in my love and to live up to the new name I have given you. Hear me now: I love you, I love you, I love you, and I have paid a great cost to woo you and bring you home."

The apostle John tells us, "God is love" (1 John 4:8 NIV). God's very nature is love. At God's core, his stance toward us is one of love. And God's love shows his wholehearted and eager readiness to secure our good. We are a mixture of virtues and vices. We exhibit love, but also selfishness; we show love, but our need for self-protection limits it; we tend to love the lovely more than the unlovely. God is not like this; his stance toward us is one of love. His love is a deep and profound cherishing of us and also a call enabling us to be all we are meant to be. His love is more profound and more significant than merely "accepting us." Oh, he accepts us and affirms our core identity, but he calls us to fullness of life. One way Jesus summed up his ministry was to say, "My purpose is to give life in all its fullness" (John 10:10 TLB).

The reality of God loving and caring for us is what the life and ministry of Jesus are about. In his ministry, we see enacted what it means that God is for us. An early Christian writer, Eusebius of Caesarea (ca. 260–340), showed how Jesus's redemptive work could be summarized under three offices—prophet, priest, and king. He said Jesus was "the true Christ, the divinely inspired and heavenly Word, who is the only high priest of all, and the only King of every creature, and the Father's only supreme prophet of prophets."[11] John Calvin developed this idea and emphasized the close bond between Jesus's character and his work. Jesus did what he did because of who he is. In other words, his death for us, to provide us life, is something he yearned to do. He

11. Eusebius, "Church History," trans. Arthur McGiffert, in *A Select Library of the Nicene and Post-Nicene Fathers*, ed. Philip Schaff, series 2 (New York: Christian Literature, 1890), 1:86.

eagerly "came to seek and to save the lost" (Luke 19:10 NIV) because it is in the character of God to care for his people—even in our rebellion. "While we were still sinners, Christ died for us" (Rom. 5:8 NIV).

As a prophet, Christ is the messenger of God's grace. But he is not just a messenger of God; he is the message. God becoming flesh is described as "the Word became flesh" (John 1:14 NIV). There was not a gap between Jesus's message and his person—no performative contradiction of any kind—so he could tell those around him that "anyone who has seen me has seen the Father" (14:9 NIV). Like the greatest prophet of old, Moses, Jesus spoke with God face to face, but his message is different: "For the law was given through Moses; grace and truth came through Jesus Christ" (1:17 NIV). He serves today for believers as their ever-present teacher—he lived it so that he can teach it. He is the king who has established a spiritual kingdom that one day will be a full earthly kingdom filled with grace, truth, beauty, justice, and abundant love. Today his kingly rule of "subduing us to himself, in ruling and defending us" is carried out mainly through the ministry of the Holy Spirit.[12] He is our priest who cleanses his people of their sin through his offering of himself as a satisfaction for our sin.

Furthermore, as our priest, he continually offers intercession on our behalf before God—he sings over us, and he prays over us. As we think of the God who is for us, remember Karl Barth's wise formula: "According to the Apostles' Creed, whatever Christ is he does."[13] It is because of who he is that God redeemed us; the act of redemption on the cross shows us the character of God through Jesus.

The spiritual reality is that God loves us with an everlasting love and desires for us to live as his beloved. And while that is the reality, we often live without a clear awareness of God's affection for us. Worse yet, many live with a sense that God is perpetually disappointed with them. How would you answer the question "What does God feel when he looks at me?" Ah, we know the "right answer," but often that is not what our hearts say. I have asked many people this question, and most often people express some form of "he's disappointed with me—I've let him down." So how do we allow our belovedness to become our life map? It is not just a matter of wanting or trying. Practice makes permanent, and we have deeply rutted mental pathways of second-guessing God's love. It is through training, not just trying, that we can

---

12. Alexander McPherson, ed., *Westminster Confession of Faith*, complete ed. (Glasgow: Free Presbyterian, 1983), 293–94.

13. Karl Barth, *The Faith of the Church: A Commentary on the Apostles' Creed according to Calvin's Catechism*, ed. Jean-Louis Leuba, trans. Gabriel Vahanian (New York: Meridian Books, 1958), 69.

learn to ever increasingly rest in God's love. I have spent many hours speaking with Christians, especially those involved in leadership and ministry, and I am convinced that we are our own worst enemies when it comes to receiving the love of God. In CSF, remembering involves unlearning habits that make our hearts Teflon to God's love and Velcro to negative accusations. And that is one of the reasons that Christian meditation should be a primary spiritual discipline taught in our churches.

Years ago, I heard a radio program that was a spoof of a consumer's guide on religion. The hosts assessed various religious options using the metric "What does it cost you, and what do you get?" This was posed as a fair cost-benefit analysis. At the end, their recommendation was for a faith that cost you very little and promised all the benefits one could hope for. I think if you asked people to dream up a religion, they would come up with something similar, something with minimal costs and lots of easily gotten spiritual goods. But in real life, we have invented something far darker.

We appear to be naturally inclined to invent religious systems in which divine acceptance is conditioned on our performance. Whether that be strictness in keeping to a sanctioned diet, performing required prayers, or living up to a moral code, we seem to have a sense that we need to earn God's favor. Now, this was not always the case. Before sin entered the world, our first parents lived in a dynamic relationship with God that precluded a sense of favor-earning performance. And notice, after sin entered the world, what is the first act of Adam and Eve? It is a performance aimed at affecting their relationship with God. When they sense their shame and vulnerability, they make clothes and hide among the trees. The impulse to hide, like the act of a guilty preschooler hiding under a table, is now so universal. This is our default response—when we feel estranged from God, we hide (deny his existence, stop praying, or try to earn his favor). It seems that we are wired to relate to God based on earning. We are all recovering Pharisees, often more concerned with our self-generated righteousness than with the grace and love of God.

Doing, working, and yearning are how we make our way in the world. We are creators and workers and doers. We are people who wield pens, shovels, trowels, and scissors. We build, we play, we worship, and we relate. We engage the world by what we do, and in many of our relationships, there is a deep-seated element of appraisal and an implicit need for performance. While in the best of families, marriages, teams, and workgroups there is an esprit de corps that dampens this appraisal-performance-acceptance cycle, we are enculturated to tie our worth to measuring up.

So here is the hard message: We seem innately disposed to relate to God as if we have to earn his favor, and much of the way we achieve our status and well-being in the world is through performance. We automatically transfer our performance orientation to our relationship with God. Our inborn tendency is to operate out of some form of legalism—through my being good or doing good, I will maintain God's favor. Yet the well-meaning corrective to this—no, you don't have to do anything to receive God's love—misses the point. To embrace and be embraced by the love of God, we need to do things. We need to do those things that open our hearts to God and express our response to his passion and character.

So, while we cannot earn God's love, we are to open ourselves to receive it through right and thoughtful effort. God's love and grace do not eliminate effort, but they do exclude striving, earning, and the arrogance that thinks, "God owes me one." Grace says you can't earn your way to God and says just as loudly, "Work out your salvation with fear and trembling" (Phil. 2:12 NIV), for transforming and healing grace is delivered through our efforts. Grace says no to earning but yes to skillful effort. "God's working in us is not suspended because we work, nor our working suspended because God works. Neither is the relation strictly one of cooperation as if God did his part and we did ours so that the conjunction or co-ordination of both produced the required result. God works in us and we also work."[14] The *Book of Common Prayer* reminds us that God is the master "whose service is perfect freedom."[15] A friend whose thought was deeply formed by the prayer book would often remind me, "Obedience will never cost you joy." Another friend used this homey illustration: "A train is free only as long as it stays on its tracks. If it jumps the tracks, it is not free to do what it was designed to do." This truth needs to be our North Star as we seek to begin exposing our hearts to God's healing grace. The pervasive myth of our day is that, in serving God, one will lose one's freedom and, hence, dignity—and with that, any pleasure life has to offer. Actually, in serving God, we discover that we don't have to do what we want to do, and by serving God, "we're no longer shackled to that domineering mate of sin. . . . We're free to live a new life in the freedom of God" (Rom. 7:6 Message). And we come to love him, "whose service is perfect freedom."

Letting the Cross Grow

It would be helpful to return to the bridge diagram (in chap. 1, see "The Gospel and the Christian" and figs. 3–4) and consider how our perception of

14. John Murray, *Redemption, Accomplished and Applied* (Grand Rapids: Eerdmans, 1975), 148–49.
15. *The Book of Common Prayer* (New York: Seabury, 1979), 69. This thought was suggested by a post on the Holy Trinity Brompton website at www.htb.org.

"the gap" relates to spiritual formation. The gap between God and humans always exists in two forms. First, there is the reality of an infinite moral, spiritual, and relational gap between God and humans, which reflects our need for God's limitless grace. Our sins, our areas of healing, our pain, and the needs of those around us require enormous amounts of grace. Second, we live as if the gap between us and God were much smaller than it is. We sometimes deliberately narrow this gap through boasting and impression management, where we seek to improve or shape our image by controlling the information we present to others. This represents a focus on trying to look good rather than seeking to be good. Still, we are blind to much of this narrowing and do it through subtle patterns of denial, ignorance, and self-protection. Here enters a simple maxim of the spiritual life: the grace of God that affects us (grace as God's transforming and healing power) generally does not exceed our perceived need for grace. People with a minimal God-human gap, meaning they have little sense of their sinfulness or brokenness, will assume that they need little grace and will receive little transforming grace.

A significant task in spiritual formation involves increasing our awareness of our need for grace. One way of doing this is by letting the cross grow larger. This means facing up to the reality of sin and growing in awe of the majestic holiness of God. We are at our best spiritually when our sin and yearnings drive us to the cross, when we cling to it and nothing else. The law, our sin, our failure, our ache for beauty, and our yearnings all can drive us to the cross. We must resist our "natural" inclination to think that *we* can handle our sin (its guilt, shame, conviction, pain, enslaving power, and so on). The cross is the place where God most clearly tells us who he is and how he feels about sin. He is holy, hates sin, and sees the pain it causes his beloved. It is also the place where God most clearly tells us what he thinks of sinners: "I would rather die than live without you; I will die to provide you a way of escape." As our appreciation of our sin grows and our appreciation of God's holiness grows, so too must our understanding of the cross.

The cumulative effect of our individual actions is a theme that runs through the writings of C. S. Lewis. In *The Great Divorce*, Lewis describes an imaginary bus trip from hell to heaven.[16] All riders have the option of not returning to hell, but only one chooses to stay in heaven and enjoy its delights. The others return to the dismal bus because, hardened and blinded as they are by repeated individual acts of pride, they are unable to see heaven's beauty and the kindness of the inhabitants who greeted them. Since the fall, humankind has suffered from poor spiritual vision. The Pharisees illustrate this because

16. C. S. Lewis, *The Great Divorce* (New York: Simon & Schuster, 1996).

they possess the same body of knowledge about God as Jesus does, but they are blinded to the complete perspective. Their myopic vision of the law leads eventually to a decline in popular opinion and immediately to the harsh judgment of Jesus: "You blind guides! You strain out a gnat but swallow a camel" (Matt. 23:24 NIV). The phenomenon of letting the cross grow is a matter of learning to see rightly. Richard Rohr captures how our perspective limits our vision: "We do not see things as they are; we see things as we are. Take that as nearly certain."[17] Figure 9 illustrates how our spiritual blindness and attempts at self-justification can cause us to view the cross through a very narrow slit. Our limited vision causes us to fail to see our need for grace.

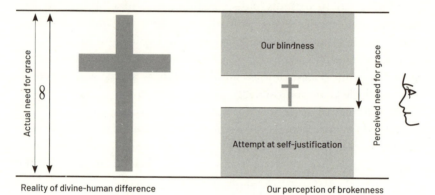

Figure 9. Need for grace

G. K. Chesterton has an intriguing section in *Orthodoxy* where he compares the numbing limits of an Eastern mindset, with its symbol of the snake chasing its tail in an eternal circle, to Christianity with its cross: "For the circle is perfect and infinite in its nature; but it is fixed forever in its size; it can never be larger or smaller. But the cross, though it has at its heart a collision and a contradiction, can extend its four arms forever without altering its shape. Because it has a paradox in its center it can grow without changing. The circle returns upon itself and is bound. The cross opens its arms to the four winds; it is a signpost for free travelers."[18]

Jesus pointed out this principle when he spoke to Simon the Pharisee about the love of those who have received much forgiveness. Simon was appalled when the woman anointed Jesus's feet at Simon's party. Jesus first asked Simon about various degrees of appreciation after certain amounts of debt were forgiven and then went on to explain that in this woman's case, "her many

17. Richard Rohr, *The Naked Now* (New York: Crossroad, 2015), 82.
18. G. K. Chesterton, *Orthodoxy* (Wheaton: Shaw, 1994), 25.

sins have been forgiven—as her great love has shown. But whoever has been forgiven little loves little" (Luke 7:47 NIV). To grow, one needs to see one's sin as clearly as this woman did. Dallas Willard advises that we seek out massive amounts of grace because we know our need: "To 'grow in grace' means to utilize more and more grace to live by, until everything we do is assisted by grace. Then, whatever we do in word or deed will all be done in the name of the Lord Jesus (Col. 3:17). The greatest saints are not those who need *less* grace, but those who consume the most grace, who indeed are most in need of grace—those who are saturated by grace in every dimension of their being. Grace to them is like breath."[19]

Saints, like the woman at Simon's party, know their need and God's provision of grace through a large, strong cross that covers their every sin, weakness, and concern. They do not delude themselves into thinking that they could ever get just enough grace to make it on their own. They are shamelessly, hopelessly, and relentlessly in pursuit of more of God's grace than they have right now.

Allow me to make this dynamic more concrete by sharing the stories of three individuals.

When I first met Sam, I was struck by his energy and evident love for his three children and his wife. He was the product of a happy, working-class, church-attending family. He was the first person in his family to go to college, and as the firstborn son, he exceeded all expectations. In college, his girlfriend urged him to attend a campus ministry, where he heard about personal faith in Christ as a present reality and power. Following Christ was more than simply trying to live a moral life—which seemed to him to summarize his church's teaching back home. Over the course of the year, he attended the meetings, and he came to relate to Christ as his Savior and Guide. He graduated from college, married his sweetheart, and started what became a very successful home-building company. For the next twenty years, he lived his life as a generous, moral, caring, and churchgoing guy. Prayer and Scripture reading marked his early days out of college, but they became less and less present. In fact, he confided to a friend that he thought personal devotional activities were a bit like a laxative: you take it when you need it, but as you try harder and get better, these "props" are less necessary. Unbeknownst to Sam, his cross was growing smaller and smaller.

Then the bottom dropped out. For Sam, it was the one-two punch, all in six weeks. He discovered that his son-in-law, the heir apparent to the business, was having an affair with a member of his staff. Amid this awkward betrayal,

19. Dallas Willard, *Renovation of the Heart: Putting on the Character of Christ* (Colorado Springs: NavPress, 2002), 93–94.

Sam ended up in the hospital with a heart attack that required a protracted rehabilitation routine. Finally, the local paper did an exposé on the business practices of some local home builders. Nothing illegal was reported, but Sam was shocked. He was humbled to see his business lumped in with all the others. He had been proud of having been "ethical" and different from the other guys.

Sam was fortunate to have a wife whose deep faith had prepared them for this time. Through her counsel and the guidance of friends, he moved from angry and despairing inactivity to a place of growth and transformation. His humility grew, and, concomitantly, so did the cross's reality in his life (see fig. 10).[20]

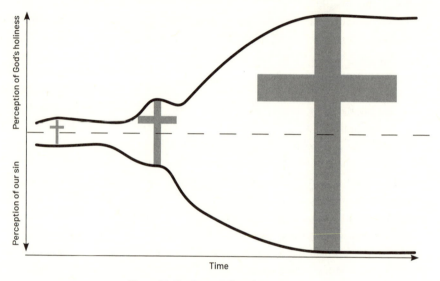

Figure 10. Sam's reception of more grace

I know Maria's story from hearing her tell it. As Horace Bushnell describes, she grew up a Christian, "never knowing a time when she was otherwise."[21] She went away to college and then on to seminary. She left seminary before completing a degree, and she and her physician husband immediately began a family. Through college, seminary, and early marriage, the cross was gradually shrinking. She was competent at all she did, loved by her friends, commended for her parenting, and deeply needed by her shy and insecure husband.

20. For a number of years, I have used a modification of the bridge diagram as a way of talking about the difference between our perceived distance from God and the reality of the chasm. I am indebted to the insights provided by the presentation of "The Cross Chart" in World Harvest Mission, *Discipling by Grace* (Jenkintown, PA: World Harvest Mission, 1996), 2.2 (p. 1).
21. Horace Bushnell, Williston Walker, and Luther Allan Weigle, *Christian Nurture*, new ed. (New York: Scribner's Sons, 1916), 4.

She was active in her church, and one day her pastor spoke to her about how her "perfectionism hindered her ministry." To her, it was a weird conversation: *Perfectionism, how could that be a problem? Wasn't that next to or the same as godliness?* she wondered. Over the next few months, she received more feedback about her "demands and expectations," "her touchiness when questioned by others," and "her put-downs of some people." This was hard to take; as she shared it with her parents and husband, they suggested that it was time to find another church where she would be appreciated. Yet the comments were consistent and came from people she respected, so she stayed. At this point, she was at a critical spiritual stage. We might say the cross was smaller than the gap. The cross can remain smaller than the gap only for a short time. She was busily filling in the gap by listening to her loved ones' affirmation and making excuses when all of a sudden she "got it." While her child was napping, she thought with anger about what her friends had said, and then suddenly, through tears, she realized that they were at least mostly right. She was broken. And the cross began to grow. Over time, she tossed aside the stuff that she had used to fill in the gap around her small cross. As Maria sat before God, more aware of her sin and far more aware of his grace than she had been in years, the cross towered over her life in an increasingly comforting way (see fig. 11).

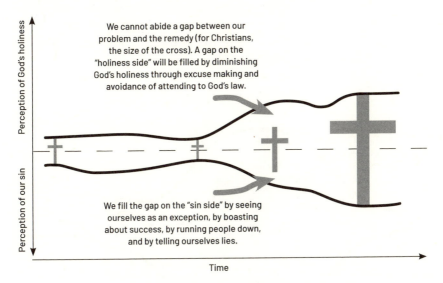

Figure 11. Maria's gap of grace

Susan's life changed immensely in college. Her goal of being a physician was set aside for the more immediate goal of fun. She did well in school, but she never let studying get in the way of a good party. One Saturday, like so many others, she was serving beer at a sorority party when she found herself outraged and disgusted by the self-centered and cruel behavior of a sorority sister. Too angry to confront her directly, she stepped aside for a minute to regain her composure, and in the quiet, she looked into an ethical mirror. The image was familiar. *She* was that girl. She had put people down like that hundreds of times. She had acted as if the world revolved around her. She was appalled at herself and walked away from the party, never to return.

Over the next months, she sought out Christian friends from high school, and by the end of the school year she had committed her life to follow Christ. She spent the summer at a discipleship-training program run by a campus ministry. She returned to college in the fall, full of enthusiasm for Jesus. She spoke of her faith and touched the lives of countless people, from janitors to professors, with her love and quick-minded defense of the faith.

She entered law school and did well, despite an enormous amount of time spent with a college ministry. She was affirmed for her teaching ministry, but the compassion, fun, and witness were not as prominent as they had been. In her adult life, she continues to be involved in ministry, much of it pro bono legal work on certain social issues on which she believes "a Christian must take a stand." All who meet her are struck by her charisma, competence, and togetherness. Over the years, as she succeeded in following a rigid pattern of discipleship, she has grown more confident of her strengths and less accepting of those who are struggling. After helping to mediate a dispute involving Susan and a ministry leader at her church, a friend confronted her: "Susan, there is no grace in you." As her perceived spiritual competence has grown, the cross has shrunk (see fig. 12).

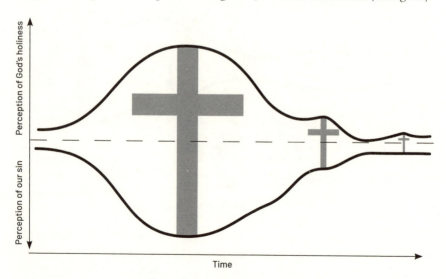

Figure 12. Susan's shrinking cross

The cross never changes, but as Sam, Maria, and Susan moved through different experiences, they came to see their need of the cross differently. For Sam and Maria, the cross became larger and far more critical as they owned their sin, need, and yearnings. As the gospel broke through and they were able to get the logs out of their eyes, they could see their own need and not be preoccupied with the shortcomings of others or their unexpected circumstances (Matt. 7:3–5). Community relationships and the words of others helped Sam and Maria to assesss their nearness to the cross. Susan's story is unfinished. We hope that she will be open to listen to her friends and seek grace for deeper and renewed formation.

Jesus healed ten lepers and sent them to the priest to have their healing confirmed. One returned to give thanks for the grace he had received. He wanted to verbalize his gratitude personally, to worship, and to prolong his encounter with his Savior. Like the woman at Simon's party, he loved much because Jesus had noticed his great need and healed his sickness. His gratitude reflects both an awareness of a deep, desperate need and the joy of new hope and wholeness. Jesus responded to him with further instructions: "Get up and go on your way; your faith has made you well" (Luke 17:19).

How often did the grateful returning leper recall the day of his healing? How long did he remember the look of pleasure on Jesus's face when he returned and worshiped? How long do we remember the grace we have received? Those with a large cross perspective take time daily to reflect on grace received. They are determined to share with others their healing and their need to remember their healing. The community disciplines of worship, confession, and learning ought to remind us that we are needy people who require enormous amounts of grace from a large cross. We will not be able to respond to this truth or relate to God and others in light of this truth if we do not first remember it.

Character: Virtues and Fruit

In chapter 3 I introduced Willard's Vision-Intention-Means formula concerning CSF. The great tradition of CSF saw the importance of providing a vision—a *telos*, or compelling goal for spiritual formation—and it boldly proclaimed that "the covenant people of God are being enabled by grace to live the holy life, hence called to holiness."[22] Paul encourages the new believers at Thessalonica to walk the path of flourishing with confidence and prayerfully reminds them, "May the God of peace himself sanctify you entirely; and may your spirit and soul and body be kept sound and blameless

22. Thomas Oden, *Classic Christianity: A Systematic Theology* (New York: HarperOne, 1992), 660.

at the coming of our Lord Jesus Christ. The one who calls you is faithful, and he will do this" (1 Thess. 5:23–24). He reminds the Ephesians that the Father chose us in Christ "before the foundation of the world to be holy and blameless before him in love. He destined us for adoption as his children through Jesus Christ" (Eph. 1:4–5). He assures the Galatians, "It is Christ who lives in me" (Gal. 2:20). "Abide in me as I abide in you," Jesus urges the disciples (John 15:4). We are united, and we are to actualize this union by abiding, which results in our lives being marked by the "fruit of the Spirit . . . love, joy, peace, patience, kindness, generosity, faithfulness, gentleness, and self-control" (Gal. 5:22–23).

One perennial issue in CSF is the temptation to turn CSF into mere moral formation.[23] This is a genuine temptation, and we can see how various Sunday school curriculums fell into this trap. Cleanliness, punctuality, and citizenship were allowed to crowd out the cultivation of abiding in Christ and putting on his character. The pull toward a behavioral moral formation focus is not the only pressure CSF faces. There is pull toward the spontaneous, impromptu, or romantic ideal that sees our spiritual formation as occurring in an intensely personal and private way, not as a particularly corporate endeavor. CSF frames the call to flourish in Christ differently: it emphasizes the call to put on the character of Christ (Col. 3:12). By underlining the reality of our union with Christ, we can encourage Christians to de-

> Our spiritual formation is intended to be the pathway to flourishing in Christ. Our flourishing comes as we take on the character of Christ through cultivating virtues. The acquisition of virtues through training and habit formation comes as we "walk by the Spirit." Sanctifying grace and virtue development are fully compatible, for all true spiritual formation is saturated by grace and human agency.

velop a character that enables them to say, more and more, "I am learning from Jesus to live my life as he would live my life if he were I."[24] The great tradition of CSF has seen the wisdom of placing an emphasis on the cultivation of virtues as we recognize our spiritual reality (we are united to Christ) and respond to the imperatives of following Jesus ("put on the Lord Jesus Christ, and make no provision for the flesh" [Rom. 13:14]). The reality of who we are in Christ and our response to the call to use this spiritual power and identity to pursue holiness should be among the themes in our teaching and pastoral ministry.

M. Robert Mulholland, whose *Invitation to a Journey* is recommended at the end of chapter 1, defines spiritual formation as "the process of being

23. John Coe, "Resisting the Temptation of Moral Formation: Opening to Spiritual Formation in the Cross and the Spirit," *Journal of Spiritual Formation and Soul Care* 1, no. 1 (2008): 54–78.

24. Dallas Willard, *The Divine Conspiracy: Rediscovering Our Hidden Life in God* (San Francisco: HarperSanFrancisco, 1998), 283.

formed in the image of Christ for the sake of others."[25] This is discipleship: to be attracted to the person of Christ and then be led into the values and lifestyle of Christ (although some are attracted to Christian values and are led through these into a relationship with the person—it works both ways). The journey of discipleship is a challenging journey into flourishing.

Christian spiritual *form*-ation is interested in forming. In the context of our unconditional welcome through Christ, we are invited to live the life of Christ as individuals and as Christian communities. The Sermon on the Mount is a programmatic declaration of where the journey of discipleship should aim; it provides a compelling picture of flourishing in Christ's kingdom.[26] And here lies the challenge: as we strive for the high call of the teachings of Christ, we face the world, the flesh, and the devil. CSF is not a way to sidestep conflict into some ethereal tranquility. We would do well to learn from the desert elders, who "believed that struggle is normal, necessary and even healthy in the spiritual life. . . . We should embrace it as one aspect of our calling."[27] Living in the reality of our union with Christ and the empowerment of the Spirit, we press on toward maturity of character, growth in love, and the imitation of Christ. CSF is marked by a clear call for the Christian to live differently from the world (a different *form*). Dietrich Bonhoeffer persuasively argues that the call to discipleship must be part of the offer of the gospel: "The cross is laid on every Christian. The first Christ-suffering which every man must experience is the call to abandon the attachments of this world. . . . When Christ calls a man, he bids him come and die."[28] At times, the enemy is not so much the world but our own flesh—our ingrained habits of self-focus. In these moments, the challenge of a discipling-oriented CSF lies within us. John Cassian captures the desert wisdom on this: "For no one is more my enemy than my own heart which is truly the one of my household closest to me."[29]

25. M. Robert Mulholland, *Invitation to a Journey: A Road Map for Spiritual Formation* (Downers Grove, IL: InterVarsity, 1993), 15. See also Kenneth Boa, *Conformed to His Image: Biblical and Practical Approaches to Spiritual Formation* (Grand Rapids: Zondervan, 2001).

26. Jonathan T. Pennington, *The Sermon on the Mount and Human Flourishing: A Theological Commentary* (Grand Rapids: Baker Books, 2017); Christopher Kaczor, *The Gospel of Happiness: Rediscover Your Faith through Spiritual Practice and Positive Psychology* (New York: Image Books, 2015).

27. Gerald Sittser, *Water from a Deep Well: Christian Spirituality from Early Martyrs to Modern Missionaries* (Downers Grove, IL: InterVarsity, 2007), 74.

28. Dietrich Bonhoeffer, *The Cost of Discipleship* (New York: Touchstone, 1995), 89. The theme of suffering as part of spiritual formation is a central element in Anabaptist spirituality. For more, see Peter Erb, "Anabaptist Spirituality," in *Protestant Spiritual Traditions*, ed. Frank C. Senn (Mahwah, NJ: Paulist Press, 1986), 80–124.

29. John Cassian, *Conferences*, ed. Philip Schaff, Nicene and Post-Nicene Fathers, Second Series (Peabody, MA: Hendrickson, 1994), 487.

There are also those seasons when we face the devil disguised as "an angel of light" (2 Cor. 11:14 NIV).

And yet CSF as a process of discipling is not all about challenge and spiritual warfare. Such was not the case with Jesus's original followers, and it is not the case for us today. CSF, as discipleship into Christ, involves every area of our lives. On the one hand, it necessarily involves a fair amount of inner examination, a kind of being aware, or noticing.[30] We pay attention to the movements of the Holy Spirit. We notice the work of spiritual enemies. We compare our lives with the life of Jesus. We pray. At the same time, any and all parts of our lives are subject to the forming work of God. Our careers, our relationships, our evangelistic and service activities—all these and more are implicated in following Jesus.[31] We learn to feel the way Jesus feels, to think the way Jesus thinks, and to act the way Jesus acts.

Similarly, CSF involves both the individual and the community. It is not merely a "me and Jesus" thing. Communities (churches, small groups, Christian companies, mission teams, intentional communities) *as communities* are in need of formation in love. Each community has its own sense of calling, its own set of enemies, and knowledge of its own journey. Reading the Bible in English, we tend to miss the emphasis on community, which is found particularly in the syntax of New Testament commands. For example, Paul urges the Roman church to "bless those who persecute you; bless and do not curse" (Rom. 12:14 NIV); all three commands are plural. Similarly, when Paul writes of his own imitation of Christ, urging the Corinthians to follow his example, his command is plural: "Follow [plural] my example, as I follow the example of Christ" (1 Cor. 11:1 NIV), which means "I want all of you to collectively follow my example." CSF is a life of following Jesus—a challenging and flourishing life of imitation, one that requires a certain amount of interior attention and ultimately incorporates all that we do and are.[32]

---

30. Richard Foster provides a clear overview of the well-regarded prayer of examen in *Prayer: Finding the Heart's True Home* (San Francisco: HarperSanFrancisco, 1992), 27–35. For suggestions on the examen, see Timothy M. Gallagher, *The Examen Prayer: Ignatian Wisdom for Our Lives Today* (New York: Crossroad, 2006); Jim Manney, *A Simple, Life-Changing Prayer: Discovering the Power of St. Ignatius Loyola's Examen* (Chicago: Loyola University Press, 2011). Journaling is a time-honored approach to self-examination; see Helen Cepero, *Journaling as a Spiritual Practice: Encountering God through Attentive Writing* (Downers Grove, IL: InterVarsity, 2008).

31. On the breadth of ongoing Christian transformation, see Richard J. Foster, *Streams of Living Water: Celebrating the Great Traditions of Christian Faith* (San Francisco: HarperSanFrancisco, 1998); Evan B. Howard, *The Brazos Introduction to Christian Spirituality* (Grand Rapids: Brazos, 2008), 254–59.

32. One of the attractive features of CSF for many is that it portrays discipleship as a total life transformation that involves one's desires and habits as well as beliefs. See Willard, *Renovation of the Heart*; Adrian Van Kaam and Susan Muto, *Formation Theology*, 4 vols. (Pittsburgh:

Grounding Our Hearts in Truth

Our first problem is that our attitude toward sin is more self-centered than God-centered.

Jerry Bridges[33]

A recovery of the old sense of sin is essential to Christianity. Christ takes it for granted that men are bad.

C. S. Lewis[34]

If remembering the Story is a conserving activity, proposing the Vision is the liberating dimension of our ministry as Christian religious educators.

Thomas H. Groome[35]

Do this in remembrance of me.

Jesus (1 Cor. 11:24)

Faith can remember that the Spirit who made his home in your heart promised to stay—whether you feel him or not.

Jack Haberer[36]

"We always give thanks to God for all of you and mention you in our prayers, constantly remembering before our God and Father your work of faith and labor of love in steadfastness of hope in our Lord Jesus Christ" (1 Thess. 1:2–3). Paul tells us that he was "constantly remembering" the Thessalonians. That is quite a testimony to his affection for them. He was always thinking about these believers. I quoted this verse at the outset of this section, which is about how to enhance churches' remembering and grounding, because we are far more likely to remember enfleshed truth—truth in the context of relationships—than mere abstract propositions. Paul's letters display a remarkable consistency, in that truth is never an abstract; it is always a very personal subject. The truth of the gospel had set Paul free and was guiding his life by changing the lives of other people who received it. Parker Palmer

---

Epiphany Association, 2003–6). Van Kaam and Muto's comprehensive series emphasizes transformation of the whole person.

33. *The Pursuit of Holiness* (Colorado Springs: NavPress, 1978), 20.

34. *The Problem of Pain* (New York: Macmillan, 1962), 57.

35. *Christian Religious Education: Sharing Our Story and Vision* (San Francisco: Harper & Row, 1980), 271.

36. *Living the Presence of the Spirit* (Louisville: Geneva, 2001), 28.

reminds us, "This distinction is crucial to knowing, teaching and learning: *A subject is available for relationship; an object is not.*"[37]

Formational Teaching

The community disciplines explored in this section fit into the broader disciplines of teaching and learning. One of the most important steps in establishing a successful, educationally based spiritual formation strategy in a local church is to shift the emphasis from teaching to learning. It's all too easy in a technology-saturated culture to begin to equate teaching with the efficient transmission of material. Spiritual formation contends that there is a need for both informational teaching (teaching that helps ground one in the content of the Christian story) and formational teaching (teaching that helps one live out the truth of the Christian gospel). Many churches exclusively focus on teaching, which tends to overemphasize informational presentations at the expense of those that are more formational.

When we emphasize learning, we highlight the experiences of individuals and communities. C. Ellis Nelson has noted the different concerns of teaching and learning as follows: "Educators often identify learning as that which a person absorbs, accepts, relates to, or identifies with, out of his or her experiences. The experience is the key to what the person learns. Teaching, however, is a deliberate act in which a leader tries to transmit knowledge, skill, attitude, or insight to someone."[38]

Matching Outcomes and Methods

Formational teaching recognizes the wide variety of learning outcomes that are needed for discipleship. Outcomes flow from both the content (e.g., the atonement or prayer) and the nature of the knowledge learned (e.g., factual knowledge, performative knowledge—learning to do something). Formational teaching recognizes that CSF needs a broad range of learning outcomes. Six types of knowledge that are present in rich CSF programs are summed up briefly below. This list is not comprehensive, but it shows the richness of what it means to "know" when we are speaking of formation. It is crucial in CSF that we do not operate as if there is "head knowledge" and "heart knowledge"; that unfortunate dichotomy can lead to learners experiencing content-laden lectures and small, touchy-feely groups as their only modes of instruction.

---

37. Parker J. Palmer, *The Courage to Teach: Exploring the Inner Landscape of a Teacher's Life* (San Francisco: Jossey-Bass, 1998), 102–3.

38. C. Ellis Nelson, *How Faith Matures* (Louisville: Westminster John Knox, 1989), 163.

Six Types of Knowledge

Type	Definition	Outcome
Factual knowledge	This knowledge ranges from relatively straightforward material (like the names of the books of the Bible) to rich, complex subjects related to theology.	What
Performative knowledge	This knowledge is skill-oriented (for example, how to pray or to explain the gospel to someone) and dispositional (having a tendency to use this knowledge or not). Both are vital to our formation.	How
Knowledge that one is part of a community	This is knowledge born of the experience of acceptance and the affirmation that one belongs.	Belong
Relational knowledge	In the Bible, to know something means to have experienced it or observed it in such a way that it has made an impact on one's life. The statement that Christ "knew no sin" (2 Cor. 5:21) does not mean that he had no intellectual comprehension of sin but that he had never sinned. The Hebraic notion that knowledge entails a personal relationship can be seen in the biblical use of "know" to describe sexual relations: "Now the man [Adam] knew his wife Eve, and she conceived and bore Cain" (Gen. 4:1). Persons can know God only if they have walked with him, worshiped him, prayed to him—in other words, if they have lived as if his existence matters.	Who
Self-knowledge	This is knowing one's strengths, weaknesses, and Spirit-given giftings. True self-knowledge is the foundation of the virtue of humility.	Self
Knowledge of God and self	Calvin begins his *Institutes* with the claim that you cannot know God without knowing yourself, and you cannot know yourself without knowing God.	Double

We begin with a sense of the content (the What) the learners need to acquire (knowledge, skills, and attitudes). And in thinking about the context, we need to consider how they should know this material. In other words, what are they going to do with this? Is this outcome a type of self-understanding or simple factual knowledge? Only once we have answered this question are we ready to think about the methods of teaching. Our method of teaching—or, better termed, our formation strategy—should be selected with an eye toward the desired outcome. A lecture or sermon can support outcomes of "What" (see the third column in the chart above) in many situations but are not the best choice for a "Self" outcome. A guided personal practice exercise will help one gain the skill mastery of "How" but will not be the best at conveying

"What." The question to guide formational teaching is, What experience will help these learners achieve the learning we desire?

The rich ways that we are to know to be fully formed in Christ call for a rich set of diverse teaching/formational strategies. To make that concrete, here are some strategies that have stood the test of time. Many involve active group learning, and that is one of the ways the church does matter in spiritual formation. It provides a learning context second to none for CSF.

Learning needs to flow from experiences in which the truths of the gospel are directly related to ordinary life and work. We should see all the disciplines in this section as aspects of the educational, learning-engendering work of the church.

Spiral Curriculum

One of the perennial problems in spiritual formation is the gap between how we profess our faith and how we live it out. We may cognitively know certain biblical and theological truths but not let them guide our lives. For

Formation Strategies

Strategy	Definition
Lecture/sermon	Clear, forceful presentation of content of the truth and demonstration of Christian thinking and analysis.
Discussion-oriented seminar	An essential format for helping people work through important but tough texts and master the material by wrestling with it.
Small group	Small caring and support groups.
Spiritual friendships	Friendships that offer spiritual support, challenge, and encouragement over the years.
Reflection-oriented experience	Can take many forms, such as a devotional tied to the church year or a journaling and reflection time during a retreat.
Therapy/coaching	Specialized support and care to assist someone with struggles relevant to their discipleship. It is a critical venue for people gaining necessary self-knowledge.
Mentoring	A long-term, supportive learning relationship of guidance in which a caring individual shares knowledge, experience, and wisdom with another.
Guided personal practice	A practice that usually takes place in conjunction with another formation strategy. For example, as homework for lectures, participants could be asked to participate in certain prayer activities and report back on their experiences.
Group practice	Opportunities to try out spiritual disciplines in a group setting. Many spiritual practices (like fasting or solitude) are best learned in a group setting and then practiced on one's own.

Learners and Learning

To learn is to integrate our awareness into our behavior in ways that influence and shape our decisions and actions. Learning is a profound event that leads to a significant change in our total lives. It involves four related steps or stages:

- An awareness of a starting point: a conscious acknowledgment of one's present state and its foundation in past experience.
- A significant experience that best takes place away from one's home environment, though shared in community with others. The experience need not always be dramatic but will usually entail a feeling of dissonance. We feel the need for change.
- Reflection: a serious confrontation with our lives as lived demands reflection in order to acquire a new sense of stability and wholeness. Prayer is an obvious, integral aspect of reflection. Reflection is best done in community with others who are also striving to resolve their dissonances.
- Assimilation: learning is not complete until we eliminate our old ways and integrate our new understandings. The end of assimilation is a public commitment to our new lifestyle and its particular behaviors.

To be Christian with others in the world through the integration of piety and politics requires such learning. And such learning is at the heart of church reform and renewal.[a]

a. Adapted from John H. Westerhoff III, *Inner Growth, Outer Change: An Educational Guide to Church Renewal* (New York: Seabury, 1979), 61–62. Used by permission.

instance, one may know Jesus's warning about improper judging ("Do not judge, so that you may not be judged" [Matt. 7:1]) but still live a life marked by racial prejudice and other deformative prejudices. Mere repetition of this command will not cause people to see the connection between Jesus's teaching and their lives. People often use the verse out of context as a defensive weapon to deny the validity of healthy confrontation. The perennial areas of struggle for Christians—racism, doubting God's love, anger, fear, worry, and not seeing their neighbor's pain—need to be addressed in creative ways that allow the message to get past our defenses.

An example of this is Nathan's creative confrontation of David through a story. David was undoubtedly aware of the scriptural teaching against adultery, lying, and murder. Still, when Nathan told a story, it caught David off guard and provided an opening for David to see the error of his ways. Similarly, drama, testimony, firsthand accounts, and immersion experiences are usually better at getting past our resistance to the very central issues of discipleship than mere direct re-presentations of the truth.

A spiral curriculum (see fig. 13) has students constantly revisiting topics and truths with the aim of working these truths deeper into the fabric of their lives. In the early twentieth century, the field of religious education adopted the linear acquisition curriculum model used in math and science instruction. In this model, students master basic material and then move on to more and more complex learning. A linear curriculum has much to commend it in many areas of study. Still, the wisdom of the ages saw a circular curriculum, analogous to the church year, as far more appropriate for spiritual formation. A circular curriculum re-presents subjects again and again and provides opportunities to go deeper into these subjects.

Palmer calls us to put obedience to truth at the heart of our teaching: "To teach is to create a space in which obedience to truth is practiced."[39] Teach-

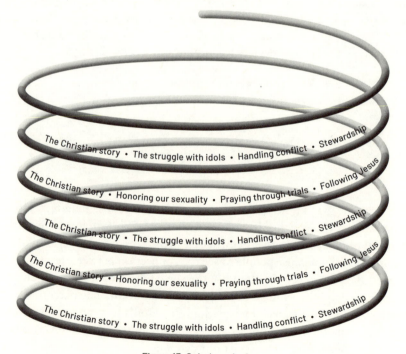

Figure 13. Spiral curriculum

39. Parker J. Palmer, *To Know as We Are Known: Education as a Spiritual Journey* (San Francisco: HarperSanFrancisco, 1993), 69.

ing that is focused on spiritual formation should not merely lay out the truth before people as just one more item to appraise; it should call for obedience to the truth of Jesus Christ as we teach the truth we have come to understand. Within the body of Christ, we teach by the way we speak and listen, the way we make appropriate claims on one another, and the way we allow ourselves to be held accountable by this learning community. We must see that our learning environment is not just a place where we present truth as so many options on a great religious smorgasbord but instead a part of the very fabric of our relationship with Christ.

Anointed Teaching

Seek Him! What can we do without Him? Seek Him! Seek Him always. But go beyond seeking Him; expect Him.

David Martyn Lloyd-Jones[40]

It is the peculiar ministry of the Holy Spirit to make the outer Word an inner experience. No other teacher can be both an outer and an inner factor.

Lois LeBar[41]

Presenting a curriculum for Christlikeness requires the integration of anointed teaching and careful curriculum development. Anointed teaching means that the Holy Spirit comes upon the teacher in a special manner. It is God giving insight and power to teachers and enabling them, through the Spirit, to do this work in a manner that lifts it beyond simple human efforts and endeavors.[42] Anointing is not just an optional enrichment to teaching but something that must mark it. The Puritan writer and preacher Richard Baxter used an apt expression when he spoke of the anointing of Christian communication as a "tincture" or dye that colors the entire communication.[43] The audience detects anointing not merely in a speaker's passion or insightful application of the text but also in the very fabric of the message and the seamless integrity between the message and the speaker's life.

God's Spirit anointed Old Testament leaders, prophets, and others for special tasks when God needed a witness to proclaim his Word, to show his providential presence, or to lead his people. Such setting apart was often indicated by actual anointing with oil, which Psalm 133:1–2 describes beautifully:

40. *Preaching and Preachers* (London: Hodder & Stoughton, 1971), 325.
41. *Education That Is Christian* (Wheaton, IL: Victor Books, 1989), 257.
42. Lloyd-Jones, *Preaching and Preachers*, 305; Thomas C. Oden, *Pastoral Theology: Essentials of Ministry* (San Francisco: Harper & Row, 1982), 139.
43. Richard Baxter, *The Reformed Pastor* (Carlisle, PA: Banner of Truth, 1974), 120.

"How very good and pleasant it is when kindred live together in unity! It is like the precious oil on the head, running down upon the beard, on the beard of Aaron, running down over the collar of his robes."

Examples of anointing include Bezalel (Exod. 31:1–5), Joshua (Deut. 34:9), Othniel (Judg. 3:10), Gideon (Judg. 6:34), Samson (Judg. 14:6, 19), Saul (1 Sam. 11:6), David (1 Sam. 16:13), Ezekiel (Ezek. 3:14), and Daniel (Dan. 5:14). These passages illustrate and emphasize that from time to time, God is pleased to sovereignly choose to come upon individuals and enable them to carry out their assigned work by the supernatural power of the Holy Spirit.

The New Testament emphasizes the Holy Spirit's enablement of believers to grow spiritually. Consequently, we can understand the interest Christian teachers have in seeking to teach with the Spirit's enablement. Galatians 5:22–23 describes the fruit of the Spirit as "love, joy, peace, forbearance, kindness, goodness, faithfulness, gentleness and self-control" (NIV), and 2 Corinthians 3 links the Holy Spirit with our transformation. Romans 5–8 teaches that the Holy Spirit pours out the love of God into our hearts and bears witness to us of our adoption. In Ephesians 6:17, the Word of God is called "the sword of the Spirit," and Paul instructs Timothy to guard the good deposit of sound teaching "with the help of the Holy Spirit living in us" (2 Tim. 1:14). First John 2:20 assures us that Christians "have an anointing from the Holy One, and all of you know the truth" (NIV). As a teacher prays over a Scripture lesson, the prayer is that the Holy Spirit would permeate the entire teaching and learning process for the spiritual growth and transformation of both the teacher and the learners.

Spirit Within, Spirit Upon, Spirit Among

It is the work of the Holy Spirit to form the living Christ within us, dwelling deep down in the deepest depths of our being.

R. A. Torrey[44]

It is the Spirit who brings gifts and giftedness for power-ministry to my life.

Jack Hayford[45]

The Spirit of God acts on people through people.

Evelyn Underhill[46]

44. *The Person and Work of the Holy Spirit*, rev. ed. (Grand Rapids: Zondervan, 1974), 122–23.
45. *The Power and Blessing: Celebrating the Disciplines of Spirit-Filled Living* (Wheaton: Victor Books, 1994), 21.
46. *Concerning the Inner Life* (Oxford: Oneworld, 1999), 55.

The privilege of being the dwelling of the Spirit was as much a group privilege as an individual one.

Jack Haberer[47]

When considering the Spirit's anointing of our communication, it is helpful to have some categories for analyzing the phenomenon. Three dimensions of the Spirit's work—the Spirit *within*, the Spirit *upon*, and the Spirit *among*—can serve that purpose. Robust conceptions of anointing expect that all three are present and active in Spirit-empowered teaching for individual and corporate formation.

The Spirit within is the cornerstone of anointed teaching. This indwelling dimension includes (1) the Spirit's work of transformation, (2) illumination of Scripture, and (3) communication of God's grace. The Spirit works to transform teachers as they are regenerate and open to the Spirit's transforming grace. The spiritual maturity of the teacher is not incidental to the teaching and learning process. Teachers can effectively teach only what they deeply understand and have grasped from experience. A teacher's spiritual experience and maturity affect what material they have mastered and their overall judgment, selection of material, and wisdom in handling class situations. Jesus captured this when he said, "A disciple is not above the teacher, but everyone who is fully qualified will be like the teacher" (Luke 6:40). Because the teacher's spiritual maturity affects the teacher's students, it is not a private matter.

The teacher must learn truth and experience being transformed by the Spirit who dwells within through prayer. E. M. Bounds makes a strong case for the connection between prayer and preaching and goes so far as to say, "Preaching which kills is prayerless preaching."[48] Bounds argues that unction (a synonym for *anointing*) flows from prayer and is essential to Christian ministry. "This divine unction is the feature which separates and distinguishes true gospel preaching from all other methods of presenting the truth."[49] The ongoing prayer of the teacher is for the anointing of the Holy Spirit and for his instruction in the study and preparation required for teaching Scripture. Prayer is needed because of the uniqueness of Scripture and the need for the Holy Spirit in understanding and explaining Scripture (1 Cor. 1–2). The teacher has the assurance that the Father will repeatedly give the Holy Spirit to those who ask him (Luke 11:13).

47. *Living the Presence of the Spirit*, 112.
48. E. M. Bounds, *The Complete Works of E. M. Bounds on Prayer* (Grand Rapids: Baker, 1990), 453.
49. Bounds, *Complete Works*, 478.

The Spirit upon, the second dimension of anointed teaching, is perhaps the most common understanding of the Spirit's work in anointing. As at Pentecost, when the Spirit descended on those gathered and they ministered in great power, the Spirit comes upon us and brings power and authority, authenticating the message and working miracles that give testimony to God's power.

The Spirit upon is a supernatural anointing of God's power; it enables our ministry and communication. Jesus taught that the purpose of the power is for witnessing. As he ascended, he said, "You will receive power when the Holy Spirit comes on you; and you will be my witnesses" (Acts 1:8 NIV). Peter preached, "God anointed Jesus of Nazareth with the Holy Spirit and power, and . . . he went around doing good and healing all who were under the power of the devil, because God was with him" (10:38 NIV). This summary in Peter's sermon is a paraphrase of Jesus's statement of purpose. When Jesus preached in Nazareth, he applied Isaiah 61:1–2 to himself and proclaimed, "The Spirit of the Lord is on me, because he has anointed me to proclaim good news to the poor. He has sent me to proclaim freedom for the prisoners and recovery of sight for the blind, to set the oppressed free, to proclaim the year of the Lord's favor" (Luke 4:18–19 NIV). The ultimate purpose of all anointing and all filling of the Holy Spirit is to proclaim and bear witness that Jesus is indeed who he said he is and that he alone can free and transform us. The effect of Peter's anointing is thus recorded: "While Peter was still speaking these words, the Holy Spirit came on all who heard the message" (Acts 10:44 NIV). These new believers give witness to the fact that the year of the Lord's favor will include Gentiles as well as Jews.

Zeb Bradford Long and Douglas McMurry note that writers often stress either the Spirit within or the Spirit upon. Long and McMurray encourage both groups to learn from each other and to understand that both elements are necessary. "Those who have matured in the character-building virtues of Christ but lack the power gifts in ministry can learn from those who have developed the power gifts, and vice-versa. . . . God wants us all to grow in both the character of Christ and in power ministry."[50] Rather than emphasizing either the Spirit within or the Spirit upon, anointed teaching must seek to integrate them.

The third dimension of anointed teaching is the work of the Spirit among. Anointing creates a new community in which the Spirit is among the participants. The Spirit among is demonstrated as the presence and anointing power of the Holy Spirit become evident in the community. The community is transformed into one marked by trust, support, loving challenge, worship,

50. Zeb Bradford Long and Douglas McMurry, *Receiving the Power: Preparing the Way for the Holy Spirit* (Grand Rapids: Chosen Books, 1996), 139.

ministry, spiritual risk-taking, and transformational learning. The Holy Spirit works to construct the church and the classroom into a loving, just, compassionate, and worshiping community that invites openness and dialogue.

The Spirit among is based on God's work with his chosen people as a group. His covenant was with a family group and not just with Abraham (Gen. 12:1–3). God tells Haggai, "This is what I covenanted with you when you came out of Egypt. And my Spirit remains among you. Do not fear" (Hag. 2:5 NIV; see also Isa. 63:11). Paul taught that we have received spiritual gifts "for the common good" (1 Cor. 12:7). The fruit of the Spirit (Gal. 5:22–23) is immediately relevant to instructions such as these: "Honor one another above yourselves" (Rom. 12:10 NIV); "Live in harmony with one another" (12:16); "Be kind to one another, tenderhearted, forgiving one another" (Eph. 4:32); and "Encourage one another and build up each other, as indeed you are doing" (1 Thess. 5:11). Gordon Fee notes that in the trinitarian benediction of 2 Corinthians 13:14 (NIV), Paul selects "fellowship" to characterize the ministry of the Spirit.[51]

The anointing of the Spirit for teaching and learning is a rich and multifaceted experience. When the Spirit comes in sovereign visitation, these dimensions are present, but often the sense of power is what is most observed. As teachers seek to cultivate the anointing of the Spirit through prayer and spiritual openness, they should be aware of the richness of this empowerment and pray with the commensurate breath for his presence and power upon their teaching and among the learners.

Cultivating the Anointing

O Lord of power and grace, all hearts are in thy hands, all events at thy disposal. Set the seal of thy almighty will upon my ministry.

Puritan prayer[52]

By means of intercessory prayer, God extends to each of us a personalized, hand-engraved invitation to become intimately involved in laboring for the well-being of others.

Richard Foster[53]

Anointed teaching is, first and foremost, an indwelling and empowering of the Holy Spirit. There are no formulas that can guarantee its coming or

51. Gordon D. Fee, *God's Empowering Presence: The Holy Spirit in the Letters of Paul* (Peabody, MA: Hendrickson, 1994), 872.
52. Arthur Bennet, ed., *The Valley of Vision: A Collection of Puritan Prayers and Devotions* (Edinburgh: Banner of Truth, 1975), 186.
53. *Prayer*, 210.

effectiveness, and yet there are patterns, practices, and dispositions that foster the presence of anointed teaching. It is our responsibility to desire it, pray for it, acknowledge our need of it, seek outcomes that require it, build a place for it, and cultivate a community that seeks its truth. Anointed teaching depends on the Holy Spirit just as much as sailing depends on the wind. All earnest sailors will mend their sails, inspect their rigging, train their crew, watch the sky, and expect the wind. They will be ready when the gust comes. They will take full advantage of even a gentle breeze to move their ship forward.

Teachers and preachers must wholeheartedly desire an anointing. Congregations and students must be open and seeking. They must all proclaim with David Martyn Lloyd-Jones, "Seek Him! Seek Him! What can we do without Him? Seek Him! Seek always. . . . This 'unction,' this 'anointing,' is the supreme thing. Seek it until you have it; be content with nothing less."[54]

The desire for an anointing ought to be the strongest in the teacher's prayer closet. The Holy Spirit guides the teacher's prayer life with an eye to the mutual concern that, in all of life, the gospel message is proclaimed and heard, Jesus is glorified, the sinner is freed, the seeker understands Scripture, and the disciple is transformed. When the teacher struggles for words or stamina in prayer, the Spirit "intercedes with sighs too deep for words. And God, who searches the heart, knows what is the mind of the Spirit because the Spirit intercedes for the saints according to the will of God" (Rom. 8:26–27). Anointing flows out of the prayer closet as the teacher's knowledge of God has been expanded and tested. To pray for unction is to pray for a specific endowment of God. As E. M. Bounds writes, "This unction comes to the preacher not in the study but in the closet."[55] Jesus set a high standard for prayer time, but he probably was tempted, like we are, to subsist on a scanty prayer diet. He sympathizes with our weakness (Heb. 4:15–16) and is the high priest who prays for the prayers of teachers and preachers.

"Piper is right when he says that all genuine preaching is rooted in a feeling of desperation. The preacher wakes up on the Lord's Day morning and he can smell the smoke of hell on one side and feel the crisp breezes of heaven on the other. He then looks down at his pitiful notes and he says to himself, 'Who do I think I am kidding? Is this all there is?'"[56] The apostle Paul had this same perspective when he wrote, "Since, in the wisdom of God, the world did not know God through wisdom, God decided, through the foolishness of our proclamation, to save those who believe" (1 Cor. 1:21).

54. Lloyd-Jones, *Preaching and Preachers*, 325.
55. Bounds, *Complete Works*, 479.
56. Arturo G. Azurdia III, *Spirit Empowered Preaching: The Vitality of the Holy Spirit in Preaching* (Fearn, Ross-shire, UK: Mentor, 1998), 92.

Once convinced of the need for complete reliance on the Holy Spirit's anointing, the teacher would be empowered to seek outcomes that require it. There is a healthy expectation and anticipation of openness, listening, and authentic change for those impacted by anointed teaching. We usually define educational outcomes as measurable and reasonable, but "when the preacher proclaims the Word of God something occurs that defies exact definition. Despair gives way to hope, lives are transformed, and changes take place that have the power to reshape history."[57] Anointed outcomes assume that the teacher has asked the hard questions: "Are you expecting it to be the turning point in someone's life? Are you expecting anyone to have a climactic experience?"[58] Anointed teaching needs a home, a truthful and holy place within the teacher's character and the classroom. W. E. Sangster goes so far as to tie both prayer and holiness to his definition of unction: "Prayer is the secret of a holy life. . . . Holiness is the secret of unction."[59]

Furthermore, the confidence that the Holy Spirit is the principal teacher and primary mover of truth must be a collective belief held by a community in order for anointed teaching to be recognized and valued in that community. Here teaching and learning are relational, and "the moment of anointed preaching is a corporate reality."[60] It is expected that learners can learn from each other and from the teacher. The teacher is humble and teachable as well as courageous, willing to listen, and willing to venture into the unknown and untried. Teachers and learners pray and seek the truth together in a loving community, upheld by the strength and courage of the Holy Spirit (Acts 9:31).

The Fruit of Anointing

Human love breeds hothouse flowers; spiritual love creates the fruits that grow healthily in accord with God's good will in the rain and storm and sunshine of God's outdoors.

Dietrich Bonhoeffer[61]

In a word, the fruit of anointed teaching is love! "The goal of our instruction is love from a pure heart" (1 Tim. 1:5 NASB). People are secure in the love of God and open to growth and care for others. "For you did not receive

57. Don Allen McGregor, "The Anointed Pulpit" (DMin thesis, Asbury Theological Seminary, 2000), 17.
58. Lloyd-Jones, *Preaching and Preachers*, 325.
59. W. E. Sangster, *Power in Preaching* (New York: Abingdon, 1958), 109.
60. James A. Forbes, *The Holy Spirit and Preaching* (Nashville: Abingdon, 1989), 86.
61. *Life Together: The Classic Exploration of Faith in Community* (Harper & Row, 1954), 37.

a spirit of slavery to fall back into fear, but you have received a spirit of adoption. When we cry, 'Abba! Father!' it is that very Spirit bearing witness with our spirit that we are children of God" (Rom. 8:15–16).

There is no room for pride or abuse in anointed teaching.[62] Pride is the opposite of humility. It seeks security in self rather than in the grace of God. Jack Deere warns that "of all people, the proud have the most difficulty hearing God's voice. They seldom seriously ask God's opinion because they are convinced they already know what God thinks."[63] In contrast, "humble people put their confidence in the Holy Spirit's ability to speak, not in their ability to hear, and in Christ's ability to lead, not in their ability to follow."[64] Humility, especially in our study of and seeking after truth, provides the opening for the Spirit to do his work.

A curriculum for Christlikeness is grounded in teaching, in diligent, thoughtful planning and study, and in careful attention to the empowering work of the Holy Spirit. We will miss the goal of spiritual transformation if we neglect any of these elements or expect them to come naturally or automatically. Including the construct of anointed teaching in our conceptualizing of a curriculum for Christlikeness represents a step toward maintaining a right focus on the Holy Spirit in spiritual formation. Such a focus is greatly aided by (1) historical studies of anointed teachers and ministries, (2) proposals of curriculum that support and create a space for anointed teaching, (3) examinations of the classroom dynamics present when anointed teaching occurs, and (4) studies in educational leadership that contribute to the presence of anointed teaching. Many perceive that Bounds's maxim "Preaching which kills is prayerless preaching" is more than just preacherly hyperbole.[65] A curriculum for spiritual formation in Christlikeness is effective only when it is saturated by a grace received through prayer, humble study, and awareness that we cannot achieve what we seek by our power alone.

Formational Patterns of Teaching and Learning

Testimonies

How can we teach and guide people so that in their remembrances, they are drawn to love and obey God? Testimonies are one of the most powerful

62. For a full discussion of spiritual abuse, see Charles H. Kraft, *I Give You Authority* (Grand Rapids: Chosen Books, 1997); David Johnson and Jeff Van Vonderen, *The Subtle Power of Spiritual Abuse* (Minneapolis: Bethany House, 1991).

63. Jack Deere, *Surprised by the Voice of God: How God Speaks Today through Prophecies, Dreams, and Visions* (Grand Rapids: Zondervan, 1996), 243.

64. Deere, *Surprised by the Voice of God*, 319.

65. E. M. Bounds, *Power through Prayer* (Springdale, PA: Whitaker House, 1982), 24.

means of drawing people into a greater love of God. The best testimonies are stories of God at work as a Lover, Healer, Savior, and Friend: good testimonies put God on display. We all love stories, and we love stories that are nothing less than tales of God's grace. Testimonies are a straightforward way of bringing the reality of brokenness into our Christian communities. In general, we can think of testimonies coming in two varieties. The first variety is resolved stories, in which the person telling the story can put it into a "from, through, to" orientation. This means that some time has passed since the person went through the struggle, and they are able to identify the lessons learned and to cast them in a way that helps others see and learn as well. The second variety of testimony is unresolved stories, which we might call "in the midst of" stories. Here the person is saying, "I got knocked off the deck of the ship, and I'm in the water; I'm not certain how much longer I can keep my head up, but in the midst of this, God is faithful." We really need a mix of both types of testimonies for them to have their real effect in the church. While testimonies seem so easy and natural, they benefit from some coaching about structure.

We begin with the assumption that a leader of the group in which testimony is given might select persons ahead of time and meet with them to help them prepare. The concern is not simply that people "get it right" but that when the proper elements are emphasized, testimonies can be a powerful means of teaching. Some of the best testimonies come from people who are not accustomed to being up front and who will feel more comfortable if they receive some help and guidance. Some people are going to be much more comfortable if their testimony is written out and they simply read it aloud. In my experience, in general, the best testimonies are given in the form of an interview in which the person giving the testimony knows the questions ahead of time. Asking people questions allows them to talk about areas of growth and victory that they might be hesitant to identify on their own.

Purpose. Make sure that you and the person giving the testimony are very clear about the purpose and the audience. Are you hoping that this testimony will engage the non-Christians in the audience, or is it intended to help move along lethargic Christians to more serious discipleship?

Sufficient information. It is very important for the person giving the testimony to share sufficient information about himself or herself. Audience members need to feel that they know the person and can understand the context in which the story is set.

Interview format. A few thoughtful questions may draw out a compelling testimony from someone who may not know where to start or what to say on their own.

Skills in Teaching to Foster Formation

Clarity of communication. Both the instructional content that is shared and the procedures to be followed in learning require clear communication. In relation to procedures, teachers share with participants the stated purposes, goals, and objectives of the instruction as a means to encourage ownership.

Flexibility and use of a variety of teaching methods. Openness is called for that compensates for change without losing sight of the original intentions and purposes of the session. Flexibility sometimes signals avoidance of key areas of learning that we should not pass over. Using a variety of teaching methods increases the possibility that the participants will be able to maintain concentration and avoid boredom.

Enthusiasm. The enthusiasm of the teacher is contagious if the instructional content is owned by the teacher in new ways. This ownership requires diligence in the preparation for teaching. Diligence in the evaluation of teaching provides new possibilities for future presentations.

Maintenance of a task orientation. Effective teachers are able to keep students focused on the tasks of learning. Sensitivity to persons in terms of care is important in the ministry of teaching, but an equal concern for the content and its potential transformative impact is required. The focus on tasks is the complementary skill to flexibility. In this maintenance of a task orientation, the teacher provides feedback to students regarding their progress in relation to the assigned tasks and reminds them of the ultimate goals of their efforts.

Inner feelings. One of the marvelous things about testimonies is that they enable people to reveal inner feelings that might not normally be shared in casual conversations. A coach or leader can help people understand what they were feeling and how that contributed to the decisions they made.

Former religion. Testimonies often involve leaving a former religion. However, spiritual heritage should be described with respect and not dismissed in a way that might offend people in the audience or diminish the important reality of Christian unity.

Chronological order. Do not be slavish to chronological order, because it will not guarantee a compelling and helpful testimony. People are interested

Ability to involve students in the teaching-learning process. This involvement includes intellectual, psychological, and physical responses. Total involvement of persons encourages the transfer of learning to other situations beyond the immediate instructional setting. In evaluation, participants reflect on and assess the levels of their involvement and suggest alternatives that may have improved their engagement with the instructional content. This skill and its evaluation foster the formation of persons as self-directed learners who have learned how to learn in other settings.

Varying the level of discourse. Discourses can be at the level of facts, explanations, evaluative judgments, justification, critical analyses and syntheses, concrete realities, and abstract conceptualizations. Variety encourages creative and critical responses. It serves to connect the instructional content with realities outside the immediate setting, and it decreases rote responses from participants.

Appropriate use of praise and criticism. The praise shared with participants must be genuine and appropriate to the instruction. This is a real concern in an age of manipulation. The criticism teachers offer to their students must be constructive, particularly in a critical and cynical age that readily dismisses others through negative critique. Affirmation centers on students as persons, and criticism is reserved for their performance or work. With criticism, it is necessary for teachers to suggest alternatives.

Self-analysis and self-evaluation. The effective teacher is capable of pursuing continuous self-study and self-analysis so that teacher's actions improve over time. It requires an integrity that models the teacher's openness toward personal transformation.[a]

a. Adapted from Robert W. Pazmiño, *Basics of Teaching for Christians: Preparation, Instruction, and Evaluation* (Grand Rapids: Baker, 1998), 89–94. Used by permission.

in hearing the "from, through, to" and a personalized understanding of how this evolved.

Wise confession. Prudent boundaries need to be set about what will be confessed. One person's confession ought not also be a confession of the sins of others. Be careful about testimonies that could embarrass family members or others in the audience.

Honesty. Because testimonies are a powerful tool, Satan will seek to supplant and destroy their effectiveness. They should not become opportunities for people to overreach in terms of what God has done in their life or for people to become spiritually proud. Be vigilant that testimonies are honest and create a climate and culture of brokenness.

Resolution. Testimonies are often criticized when they are "all wrapped up in a neat little package." The "from, through, to" understanding of a person's predicament and a realistic assessment of where they ended up are higher priorities than excessive language of victory. When stories are told, the human heart yearns for a celebration of grace and a sense of resolution of life's problems. The call is not for more unresolved stories, because many listeners will be able to identify with the "through" or "still in the midst of it" turbulent state of affairs. When stories have a happy ending, an interviewer can ask simple follow-up questions or make some appropriate comments that help put this in a context of truth.

What we remember about ourselves and God affects how we serve and love. One of the most important ways we can affect what we remember and act on is through teaching and learning. When we remember the love and grace God has shown us through Christ, we are far more likely to pattern future responses after that kind of love.

Scripture

"Seek God, not happiness"—this is the fundamental rule of all meditation. If you seek God alone, you will gain happiness: that is its promise.

Dietrich Bonhoeffer[66]

Meditation is the aspect of spiritual reading that trains us to read Scripture as a connected, coherent whole, not a collection of inspired bits and pieces.

Eugene H. Peterson[67]

The Bible itself performs certain actions when told, heard, and remembered.

Craig Dykstra[68]

As people of the book, we are to be growing in biblical literacy. Such a working literacy should include an outline of the flow of biblical history, knowledge of the main characters and stories in the Bible, and comprehension and internalization of the biblical symbol system. The Christian story found in the Bible should form our lives. An important part of spiritual formation is the systematic teaching of the Bible, equipping people to read the Bible on their own in a thoughtful and spiritually engaging way.

66. *Life Together*, 84.
67. *Eat This Book: A Conversation in the Art of Spiritual Reading* (Grand Rapids: Eerdmans, 2006), 100.
68. *Growing in the Life of Faith: Education and Christian Practices*, 2nd ed. (Louisville: Westminster John Knox, 2005), 58.

It is difficult to clearly remember our identity in Christ when we only vaguely remember the words of assurance of God's love, given to us by our Savior. One of the most powerful spiritual disciplines that Christians can engage in is regular memorization of Scripture. We often think of Scripture memory as something that is completely private, but the community can foster and encourage it.

A church can identify key verses that it believes members should commit to memory. A church can also present these in the worship service and provide opportunities and encouragement for people to repeat them from memory. People in church often recite Scripture passages like the Lord's Prayer and Psalm 23 almost from memory. Why not other intentionally memorized passages? Why not a collection of biblical passages that have special meaning to that local congregation? I am aware of a church in Wisconsin that chose one of Paul's prayers for the believers in Ephesus and made it their "church life-verses." Visitors have often admitted to a powerful awareness of God's presence when the congregation spontaneously joins the pastor in the benediction with these words:

> We pray that Christ will be more and more at home in our hearts, living within us as we trust in him. May our roots grow down deep into the soil of God's marvelous love. And may we be able to feel and understand, as all God's children should, how long, how wide, how deep, how high his love really is. And to experience that love for ourselves, though it is so deep that we will never see the end of it, or fully know or understand it, and so at last we will be filled up with God himself. (based on Eph. 3:17–19)

Another advantage that comes from encouraging memorization in a community context is that people learn truth that they might not have gravitated to on their own. At various points on our journey, we tend to emphasize certain truths that bring us comfort and solace and are compatible with our outlook. Yet as Martin Luther taught us, we need the whole counsel of God. When we learn to memorize passages in a community context, we learn verses that emphasize the love of God, our need to participate in building a just community, the importance of prayer and worship, assurance of our salvation, the value of godly family relationships, and much more.

A church that has learned Scripture is also able to engage in worship in a more meaningful way. A part of worship is a purposeful response to God. When the community knows Scripture, God's Word can have a greater place in the singing, exhortation, comforting, teaching, preaching, and care. Paul encourages believers, "Let the Word of Christ—the Message—have the run

Life Together

Is the invisible presence of the Christian fellowship a reality and a help to the individual? Do the intercessions of others carry him through the day? Is the Word of God close to him as a comfort and a strength? Or does he misuse his aloneness contrary to the fellowship, the Word, and the prayer? The individual must realize that his hours of aloneness react upon the community. In his solitude he can sunder and besmirch the fellowship, or he can strengthen and hallow it. Every act of self-control of the Christian is also a service to the fellowship.

On the other hand, there is no sin in thought, word, or deed, no matter how personal or secret, that does not inflict injury upon the whole fellowship. An element of sickness gets into the body; perhaps nobody knows where it comes from or in what member it has lodged, but the body is infected. This is the proper metaphor for the Christian community. We are members of a body, not only when we choose to be, but also in our whole existence. Every member serves the whole body, either to its health or to its destruction. This is no mere theory; it is a spiritual reality. And the Christian community has often experienced its effects with disturbing clarity, sometimes destructively and sometimes fortunately.

One who returns to the Christian family fellowship after fighting the battle of the day brings with him the blessing of his aloneness, but he himself receives anew the blessing of the fellowship. Blessed is he who is alone in the strength of the fellowship, and blessed is he who keeps the fellowship in the strength of aloneness. But the strength of aloneness and the strength of the fellowship is solely the strength of the Word of God, which is addressed to the individual in the fellowship.[a]

a. Bonhoeffer, *Life Together*, 88–89.

of the house. Give it plenty of room in your lives" (Col. 3:16 Message). In the context in which Paul was writing, the emphasis was on corporate worship that flowed from the group's knowledge of Scripture.

When the community has memorized and "bought" Scripture, the Bible can have a higher authority in members' lives. Before we hear a word of correction based on Scripture, we have already committed ourselves to the truth of that Scripture passage when we memorized it; therefore, we are more likely to abide by an admonition based on a Scripture passage that we thought was worthy of our time to memorize.

Bible memorization is also foundational to many other key spiritual disciplines. For example, Scripture encourages us to meditate on the Word of God continually, and Scripture-based meditation requires knowledge of Scripture. Praying Scripture has been a source of comfort and guidance for Christians throughout the centuries and requires an intimate understanding of the Bible. Thoughtfully using the Bible for guidance and discernment also requires an ability to reflect on a wide range of verses that one has come to know and understand through Bible memorization.

In corporate and individual meditation, we can revisit passages that we have memorized. This discipline provides opportunities for us to go deeper into the meanings and applications of Scripture. We grow as Christians by learning and relearning a somewhat limited set of material and learning how to live it out. Insight comes from sustained, thoughtful attention rather than occasional glances. Then, through that living out, we recognize new opportunities to apply the gospel and to bring Jesus's perspective to bear on our life situations. Scripture's power to teach repeatedly over a lifetime through a myriad of experiences is inherent within a passage, which highlights the fact that Scripture is the fusion of words and Spirit. Jesus reminds us, "The words that I have spoken to you are spirit and life" (John 6:63).

Finally, we need to acknowledge that community-oriented Bible memorization often has been quite deformative. Prizes, rewards, and competitions have distorted why we are learning Scripture. It is a tragedy when this good gift is so trivialized and belittled. Community-oriented Scripture memorization need not have these deformative aspects. Through using Scripture in worship, in both singing and congregational responsive readings, people can memorize Scripture in an effective but subtle way over time.

Jesus's Teaching Methods

The discipline of learning helps us to be *intentional* learners, not accidental learners.

Donald S. Whitney[69]

You call me Teacher and Lord—and you are right, for that is what I am.

Jesus (John 13:13)

Remembering is deeply related to the life of learning that Jesus engaged in through his teaching ministry. Jesus's disciples were his students, his apprentices,

69. *Spiritual Disciplines for the Christian Life* (Colorado Springs: NavPress, 1991), 219.

Jesus's Teaching Methods

Jesus is universally accepted as a master teacher. As a communicator, he presented truth to people who had heard it before but who had lost the meaning of the truth. The people already had a structure for education, and they had heard five hundred sermons on a given topic before. Jesus and the Pharisees were both building fundamental theology on the foundation of the Old Testament. However, Jesus injected a new approach for thinking and considering questions.

Jesus used the vocabulary of the people who were listening. He was clear, simple, and direct, and he did not use unfamiliar jargon. When talking with the Pharisees, Jesus used language and jargon that suited them. He knew how to read their questions. Some questions were simple and serious, and others were loaded or trick questions. Jesus adjusted vocabulary to the audience and to his concern that they hear afresh.

Jesus knew that the people were not really listening or thinking deeply and that their minds were "in neutral." He forced them to think and question by speaking the truth just below the surface of the language. They would walk away wondering what he really meant and what the truth was. His parables are a prime example of this approach. Parables reveal and conceal at the same time. To reveal is to draw in and ask questions. To conceal is to encourage searching and thinking and not to spoon-feed. Jesus often called them "parables of the kingdom," and the design is that the Jews are blinded until the Gentiles can be drawn in as well. In an example from Mark 10:13–15, Jesus explains that we are to receive the kingdom as a little child. This is not a call to become immature but to grow up. Jesus says, "Consider carefully how you listen. Whoever has will be given more; whoever does not have, even what

and he often asked questions that challenged them to remember, to learn, and to form new meanings. He is continually addressed as "Rabbi" and "Teacher" (Matt. 8:19; 12:38; 23:7–8; Mark 9:5; Luke 22:11). He surely was a teacher. The Gospels are filled with his teaching, and he invites his disciples to embrace a life of learning.

Much of the learning Jesus invited his first followers to absorb was decidedly corporate. They were gathered together when he taught them to pray (Luke 11:1–4), and his discipleship program required his learners as a group to "follow me" (5:27).

In terms of emphasis, learning is the spiritual practice that receives the greatest attention in the Gospels. Jesus is continually teaching and calling his disciples to greater understanding, which is measured by their heartfelt they think they have will be taken from them" (Luke 8:18 NIV). In the kingdom, one is either receiving or losing. There is no neutrality in the kingdom. In another parable, Jesus says, "Wherever there is a carcass, there the vultures will gather" (Matt. 24:28 NIV). He is teaching about the second coming. When certain things happen, then certain other things happen. The second coming will happen when the situation is right.

Jesus's vocabulary also made use of highly graphic wordings, paradoxical language, and hyperbole. Jesus used graphic wording to describe faith as being like the tiny mustard seed (Luke 17:6). We think bigger is better. Jesus thinks size is irrelevant. There is no correlation between the size of my faith and what happens. Even if we can only rise to the faith of a mustard seed, God can move through it. The issue is the power of God and not the size of my faith. Using paradoxical language makes us think because the ideas presented sound self-contradictory; Jesus says, "Many who are first will be last, and the last will be first" (Mark 10:31), and, "Whoever wishes to be first among you must be slave of all" (10:44). A hyperbole is an overstatement used for its shock effect. Jesus suggests that if a body part causes one to sin, it ought to be cut off (9:42-48).

Jesus's teaching methods were much like those of the rabbis. He used the familiar method because he did not want the method to offend or distract. He used parables, illustrations, object lessons, commands, proverbs, quotations from the Old Testament, actions, humor, puns, and riddles. His illustrations and object lessons were authentic, and they dealt with general issues from ordinary life such as animals, work, fields, marriage, trees, children, money, and weather.[a]

a. Adapted from Walter Elwell, class lecture on Jesus's teaching methods (November 2002, Wheaton College, Wheaton). Used by permission.

demonstration of embodied responses. The task of learning to love one another is mastered only when one does, in fact, love the other (John 13:34–35). The learning he desires is holistic knowledge that leads to obedience.

A Focus on the Gospel and Double Knowledge

In the earlier chapters, I mentioned the need for the gospel to be a road map to guide our lives. When we look at Paul's letter to the Galatians, we realize that it is easy for us to follow false gospels of various kinds. We need to remind ourselves that all of us follow and lean on various false gospels. Detecting them is difficult because they often are below our theological radar. Few well-churched Christians would claim that good parenting, punctuality,

etiquette, physical fitness, and active church involvement are ways of achiev-
ing peace with God. Still, we live as if these are proven ways of gaining God's
love and favor. We need to begin with an assumption that daily appropriating
the gospel will be a struggle for Christians, and we continuously need to be
retrained to rely on the grace of Jesus Christ as offered in the gospel for our
salvation and hope.

Training that appropriates the gospel will require a concrete look at subtle
patterns of self-reliance and defensiveness. This requires cultivating the kind
of double knowledge that John Calvin speaks of in the first chapter of his
Institutes of the Christian Religion. He holds that "without knowledge of
self there is no knowledge of God," and "without knowledge of God there is
no knowledge of self."[70] For Calvin, double knowledge leads him to conclude
that without self-consciousness there is no consciousness of God and without
consciousness of God there is no true self-consciousness. True spiritual formation does require the growth and knowledge of self and the knowledge of God.

Since Calvin, other spiritual writers have expressed an awareness that
without proper double knowledge, we will not grow in the joy and peace of
Christian discipleship. An example is Ruth Barton, who links one's self-worth
in Christ with self-knowledge: "First of all, he [Christ] wants us to know how
much we are worth. . . . Key to a woman's self-esteem is knowledge of herself
as an individual who is unique and separate from others, balanced by a sense
of how she fits into her community. Many women lack self-esteem precisely
because they know so little about themselves."[71] Similarly, David Benner is
concerned for the connectedness and growth of spiritual and psychological
wholeness that is embedded in Calvin's position. Benner claims that "people
who are afraid to look deeply at themselves will, of course, be equally afraid
to look deeply and personally at God."[72] Finally, Howard Rice works with
Calvin's use of the word *knowledge*. He "maintain[s] that 'experience' is a
better word than 'know' to point to the way believers apprehend God's acts
in the world."[73] When we aim for a strong double knowledge that highlights
experience, we are circling back to a previously stated priority to emphasize
learning over teaching because learning involves what "a person absorbs, accepts, relates to, or identifies with, out of his or her experiences."[74] I might

70. John Calvin, *Institutes of the Christian Religion*, ed. John McNeill, trans. Ford Lewis
Battles (Philadelphia: Westminster, 1960), 1:35, 37.

71. Ruth Haley Barton, *The Truths That Free Us: A Woman's Calling to Spiritual Transformation* (Colorado Springs: Shaw Books, 2002), 26–27.

72. David Benner, *Care of Souls* (Grand Rapids: Baker, 1998), 99–100.

73. Howard L. Rice, *Reformed Spirituality: An Introduction for Believers* (Louisville: Westminster John Knox, 1991), 26–27.

74. Nelson, *How Faith Matures*, 163.

The Gospel and Christian Education

Is there an element that will bring the Bible, Christian doctrine, all human problems, life, experience, the child, the person, the church, and the Redeemer of mankind all into bold relief? I believe that there is such an element and that it is the gospel of God's redeeming activity in Jesus Christ. My conviction is that Christian education can center in the gospel and use the gospel as its guiding principle with assurance of its complete adequacy, both theologically and educationally, and with assurance of its simplicity and clarity.

The suggestion that the gospel be used as the basic guide for Christian education theory is supported by five arguments:

1. Revelation—the Word of God—is central in Christian education theory.
2. The gospel—God's redeeming activity in Jesus Christ—is the very heart and point of the Word he has spoken to men in their self-centered helplessness throughout the ages, and the very heart and point of the Word he speaks to men today.
3. The gospel is the clue to the meaning of history.
4. The gospel is the clue to the meaning of existence.
5. The gospel is the reason for the church's existence: it brings the church into existence; it sustains the church; it informs, directs, and corrects the church.[a]

a. D. Campbell Wyckoff, *The Gospel and Christian Education: A Theory of Christian Education for Our Times* (Philadelphia: Westminster, 1958), 92, 98, 108.

say that without learning about and experiencing myself, there is no experience of God, and without learning about and experiencing God, there is no experience of myself. I define myself as a person in light of my experience with the Other Person.

Cultivating a Disposition of Awe

Awe comes when we understand our place as humans and know our dependence on a God whom we can never fully understand. Children are blessed with the ability to wonder and to live with mystery because they trust their parents and are not troubled by their dependence. David wonders at "the moon and the stars, which you have set in place" (Ps. 8:3 NIV), and at God's mindfulness of humans. How could such an awesome God care for a human or be so lavish toward him? When I am struck by the grandeur of my God and by my puny, undeserving weakness and inabilities, the contrast is staggering and raises a question about God's motives. Yet God does love me beyond measure, and I can easily join in David's refrain of praise: "LORD, our Lord, how majestic is your name in all the earth!" (8:1 NIV). Awe naturally leads to praise.

Childlike awe and wonder are our allies in the darkness and confusion of brokenness. When we are overcome by the tragic, it is easy to doubt and question God. If in tears and despair we can ponder that God's awesome vastness is beyond us and know, like a child, that we do not and cannot understand his majesty, then, like a child, we can depend on a love that we also cannot understand. In accepting the love we do not understand, we can have trust that in the majesty we do not understand, there is a purpose for the tragedy we do not understand. We must embrace the mystery in the sovereign power and love of God and also in the particular trials and brokenness of our lives. In childlike awe and dependence, we accept God's grace and are free of the pressure to hold ourselves and our faith together by the strength of our faith. Ruth Tucker says, "This is my faith, and I will never abandon it—nor will God abandon me. But do I believe it? If everything depended on my belief, there are some days when I think I would be doomed. But my salvation does not depend on the strength of my faith; it depends only on God's grace. Even when my faith is weak, I have confidence in God's hold on my life."[75] Her awe and wonder at a God who is vastly beyond her, more than her knowledge and understanding, open a way to confidence in God's gracious hold on her life.

Similarly, Adrian Van Kaam uses the term *appreciative abandonment* to describe a positive outlook in which at all times, under all circumstances, one chooses to live in praise of the embracing, never-failing care of the mystery.[76] This attitude instills in one's heart a disposition of awe-filled appreciation for anything praiseworthy, despite the darkness of the hour. It encourages a joyous outlook without denying the pain one is going through.

> Christian Spiritual Formation should always be more than the teaching ministry of the church but never less. True formational teaching is compressive, deeply orthodox, healthy, and anointed by the Spirit of God.

Paul also expressed this attitude when he wrote, "The saying is sure: If we have died with him, we will also live with him; if we endure, we will also reign with him; if we deny him, he will also

75. Ruth Tucker, *Walking Away from Faith: Unraveling the Mystery of Belief and Unbelief* (Downers Grove, IL: InterVarsity, 2002), 26.

76. Adrian Van Kaam, *Fundamental Formation*, vol. 1 (New York: Crossroad, 1989), 240–41.

deny us; if we are faithless, he remains faithful—for he cannot deny himself"
(2 Tim. 2:11–13).

Solitude

The Word of God is the fulcrum upon which the lever of prayer is placed and
by which things are mightily moved.

E. M. Bounds[77]

Christian love between persons is reborn in solitude.

Susan Muto and Adrian Van Kaam[78]

Silence has the power to force you to dig deep inside yourself.

Paul Tournier[79]

The quest for spiritual formation has included the development of a disciplined prayer life frequently called "centering prayer." Centering prayer is
a quiet, Scripture-based, meditative prayer designed to replace worry and
anxiety with a focus on our ever-present Savior and guide, Jesus Christ.[80]
Again, many see centering prayer as something done by an individual in
private. Under this view, centering prayer is a quite personal and intimate
activity. When people have learned the discipline, they undertake it as a way
of casting their cares on Christ as Scripture admonishes us, and they often
do this in a quiet, private setting.

Many of us have found that although centering prayer is often practiced in
private, it is best learned in a group setting. Quiet, meditative prayer is very
countercultural. While it enjoys biblical and historical support, many contemporary Christians find a slight guardedness about it and therefore would
be inclined to give it up easily if it does not work when first tried. A retreat
setting can be an ideal way to help people become established in this pattern
of casting cares on Christ as they gently and quietly pray over Scripture.

77. *Complete Works*, 66.

78. *Tell Me Who I Am: Questions and Answers on Christian Spirituality* (Denville, NJ:
Dimension Books, 1977), 16.

79. "The Power of Listening, the Power of Silence," in *Spiritual Classics: Selected Readings
for Individuals and Groups on the Twelve Spiritual Disciplines*, ed. Richard J. Foster and Emilie
Griffin (San Francisco: HarperSanFrancisco, 2000), 161.

80. *Centering prayer* has unfortunately become a widely used term in the internet spirituality
sphere, where it has lost all its deep Christian connections. I use this term here in respect to its
Christian origin, but it may be better replaced with terms like *waiting prayer* or *contemplative
prayer*.

Small Groups

Problems that seem insoluble when individuals ponder them alone are viewed in a much more optimistic light when the Spirit of God is free to move a group in the direction of God's will.

Lois LeBar[81]

Small groups can provide a marvelous environment for us to remember who we are in the midst of challenges and for the community to love its members. Small groups give us the opportunity to learn and to reflect on our situation. They can be the place where double knowledge (i.e., knowledge of God and self) is refined. Small groups are the perfect environment to provide both the support and the challenge we need to live the Christian life well.

Small groups are a gift of grace from God to a group of people committed to learning and growing together. For many people, these small gatherings provide the best examples of Christian community. They are contexts in which Larry Crabb's characteristics of spiritual community are often most clearly seen: "1) celebrating people as created and forgiven by God; 2) visioning what another is becoming and trusting God to accomplish such; 3) discerning happenings as climates for growth; 4) empowering others to fully become what God is desiring for them to be."[82]

Pastoral Care

Personal loss, tragedies, changes, and disruption can contribute to spiritual formation. These events have the effect of stripping away our self-reliance and reminding us of what is truly important in life. They can also be times of great embitterment and loss. We need to put structures in place that emphasize deep compassion, care, and empathy as well as formative guidance. In general, our churches are better at providing compassion than formative guidance, and youth programs are far more prone to emphasize diversion than direction. Formation implies in its language that there is a form (an image) to which we are seeking to conform—the character of Christ.

The religious instruction described in the Bible is remarkably God-centered, and yet not God-centered in the way we might first imagine. It is not God-centered in the sense that it focuses on theology; rather, the focus is on God himself. Significantly, in several Old Testament occurrences of a common Hebrew word for "teach" and "learn" (*lāmad*), it is the Lord himself who is the teacher. God taught his people through his interactions with them in

---

81. *Education*, 303.
82. Larry Crabb, *The Safest Place on Earth* (Nashville: Word, 1999), 136–40.

day-to-day living. Furthermore, the great and powerful teachers of the Bible, like Isaiah and Jesus, always had a message directly related to the lives of their learners, but, even more important, it was a God-centered message. True spiritual formation constantly shows people that righteous and joyful living is available only to those who look at life from God's perspective rather than, as is the usual case, judging God by viewing him through the perspective of their own lives.

The Lord's Supper

The Lord's Supper is a great antidote to the toxic individualism of our age. Sharing in this sacramental mystery these many individuals become one body, bearing each other's burdens and heartaches and multiplying each other's joys.

Harold Senkbeil[83]

In our Western (Greek) intellectual heritage, "remembering" means "recollecting": recalling to mind something that is no longer a present reality. Nothing could be further from a Jewish conception. For example, in the Jewish liturgy, "remembering" means participating here and now in certain defining events in the past and also in the future.

Michael Horton[84]

The Lord's Supper is a means of grace, a way that Christians are strengthened, and it is a powerful tool to aid our remembering whose we are and who we are. One of the main goals of Hebrew education was to make sure the people would not forget their identity and would therefore always fear God and obey his commandments. The dark period of Israel's history during the time of the judges is explained as being the bitter fruit of forgetfulness: "That whole generation also died, and the next generation forgot the LORD and what he had done for Israel" (Judg. 2:10 GNT). In Hebrew thought, the chief spiritual malady was forgetfulness. In Deuteronomy 4, the practical consequences of God's great deliverance are clearly set out and an overwhelming concern is that Israel remember what they experienced: "But take care and watch yourselves closely, so as neither to forget the things that your eyes have seen nor to let them slip from your mind all the days of your life; make them known to your children and your children's children" (4:9).

---

83. *The Care of Souls: Cultivating a Pastor's Heart* (Bellingham, WA: Lexham, 2019), Kindle Loc. 4803.

84. *The Christian Faith: A Systematic Theology for Pilgrims on the Way* (Grand Rapids: Zondervan, 2011), 799.

We are indeed forgetful pilgrims, and we need to be reminded of the good things that God has done in our lives, in the lives of our brothers and sisters in Christ, and in salvation history. Accordingly, in our spiritual formation, we must take time for testimony, reflection, and remembrance. The Lord's Supper must not be reduced to a formational practice but should remain a communal Christian activity that has a goal of helping believers remember.

Conclusion

[People] are more eager to hear what the world has to say than to listen to God.

Thomas à Kempis[85]

Studying the Master is a critical part of remembering what we have received. In our information-saturated society, it is easy to believe that the most pertinent information for guidance and decision making comes from one of our much-vaunted experts. The sentimentalized picture of Jesus that is so prevalent leaves the impression that he is an expert on weakness and ineffectiveness. That is a far cry from the picture of Jesus in the Gospels. Here is a man who, as a boy, kept the intelligentsia of his day occupied for three days when he paid them a visit. He was a spellbinding speaker, a master at verbal repartee, a conversationalist, a counselor of great skill and insight, and the life of the party. There is much we can learn from this man, and we can learn to imitate Jesus only after we have a grasp of his life and teaching.

Rightly remembering is a basic move in spiritual formation. Remembering requires experiences, content, and a way of seeing the world as well as an opportunity to disengage from the rush of life in order to reflect. Spiritual formation has the task of building up memories and providing structures for people to reflect on what they know/remember about God's work in their lives and then to live out of that reality.

Before moving on to the chapters on responding and relating, it is helpful to recall what has gone before. Most basically, remembering in community is tied to patterns of communal learning and teaching. Teachers and learners must work together to create and maintain spaces where the truth of the gospel is creatively presented. Wisdom is needed in the search for an expanding self-knowledge based on a clearer knowledge of God. The communal or group effort to learn together enriches pastoral care in times of struggle. The

85. *The Imitation of Christ*, ed. and trans. William Creasy (Notre Dame, IN: Ave Maria, 2004), 86.

joint effort deepens each personal story as it is connected with the stories of peers and with the stories of spiritual heroes and forebears.

Remembering is critical, as it recalls the grace we have received. The gospel is necessary for spiritual formation as one first understands the call to salvation and then, in a day-to-day recalling of the gospel's power, as one persistently seeks to grow in Christlikeness. Jesus invites us to love and obey God and also to love one another. We can answer these invitations only as we remember the grace we have received and use that grace as the driving force in a desire to grow and be formed like Christ. Spiritual disciplines help to place one in spiritual, emotional, and physical places where the desire to grow can be watered and nourished.

We strengthen and expand remembering in community as individuals work together in Bible memory and study, storytelling, and catechesis. A primary goal of remembering in community is to focus on grace received, with an eye to taking grace as the major driver or impetus in responding and relating in a Christlike manner. Receiving, remembering, responding, and relating are a package. Responding is the work within the individual heart, where one remembers and internalizes what one has received. Relating is the outer demonstration or working out of one's responses. Again, it is critical that receiving, remembering, responding, and relating work together to build and reinforce each other. Sharing our lives and effort with one another other in community provides connection, challenge, compassion, and celebration. This sharing is built on the premise that we serve as priests to one another, and it stands in contrast to the culture's preference for individualism.

For Further Reading

Bounds, E. M. *The Complete Works of E. M. Bounds on Prayer*. Grand Rapids: Baker, 1990. This brief volume argues that life-giving and anointed preaching flows out of a preacher's prayer life. While we can learn much from Bounds' writing and ministry, readers may find the male-oriented language quite jarring. Readers should also be aware that Bounds served as a chaplain in the Confederate army during the Civil War.

Gorman, Julie A. *Community That Is Christian*. 2nd ed. Grand Rapids: Baker Books, 2002. A book that examines the role, definition, and dynamics of small groups for corporate spiritual formation.

Lloyd-Jones, David Martyn. *Preaching and Preachers*. London: Hodder & Stoughton, 1971. A book that contains a chapter on anointed preaching that is a wise, balanced, and compelling presentation by a widely acknowledged, anointed preacher.

Lovelace, Richard F. *Dynamics of Spiritual Life: An Evangelical Theology of Renewal*. Downers Grove, IL: InterVarsity, 1979. A comprehensive theological treatment of Christian growth with a strong community orientation.

Nelson, C. Ellis. *How Faith Matures*. Louisville: Westminster John Knox, 1989. A book that explains how a person's faith matures when ordinary life experiences are interpreted in the light of the gospel and when the congregation is the context for maturing.

Nouwen, Henri J. M. *Creative Ministry*. Garden City, NY: Doubleday, 1971. A brief book with a thoughtful essay titled "Beyond the Transference of Knowledge."

Oden, Thomas C. *Pastoral Theology: Essentials of Ministry*. San Francisco: Harper & Row, 1982. A theologically rich but brief exploration of unction.

Osmer, Richard Robert. *The Teaching Ministry of Congregations*. Louisville: Westminster John Knox, 2005. A book that sets forth a practical theology of the teaching ministry grounded in the practice of the apostle Paul. The author sees the central tasks of the teaching ministry to be catechesis, exhortation, and discernment.

Packer, J. I. *Knowing God*. Downers Grove, IL: InterVarsity, 1973. An invitation to pursue the knowledge of God and a demonstration of the power of theology in personal formation.

Palmer, Parker J. *The Courage to Teach: Exploring the Inner Landscape of a Teacher's Life*. San Francisco: Jossey-Bass, 1998. A book that argues that good teaching comes from the identity and the integrity of the teacher.

Thune, Bob, and Will Walker with World Harvest Mission. *The Gospel Centered Life*. Greensboro, NC: Growth, 2011. A model presentation for how to help Christians remember the gospel.

Wilhoit, Jim, and Leland Ryken. *Effective Bible Teaching*. 2nd ed. Grand Rapids: Baker Academic, 2012. A call for teachers to give more attention to their preparation through observing the literary dimensions of the text.

FIVE

Responding

Love and Service to God and Others

Therefore, go and make disciples of all the nations, baptizing them in the name of the Father and the Son and the Holy Spirit. Teach these new disciples to obey all the commands I [Jesus] have given you. And be sure of this: I am with you always, even to the end of the age.

Matthew 28:19–20 NLT

But the goal of our instruction is love from a pure heart, from a good conscience, and from a sincere faith.

1 Timothy 1:5 NASB

The spiritual life, however, is prior to the moral life, for we can love the neighbor as God loves us only if first we have experienced that love affair with God. More important, we cannot love God except in response to God's love for us. This love affair with God is the one and only end of human life.

John H. Westerhoff III[1]

What are we to respond to? We are to respond to God's gospel of love and forgiveness with love and service to God and those around us.

1. *Spiritual Life: The Foundation for Preaching and Teaching* (Louisville: Westminster John Knox, 1994), 1.

How do we do this? The gospel changes us, and our responding is an outflow of a changed heart. We also learn that God changes us as we live our lives well and reach out in love and service to God and others.

What stance does this require? Marveling at grace. Realizing we are pipes to carry his grace to others and not buckets content to hoard it. Grace comes to us to go through us to others.

Many resources aimed at promoting spiritual growth offer personal growth, competence, and fulfillment and urge one to be on the right side of the day's hot-button moral issues; in short, they are narcissistic at their core. They focus on the individual and on empowering the individual with little regard (unless the individual so chooses) for the good of the community and society at personal cost. In contrast, CSF ultimately enables people to love others more fully and to contribute to fostering a more just, lovely, and well-ordered community.

Appropriate responses to the gospel come in many forms. At times, a quiet prayer is the fullest and most appropriate response. At other times, the appropriate response may be costly and dramatic. What is crucial is that we see that following Christ requires us to cultivate a lifestyle of response. Well-formed believers do not let circumstances have the final word. They do not merely react to crises but learn to respond with a gospel-grounded response. Their response in a crisis is not different from their usual response: telling the truth, though now it is quite costly; loving the outcast, though now that seems to betray one's race/class; praying, though now that is forbidden by their persecutors.

Formed to Serve, Formed by Serving

In doing we learne.

George Herbert[2]

Of this gospel I have become a servant according to the gift of God's grace that was given me by the working of his power.

Ephesians 3:7

Cultivating the instinct to act on gospel teaching is crucial to our transformation. Our instruction is not complete until we have nurtured in learners a tendency to act.[3] Cultivating a tendency toward responsible action and

2. *The Works of George Herbert*, ed. F. E. Hutchinson (Oxford: Clarendon, 1941), 347.
3. Nicholas Wolterstorff, *Educating for Responsible Action* (Grand Rapids: Eerdmans, 1980), 4–6.

engagement is part of the culture of effective spiritual formation programs. Douglas Hyde has aptly illustrated the reinforcing interplay between doing and being. In his book *Dedication and Leadership*, he describes how the Communist Party in Great Britain, of which he had been a member, effectively used party service as a way of generating interest in learning. A new convert, for example, was not immediately put into classes to learn about Communism but was assigned to a street corner. As the recruit distributed Communist papers and pamphlets, people asked questions about the Soviet Union and Communism that the recruit could not adequately answer. Inevitably, this green recruit found the defense of Communism to be less convincing to the passersby than they had imagined. The recruit left this curbside propaganda work with a thirst to learn to serve the cause better the next time they had the opportunity. Hyde comments,

> Those who sent him into this form of activity did not expect him to have all the answers. He has let down neither the Party nor himself. In the process he has learned a good deal. When he next takes up his stand at the side of the road, he will come determined to do better. Most probably, he has been reading Communist papers in a different way, looking for the answers to the questions he was asked last time. Gathering shot and shell in readiness for the next fight. This is when he really begins to learn—and the desire to learn now comes from within himself.[4]

Service predisposes a person to learn. The Communists, at times, understood this truth very well. Hyde documents how service leads to teachableness and a genuine motivation to learn. John Dewey understood well this interplay of learning and engagement: "To 'learn from experience' is to make a backward and forward connection between what we do to things and what we enjoy or suffer from things in consequence. Under such conditions, doing becomes a trying; an experiment with the world to find out what it is like; the undergoing becomes instruction—discovery of the connection of things."[5]

As Christians, we can take Dewey's phrase "an experiment with the world" and enrich it to "an experiment with the world in partnership with God." I made far more progress in prayer when I realized that while prayer is a powerful spiritual tool, it is not something I could break—I could, in partnership with God, make my practice a holy experiment. Even inappropriate

4. Douglas Hyde, *Dedication and Leadership: Learning from the Communists* (Notre Dame, IN: University of Notre Dame Press, 1966), 44–45.

5. John Dewey, *The Middle Works, 1899–1924*, ed. Jo Ann Boydston, vol. 9, *1916: Democracy and Education* (Carbondale: Southern Illinois University Press, 1980), 147.

prayer exposes us to valuable lessons when we engage with a teachable spirit. I was encouraged by a spiritual mentor to experiment with practiced reflection on biblical teaching and spiritual masters' teaching on prayer. In this context, Dallas Willard's insight that "prayer is talking to God about what we are doing together" makes so much sense.[6] As with every significant endeavor in life, we do not know how well we have understood or observed until we try to do what we have learned.

Woven into the fabric of formation is an emphasis on the learner discovering their "unique-communal life call."[7] The discovery of and the attentiveness to guarding and developing one's unique-communal life call are a lifelong project, not something accomplished fully in a single class or seminar. Adrian Van Kaam's notion of "unique-communal life call" captures the twofold truth that our calling is unique to us and that it is compatible with our unique gifting, training, life story, and current situation. And our calling is discovered within, affirmed by, and useful to the community of faith. It also is a life calling, not just a passing whim or passing interest but something that provides a life direction.

Part of the foundation for cultivating a tendency to respond can be seen in communities that provide Christians with a deep sense that they are equipped to respond and to serve God at this very moment. New Christians can be slow to engage in areas of service because they feel inadequate to the task. Satan exploits this normal and understandable hesitancy with his accusations (Rev. 12:10) and his lies. As Jesus said, "When he lies, he speaks his native language, for he is a liar and the father of lies" (John 8:44 NIV). Often an early victory in proper spiritual listening occurs when Christians give attention to God's affirming voice calling his beloved to creative service, which fits who they uniquely are. They discover the strength to ignore the accusations of Satan, which breed self-doubt and fear. Wise communities of believers do not push new Christians into merely serving out of dutiful obligation in a ministry that "does not fit." A faithful, persistent call to "listen to God" through Scripture and wise counsel will accomplish more for the kingdom than compiling another list of "tasks that need doing—please do one."

Self-acceptance is often not well understood in many Christian communities. The misuse of statements like Jesus's command to deny ourselves has not helped. Even the linchpin statement in the Great Commandment that the degree of love we must have for our neighbor ought to parallel our love for

---

6. Dallas Willard, *The Divine Conspiracy: Rediscovering Our Hidden Life in God* (San Francisco: HarperSanFrancisco, 1998), 243.

7. Adrian Van Kaam and Susan Muto, *Formation Theology*, vol. 3, *Foundations of the Christian Heart* (Pittsburgh: Epiphany Association, 2006), 201–10.

ourselves does not receive the serious attention it deserves. Historically, self-acceptance was taught as part of the formation process. An emphasis was placed on appropriate patience with oneself. This patience and self-acceptance were grounded in the conviction that God created me to be exactly as he wants me to be. In creating me in this way, he created a wonderful and magnificent being. Psalm 8:5 instructs, "You have made them a little lower than the angels and crowned them with glory and honor" (NIV). This truth is captured in the popular expression "God don't make no junk!"

Christians have seen the adverse effects of the popular self-esteem movement and sometimes discount the importance of teaching self-acceptance, but what should we teach in its place? Certainly not self-hatred, which is simply a rejection of God's providence and a rebellion against the creation that he declared to be good. At times, believers have taken Jesus's words "Let him deny himself" as an encouragement toward self-hatred, when that is certainly not their message. I do not hate myself when I deny myself any more than I would hate my child if I said no to her when she made an unwise request. Some of the godliest acts of self-acceptance come at precisely those times when we deny ourselves. Self-acceptance is not something that comes easily, and it is something that must be taught and nurtured because we confront plenty of negative data about ourselves. Negative accusation is one of Satan's most effective tools. Richard Lovelace gives this assessment of God's acceptance of us as a lived reality: "There is endless talk about this in the church, but little apparent belief in it among Christians." He develops this further:

> It is often said today . . . that we must love ourselves before we can be set free to love others. This is certainly the release which we must seek to give our people. But no realistic human beings find it easy to love or to forgive themselves, and hence their self-acceptance must be grounded in their awareness that God accepts them in Christ. There is a sense in which the strongest self-love that we can have, in the sense of *agapē*, is merely the mirror image of the lively conviction we have that God loves us. There is endless talk about this in the church, but little apparent belief in it among Christians, although they may have a conscious complacency which conceals the subconscious despair which Kierkegaard calls "the sickness unto death."[8]

This subconscious despair eviscerates Christian service because it leads believers to doubt that they have a significant contribution to make. Serving has such a formative effect because it provides clear evidence that my contribution

---

8. Richard F. Lovelace, *Dynamics of Spiritual Life: An Evangelical Theology of Renewal* (Downers Grove, IL: InterVarsity, 1979), 212.

matters. One can see the church cleaned, people fed, children cared for, and the words of witness spoken. We have done something not because of how we expected to feel but simply because Jesus asks us to do it. Appropriately motivated service affirms our contribution to the body of Christ.

Responding as an Outflow of the Priesthood of All Believers

The doctrine of the priesthood of all believers is central to how I am construing spiritual formation. This ancient doctrine mandates and enables spiritual formation and serves as part of its implicit theological foundation. When properly understood, the biblical principle that all believers are priests has infused spiritual formation with a refreshing vitality and a spirit of renewal; at other times, however, it has been used to excuse individualism, intellectual lethargy, and a lack of respect for the teaching office of the church. A balanced concept of the priesthood of all believers will affirm the personal spiritual responsibility of all Christians, their right and duty to minister in Christ's name, and the truth that one does not abide in Christ apart from abiding in the body of Christ, the church.

Spiritual Responsibility and Responding

It is he whom we proclaim, warning everyone and teaching everyone in all wisdom, so that we may present everyone mature in Christ. For this I toil and struggle with all the energy that he powerfully inspires within me.

Colossians 1:28–29

Martin Luther recognized that if all Christians are called to be responsible servants and worshipers, they must be trained and equipped to fulfill this calling—they must be prepared to respond to the gospel. Hence, he became involved in Christian education. His Small Catechism stands as a reminder of this interest. This catechism was written after he visited nearby country parishes, where he was appalled by the ignorance he found. Luther was keenly aware that each believer must ultimately answer to Christ concerning their spiritual condition. If these people were to be accountable for their faith, Luther reasoned, they had to be instructed in spiritual matters.

All Christians are called to worship God, utilize their gifts, and minister to others according to God's principles as set forth in Scripture. Good intentions or ignorance of divine requirements do not absolve the believer of the responsibility to live out the gospel.

Philipp Jakob Spener (1635–1705) and some like-minded Lutheran Pietists developed further the ramifications this doctrine has for Christian education.

Spener, a brilliant and sensitive Lutheran pastor who held a doctorate in theology and was fluent in several languages, firmly believed that a vital faith is as important for ministry as is ordination and formal training. He did not disparage theological training (although he wanted to reform it), but he genuinely felt that to be fit for ministry, one needed a renewed heart and mind. Though Lutheranism taught the ministry of all believers, he was aware that people still looked to the pastor as the spiritual center and theological expert in the church. Most of the laity were passive recipients of sermons and sacraments. To correct this situation, Spener, in his book *Pia Desideria*, called for an increased and "diligent exercise of the spiritual priesthood."[9]

According to Spener, the responsibilities of the spiritual priesthood fall into three general areas: (1) It is the duty of every Christian "industriously to study in the Word of the Lord." By spending time in the study of Scripture, we can order our lives by its priorities and minister the word of truth to those around us. (2) As Christians, all of us have a responsibility "to teach others, especially those under [our] own roof, to chastise, exhort, convert, and edify them, to observe their life, pray for all, and in so far as possible be concerned about their salvation." Like the writer to the Hebrews (5:12), Spener believed that all Christians have a responsibility to teach in the sense of speaking the word of truth and influencing people to walk in the paths of righteousness. (3) "Every Christian is bound not only to offer himself but also what he has, his prayer, thanksgiving, good works, alms."[10] The wonderful privileges of the universal priesthood enable us to serve others with a renewed vigor and enthusiasm and with a full array of spiritual tools. Through intercessory prayer and acts of mercy, believer-priests serve one another and their world.

Spener saw his emphasis on the universal priesthood as a restatement of Luther's emphasis: "Nobody can read Luther's writings with some care without observing how earnestly the sainted man advocated this spiritual priesthood."[11] Spener thought that a focus on the universal priesthood of believers is necessary for the church to fulfill its biblical obligations of service, worship, care, witness, and prayer. He did not see such a priesthood as competing with the ordained clergy; instead, together, they can accomplish what neither one can do alone: "No damage will be done to the ministry by a proper use of this priesthood. In fact, one of the principal reasons why the ministry cannot accomplish all that it ought is that it is too weak

9. Philipp Jakob Spener, *Pia Desideria*, trans. and ed. T. G. Tappert (Philadelphia: Fortress, 1964), 92.

10. Spener, *Pia Desideria*, 94.

11. Spener, *Pia Desideria*, 92.

without the help of the universal priesthood."[12] Without an emphasis on laypersons teaching other laypersons, modern Christian education would not have developed. The tasks of Christian education and spiritual formation can never fall entirely on professionals because the financial cost would be prohibitive and because we gain much through the process of mutual teaching and learning. A somewhat bookish academic has frequently told me how encouraged he is by hearing faithful laypeople teach the Bible. Teachers strengthen their credibility when they reveal a life of integrity as they teach.

Equipping to Respond to the Gospel

Crossing cultural boundaries has been the life blood of historic Christianity.

Andrew F. Walls[13]

Few developments in our day have been more striking and less anticipated than the emergence of Christianity as a world religion. . . . By contrast, Europe and, to some extent, North America, once considered Christian strongholds, are in marked recession or retreat.

Lamin Sanneh[14]

Equipping the priesthood of all believers for spiritual service must be at the heart of the church's formational ministry. We must emphasize this focus of Christian education and formation for all ages. To live as a Christian entails carrying out a believer-priest's responsibilities, and this is as true for an elementary-school child as for an adult. Three emphases have historically provided Christians with everyday opportunities to respond to the gospel.

Forming World Christians

When Christians learn to recognize a deep connection with believers worldwide, they see the world through a whole new lens. Stories of persecution become stories about family members. We learn to "pray the newspaper" as we see the spiritual implications of the news. We certainly understand that our connection to other Christians is as deep as any other bond.

12. Spener, *Pia Desideria*, 94.
13. *The Cross-Cultural Process in Christian History: Studies in the Transmission and Appropriation of Faith* (Maryknoll, NY: Orbis Books, 2002), 32.
14. Introduction to *The Changing Face of Christianity: Africa, the West, and the World*, ed. Lamin O. Sanneh and Joel A. Carpenter (New York: Oxford University Press, 2005), 3–4.

In the early church, as people from various races, classes, and conditions came to faith in Jesus Christ and were reconciled to God, they were called to live out this reconciliation with one another. As world Christians, we seek to learn from our brothers and sisters in Christ in different parts of the world. We adopt a stance of respect, learning, and curiosity as we connect with these Christians.

Learning to Witness to God's Love and Provide Spiritual Care

All Christians should be prepared to speak of God's gracious dealings with them. Too often, we speak of this as "evangelistic witnessing" in terms that mostly fit highly verbal extroverts. We need to teach and encourage people to witness to God's love and provide spiritual care for those in their relational networks. All of us can learn to pray with and for people, offer spiritual guidance and comfort, and patiently and carefully offer words of discernment. A friend remarked that at a local county hospital, the most effective spiritual care was provided by the Jamaican housekeeping staff, who by speaking openly of God brought comfort and guidance to so many. When the bar is set at "present the gospel," many Christians remain silent. Many more will respond if we invite them to witness to God's love and provide spiritual care to those who cross their paths.

Cultivating the Spirit of Hospitality

Christians need to extend hospitality to others, especially those who are lonely, mentally ill, needy, and on the margins (Rom. 12:13). We will read the Bible differently when we keep in mind that hospitality is usually described rather than prescribed. Hospitality was a cultural expectation in biblical times. Today it must be intentional. Offering hospitality provides Christians with many opportunities to respond to the gospel's call to love and care. Hospitality means that we must address the racism that so often thwarts the biblical call to hospitality.

The consumer emphasis in modern American religion is opposed to the Reformation concept of the believer-priest. The formational ministry of a church will never be fully effective if people come to the church simply to consume spiritual benefits in exchange for their money and loyalty. By contrast, equipping means training people "to do." In the church, we must train people for responsible priestly service. This means that we cannot be content simply to urge people to pray; instead, we must teach them how to pray. And we must not merely talk about evangelism; instead, we must train people to share their faith.

In equipping for spiritual service, the church should give attention to the main contexts in which people live out their faith: the home, neighborhood, and marketplace. The church must enable Christians to bear witness to their faith in all those contexts: to minister in and through their families and to genuinely serve their coworkers.

Responding with God's Transforming Grace

The practices of faith are not ultimately our own practices but rather habitations of the Spirit, in the midst of which we are invited to participate in the practices of God.

Craig Dykstra[15]

Only if we experience the mysterious attraction of God will we be able to impart it to others.

John H. Westerhoff III[16]

It is God who is at work in you, enabling you both to will and to work for his good pleasure.

Philippians 2:13

In our discussion of the priesthood of all believers, we have looked at only one half of the equation: our access to God and its attendant responsibilities. The Old Testament priests not only approached God but also ministered as agents of God's grace to his people. Priests make God's grace available to others. God has called us as believer-priests to administer his transforming power to others. "Like good stewards of the manifold grace of God, serve one another with whatever gift each of you has received" (1 Pet. 4:10). That we can become agents to minister God's sustaining grace to others should transform our view of everyday activities. Our service in the home, our empathy with coworkers, our prayers, our conversations, and our online presence are not just ways of being kind or speaking words of truth; they also are ways of ministering God's grace. Paul urged the believers to whom he ministered to adopt this aim in life. He encouraged them by noting that something as simple as an ordinary conversation can be a way of dispensing God's power: "Your speech must always be with grace, as though seasoned with salt, so that you will know how you should respond to each person" (Col. 4:6 NASB). Grace

15. *Growing in the Life of Faith: Education and Christian Practices*, 2nd ed. (Louisville: Westminster John Knox, 2005), 78.
16. *Spiritual Life*, 76.

is a verb: grace brings change. Grace is God's sustaining and transforming power, which we have the privilege to bring to others.

The grace of God that has reconciled us and saved us is not just God's kindness but also his marvelous power that can remake us into new people. In the book of Acts, grace essentially equals power. Those persons who were full of grace were also full of God's power to preach and to work mighty miracles. Notice what is said of Stephen: "Now Stephen, a man full of God's grace and power, performed great wonders and signs among the people" (Acts 6:8 NIV). God's powerful sustaining grace brings about transformation and healing in our lives. The writer to the Hebrews urges readers to walk closely with Christ, warning them not to try to hasten their Christian development through futile means such as ceremonial foods, strange teachings, and mysterious ceremonies. Instead, Hebrews advises, "It is well for the heart to be strengthened by grace" (13:9).

In the church, there are many ways that we can strengthen our hearts through grace. One of the most effective is wise and biblically grounded personal ministry of one believer to another. It is eye-opening to see how many passages in the Bible include the phrase "one another":

Thus says the LORD of hosts: Render true judgments, show kindness and mercy to one another. (Zech. 7:9)

Have we not all one father? Has not one God created us? Why then are we faithless to one another, profaning the covenant of our ancestors? (Mal. 2:10)

So if I [Jesus], your Lord and Teacher, have washed your feet, you also ought to wash one another's feet. (John 13:14)

I [Jesus] give you a new commandment, that you love one another. Just as I have loved you, you also should love one another. By this everyone will know that you are my disciples, if you have love for one another. (13:34–35)

Love one another with mutual affection; outdo one another in showing honor. (Rom. 12:10)

Live in harmony with one another; do not be haughty, but associate with the lowly; do not claim to be wiser than you are. (12:16)

Owe no one anything, except to love one another; for the one who loves another has fulfilled the law. (13:8)

Let us therefore no longer pass judgment on one another, but resolve instead never to put a stumbling-block or hindrance in the way of another. (14:13)

Welcome one another, therefore, just as Christ has welcomed you, for the glory of God. (15:7)

I myself feel confident about you, my brothers and sisters, that you yourselves are full of goodness, filled with all knowledge, and able to instruct one another. (15:14)

I appeal to you, brothers and sisters, in the name of our Lord Jesus Christ, that all of you agree with one another in what you say and that there be no divisions among you, but that you be perfectly united in mind and thought. (1 Cor. 1:10 NIV)

With all humility and gentleness, with patience, bearing with one another in love . . . (Eph. 4:2)

And be kind to one another, tender-hearted, forgiving one another, as God in Christ has forgiven you. (4:32)

. . . speaking to one another with psalms, hymns, and songs from the Spirit. Sing and make music from your heart to the Lord. (5:19 NIV)

Be subject to one another out of reverence for Christ. (5:21)

Bear with one another and, if anyone has a complaint against another, forgive each other; just as the Lord has forgiven you, so you also must forgive. (Col. 3:13)

Let the word of Christ dwell in you richly; teach and admonish one another in all wisdom; and with gratitude in your hearts sing psalms, hymns, and spiritual songs to God. (3:16)

Therefore encourage one another and build up each other, as indeed you are doing. (1 Thess. 5:11)

Salvation begins with our being called by God and is consummated with our glorification. The grace of God is working throughout this entire process to bring about our transformation into Christlikeness. Paul, highly disciplined as he was, celebrated the movement of grace in his life: "By the grace of God I am what I am, and his grace toward me has not been in vain. On the contrary, I worked harder than any of them—though it was not I, but the grace of God that is with me" (1 Cor. 15:10). Ultimately, God's grace brings about human transformation, and we must avail ourselves of the means that God has established to make his grace available to us and others. We respond to his grace, and we respond with his grace as we minister. Christian formation includes a grace-oriented inculcation of the tendency to respond, through training, in a Christ-imitating way, to the gospel.

Personal Holiness Fosters Healthy Responding

> Every Christian community must realize that not only do the weak need the strong but also that the strong cannot exist without the weak. The elimination of the weak is the death of the fellowship.
>
> Dietrich Bonhoeffer[17]

> The community of believers represents a prophetic counterculture that challenges the gods and myths of the day with regard to which world and life view best fulfills humanity.
>
> Kevin Vanhoozer[18]

> A spiritual community, a church, is full of broken people who turn their chairs toward each other because they know they cannot make it alone.
>
> Larry Crabb[19]

There's a deep yearning within us for wholeness, and we find wholeness in the life of holiness. Holiness does not come simply by avoiding certain actions but by our becoming a channel for God's empowering presence—living as a pipe, not a bucket. Holiness begins with our being made new by God and grows as we open ourselves to the work of God. When we see holiness as merely avoiding bad actions, we become passive and wall ourselves off from the world. True piety leads to service, but false piety leads to self-protection. True piety produces a depth of soul; false piety yields shallow hypocrisy. We have centuries' worth of faithful witnesses to the possibility of authentic piety. "Lot went to Joseph and said, 'Abba, as far as I can, I keep a moderate rule, with a little fasting, and prayer, and meditation, and quiet: and as far as I can I try to cleanse my heart of evil thoughts. What else should I do?' Then the hermit stood up and spread out his hands to heaven, and his fingers shone like ten flames of fire, and he said, 'If you will, you can become all flame.'"[20]

In an earlier age, holiness was seen as something possessing substance—a transcendent quality that flowed out of our deep inner essence, from our very souls. Many churches have lost sight of the holy and the soul, and the results are tragic. This change has allowed people to replace the idea of growing in

17. *Life Together: The Classic Exploration of Faith in Community* (Harper & Row, 1954), 94.
18. *First Theology: God, Scripture and Hermeneutics* (Downers Grove, IL: InterVarsity, 2002), 334.
19. *The Safest Place on Earth: Where People Connect and Are Forever Changed* (Nashville: Word, 1999), 32.
20. Benedicta Ward, *The Desert Fathers: Sayings of the Early Christian Monks* (New York: Penguin, 2003), 131.

holiness (as the presence and power of God increasingly permeate our lives) with the notion of sin management. As explained earlier (see the section titled "The Depth of our Yearnings" in chap. 3), sin management claims that people are basically "okay." Such a view rejects the biblical assertion that the human heart—the core of our beings—is bent away from God and others; it replaces that biblical insight with the notion of sin as personal impairment. The idea is that people need to employ a variety of techniques to reduce the amount of overt sin in their lives because it stifles their growth, hampers their witness, tends to be personally unpleasant, and harms others. The desire for holiness remains, but the primary means become "cheap" (to use Bonhoeffer's language). We want cheap holiness. We want holiness that relishes God's forgiveness and grace without actually admitting that we have anything for which we need forgiveness. We demand the right to claim holiness (at least internally) without having to be holy.

Holiness begins with our being made new by God. Through regeneration, we receive spiritual life: we are brought from spiritual death to life. With this new life comes the possibility of spiritual growth and growth in gospel virtues. Through this act, we receive a new set of governing tendencies and values, begin to perceive and cherish spiritual truths, and seek to live as faithful followers of Christ.

Jesus provides us with a clear picture of holiness. We marvel at Jesus not because he avoided a particular set of negative actions ("him who had no sin" [2 Cor. 5:21 NIV]) but because he lived a life full of spiritual power, vitality, and love. Though he kept the law fully, he was a constant irritation to his day's religious leaders because of his teachings, challenges to their authority, and refusal to follow all the ritual regulations. He firmly rejected the surrounding shift in the definition of sin and pointed his listeners back to their ultimate spiritual accountability before a holy God. His confrontations were scathing: "And so you cancel the word of God in order to hand down your own tradition" (Mark 7:13 NLT). For guidance, we go back to Jesus's life, in which spiritual power and love shine forth like a beacon across a barren spiritual terrain, and holiness is much more than moral rectitude.

In his public ministry, we see his power demonstrated repeatedly. Jesus resisted Satan's direct attack during his time of wilderness temptation (Matt. 4:1–11) and his subtle assault through Peter's concern (16:22–23). He cast out demons by a simple command, healed various infirmities, quieted a storm, turned water into wine, multiplied bread, and showed love in the face of brutal opposition and hatred. His insight showed in his penetrating teaching. With perfect accuracy, he discerned the motives and longings of those

Transformations of the Heart

As our hearts are transformed by faith, we will move

- from self-absorption to concern for God's kingdom (Matt. 6:33);
- from defiance to submission (1 Sam. 15:19-22);
- from self-reliance to God-reliance (Jer. 17:5-8);
- from squandering resources to stewarding them (Matt. 25:14-30);
- from expecting and taking for granted to accepting and gratitude (Luke 17:11-19);
- from spiritual indifference to spiritual growth and vitality (2 Pet. 1:3-8);
- from concern with externals to concern for character (1 Sam. 16:7);
- from conformity with the culture to conformity to God (Rom. 12:1-2);
- from concern for self to concern for others (Phil. 2:3-4);
- from lording [it] over others to serving others (Mark 10:42-45);
- from quarreling to cooperation (James 3:13-17);
- from independence to community (Eccles. 4:9-12);
- from envy, competition, and self-protection to love (1 Cor. 13:4-13); and
- from harboring hurt and resentment to extending forgiveness and seeking reconciliation (Eph. 4:32-5:2).[a]

a. David Henderson, "The Art of Voice Recognition," *Discipleship Journal* 25 (November/December 2005): 61.

he talked with, predicted future events, and offered words of challenge and direction in strikingly artistic sermons. His love shone forth as he associated with unpleasant and marginalized individuals, turned away unkind words with a gentle response, and forgave those who wronged him. And Jesus's willing sacrifice on the cross stands as the greatest act of love that history will ever know.

A simple event during Christ's last week typifies his genuine and unique holiness. Jesus rode into Jerusalem on a colt that had never before been ridden. Beasts of burden require some process of breaking in and do not immediately take to being ridden or harnessed. Yet Jesus simply rode, apparently without any objection from the colt. He possessed great spiritual power that could calm a sea, quiet a crowd, or reassure an untrained animal. His spiritual power was not marked by noise and bravado but by an understated authority. He did not need to raise his voice or give the impression of being in control because he *is* in control. Jesus did not do miracles to prove he is the Son of God but because he *is* the Son of God. This example of holiness as flowing out of a person's depths has been replicated in succeeding generations by those who have responded and turned from regeneration toward holiness. It is in marked contrast to the picture of holiness set forth in so many contemporary writings on ministry, in which holiness/maturity is simply a cluster of external competencies and others-oriented values.

We face a critical question: How do we live so that Jesus's experience of holiness is appropriately present in our lives? The answer: There is nothing we can do to generate the holiness seen in Jesus, but there are things we can do to receive it. As Christians, we no longer have to do what impulse tells us. These misdirected longings of our hearts exert inordinate and persistent influence on us not only by attaching to the wrong objects but also by profoundly disordering our interiors.

Biblical teaching about the heart, or the human interior, is vibrant. Without a clear connection to the heart, religion will degenerate into legalism (a system of impression management), superstition (a system of external acts designed to control deity), or emotionalism (a system that equates faith with positive emotions and a sense of being "inspired"). Within all of us is a tendency to distort our faith in one of these directions. Maturity requires that we understand how we distort our spiritual lives and then cultivate spiritual practices that help us resist this distortion.

In considering how to pattern our lives after Christ, we need to realize the power of our core being (in biblical language, our heart, soul, mind, will) to shape our lives. The biblical writers continually give attention to the interior. In fact, the metaphor of "roots" is one of the primary images for the hidden but essential spiritual life. Those who trust the Lord are like a well-rooted tree planted by a stream (Jer. 17:7–8). Even during hot weather and drought, the leaves of this deeply rooted tree remain green, and it continues to produce fruit. Believers are to stay rooted in the Lord Jesus (Col. 2:7) and his great love (Eph. 3:17–19) so that they might remain stable. A fundamental spiritual principle emerges: the aspects of spiritual life that are out of sight deserve our closest attention. "Spiritual growth consists most in the growth of the root, which is out of sight."[21] Jesus certainly taught and demonstrated public prayer, but he also spent extended private times with his heavenly Father.

21. Robert Jamieson, A. R. Fausset, and David Brown, *A Commentary, Critical and Explanatory, on the Old and New Testaments* (Grand Rapids: Zondervan, 1934), 663.

He did not hesitate to send his followers alone to the prayer closet (Matt. 6:5–6).

The will is immensely important in our spiritual transformation, but it is of very limited power and is best used to marshal other spiritual resources at our disposal. Our wills inherently suffer from a kind of spiritual attention deficit disorder; they cannot sustain long-term direction without training, but they are marvelous at making conscious and informed choices to bring other resources to bear. For example, one may find it difficult to resist the allure of drugs and alcohol at a party. Untrained willpower alone will often prove ineffective at keeping a person sober in the face of temptation. Still, one can use willpower to relocate (remove oneself from temptation) and thereby avoid the temptation that seems irresistible when among peers. An important maxim of the spiritual life is that we should never expect our will to work by itself. Do not use your will to simply "say no." Use your will to marshal spiritual resources available to you. Remember: "At the crucial moments of choice, most of the business of choosing is over."[22]

The soul as "who we are" but also "capable of being programmed" is evident in the biblical perspectives on meditation and CSF. Developing a tendency to respond to others' needs will undoubtedly mean training and equipping to both "do" and "be." Practices like meditation and contemplative prayer can enable us to learn to respond to the needs we see rather than react out of anger, fear, or self-protection. Jesus responded to the needs around him but did not react. He could say at the end of his ministry, "I have brought you glory on earth by finishing the work you gave me to do" (John 17:4 NIV), yet he had not preached to all those who lived in Israel, nor had he healed all the lepers or comforted all the sorrowful. He had a clear sense of mission and was a whole person who ministered out of his full relationship with God, so that he did not see every need as a calling. Independence from the approval of others and connection with the Spirit's power and heart for God lead to creative ministry and action.

Community Practices That Encourage Responding

The tendency to respond with grace-filled action is something that seems more often caught than taught. This is not to say that a church should not be intentional about seeking to instill this tendency in its members. We can look at churches where this active other-orientation is present and find some community practices that are in place.

22. Iris Murdoch, *The Sovereignty of Good* (New York: Schocken Books, 1971), 37.

Teaching and Preaching That Encourage Responding

Sermons should shape hearers by bringing the transforming Word to nurture
the development of their character in the pattern of Christ.

                                                                    Marva Dawn[23]

It is a long-acknowledged truth that teachers teach the lessons they most need
to learn and writers write about the very things that they are most in need of
understanding.

                                                              Ruth Haley Barton[24]

There is a way of viewing life that supports a compassionate response to
ourselves and those around us. The teaching and preaching ministry of the
church plays a vital role in helping form this life orientation. In this area,
proper teaching and preaching form an essential but insufficient foundation
for cultivating this disposition to respond. Here are some key themes I have
observed in the teaching and preaching ministries of churches that support a
widespread responding orientation:

Biblical focus. Not only is the proclamation of these churches grounded
    in Scripture, but the teaching ministry also has the effect of making the
    congregation "people of the book." Page after page of Scripture invites
    us to join the work of God in the world. When people are taught to turn
    to Scripture for guidance, they are more likely to be people who live out
    the gospel. The atmosphere is one in which Scripture, rather than the
    interpreter, is honored with the last word.

It is not all about me. Through our teaching and preaching, we need to
    invite people into God's kingdom work and perspective. They have
    gained citizenship in his kingdom through regeneration and need to
    see that life in the kingdom may cost convenience but never joy. It is the
    life we truly want to live.

Gratitude. Our response to the gospel should flow out of a heart that is grate-
    ful for grace and a life that has been transformed by God's grace. Deep-
    seated gratitude is the best motivation for our serving and witnessing.

Empathy. Christians live as broken people in a broken, hurting world. Our
    observation and assessment of the dominant culture should emphasize

23. *Reaching Out without Dumbing Down: A Theology of Worship for the Turn-of-the-
Century Culture* (Grand Rapids: Eerdmans, 1995), 211.
    24. *Truths That Free Us: A Woman's Calling to Spiritual Transformation* (Colorado Springs:
Shaw, 2002), xviii–xix.

our empathy for the pain and disorientation we see around us. We should not shy away from the prophetic cultural critique. In speaking out, our emphasis should be on an empathetic understanding of this brokenness rather than merely a judgment of it. And we must emphasize that our empathy prompts us to ministry, but at the end of the day, only God can heal and restore, so we do not offer our empathy but the tangible love and truth of God.

Yearning for justice and flourishing. Two foundational strengths of evangelicalism are its attention to the heart and its personal commitment to Christ. This in no way diminishes our desire for justice to mark our nation and communities and for us to promote human flourishing. We realize that the Bible tells of the pervasive presence of sin, and we address it by proclaiming the gospel and seeking justice in our land.

Evangelism. We need to teach Christians how to share the gospel with those in their relational web. Life in the kingdom involves more than a personal witness to the reality of Christ; that reality is a core disposition on which we need to build a life of responding.

Responding out of love is foundational to accepting the two great invitations of Jesus: love God, love neighbor. Ironically, love is a topic that church teaching often dodges. In my fifty years as an adult Christian, I do not recall a single course or small-group series that specifically explored the nature of Christian love. We seem to be attracted to the lofty ideal and our glimpses of its presence, but we are repelled by the sentimentality and naive judgments that are born of "love." The approach of avoidance is spiritually deadly because, through it, we may have hardened our hearts to the Bible's clear message to love. Scripture always places a call to love in balance with other virtues: "This is my prayer, that your love may overflow more and more with knowledge and full insight" (Phil. 1:9).

Discernment That Fosters Responding

Covetousness we call ambition. Hoarding we call prudence. Greed we call industry.

Richard Foster[25]

Responding to the gospel in healthy, loving, and life-giving ways requires that we follow the path of wisdom and practice the discipline of discernment. A

25. *Celebration of Discipline: The Path to Spiritual Growth*, 3rd ed. (San Francisco: Harper-SanFrancisco, 1998), 81.

person whose heart is alive with the gospel and brims with gratitude to God is disposed to reach out to others. That is good, and it is best done when guided by wisdom and in accordance with one's unique-communal life calling. Letting people see that simple faithfulness (e.g., work in the home, honesty in the shop, integrity in one's work) as they carry out their vocation is the context for much of our response to the gospel. Discernment is foundational to responding because we want to do that which is good and right, and the challenge of living well brings with it questions about the best path to take. The confidence in continuing to do good is enhanced by plans that are shaped in times of discernment.

The message of the gospel is that when we were far from God, when we were seeking to manage our lives to bring the pleasure and peace we desired, when we were utterly lost in our plans and self-protection, God reached out to us and all humanity collectively through Jesus Christ. The message of the gospel is that of God reaching out to us, and that invites us to reach out to those who are on the margins. The human instinct is to seek the inner circle in a group, to break in and be part of the group that is affirmed and is seen as the center of things.[26] Life teaches us that the "inner circle" is illusory and that being there is seldom worth the price extracted to get there. Christians should cultivate a disposition not of seeking to break in to the inner circle but of reaching out to those who are on the margins, such as those who are lonely or struggling with mental illness—people whose life situations and struggles leave them vulnerable.

A Filipino-American pastor told me that American society views most of the members of his congregation as "machine people." Such people are invisible to busy professionals, who view them as merely an extension of service machinery that performs the duties we want done. They are an extension of dish washing, dry cleaning, or hotel services. He challenged me to simply pay attention to these invisible "machine people" that I, as he correctly predicted, encounter every day and yet overlook. He urged me, as an act of following Jesus, to engage these people with eye contact, affirmations, and questions about their lives and well-being. Part of the call here for compassion is simply developing a way of seeing. The early desert writers of Christianity were willing to say that the essence of spirituality was adopting a new way of seeing. Regarding or showing compassion and cultivating an ability or disposition to see those who are lonely and in need are the first significant steps toward loving them. Yes, we must be willing to do "big things," but we are to be kind and available to those we meet too.

26. C. S. Lewis discusses with pastoral brilliance the false allure of the inner circle in "The Inner Ring," in *The Weight of Glory* (New York: Macmillan, 1980), 93–105.

Racial and ethnic prejudice is endemic to the fallen human race. It creates needless divisions, fuels hatred, and, when present among Christians, destroys the kingdom community of Christ. So we know that one response to the gospel we are called to is to address this issue at the levels we face it. The problem of our prejudice is illustrated by the godly prophet Samuel, whom God told to anoint the new king of Israel. Samuel searched for a king and looked for what he thought would be a "kingly type." But God had something different in mind; his choice was the youngest boy, whom his father had not even called to meet Samuel. Samuel was ready to decide based on physical prowess, but God told him, "Do not look on his appearance or on the height of his stature, because I have rejected him; for the LORD does not see as mortals see; they look on the outward appearance, but the LORD looks on the heart" (1 Sam. 16:7). Christians need to be taught to walk free of prejudices, which distort our ability to see people's worth and discern their hearts. Our dream should be that of Martin Luther King Jr.: "I have a dream that my four little children will one day live in a nation where they will not be judged by the color of their skin but by the content of their character."[27]

One of the great thinkers in CSF is Ignatius of Loyola. In his *Spiritual Exercises* he shows how discernment, an intentional decision-making process whereby we seek to understand what God wants us to do, is foundational to discipleship.[28] We need to have the humility to be constantly seeking to discern how God is active in our life and what we are being called to do. Christians need to understand that one of the first ways to respond to the gospel well is by practicing discernment about what we "hear" about ourselves. In the course of the day, it is easy for a person to encounter myriad negative messages: we are not wearing the right clothes, we do not smell just right, our hair is not the way it should be, our car is not cool, and we have not gone to the right place on vacation. When this is coupled with work and family situations marked by negativity, it is easy for a person to take in harmful negative messages. The gospel calls us to see ourselves as sinners, but it never calls us to embrace self-hatred. An essential step in discernment is learning to listen to the voice of God, who sings a song of affirmation and love over us. This is something that the community must encourage. Going to church should not load one with guilt but leave one marveling at God's grace and standing in awe at the magnificence of his love.

27. Martin Luther King Jr., *A Testament of Hope: The Essential Writings of Martin Luther King, Jr.*, ed. James Melvin Washington (San Francisco: Harper & Row, 1986), 219.
28. David L. Fleming, *Modern Spiritual Exercises: A Contemporary Reading of "The Spiritual Exercises of St. Ignatius"* (Garden City, NY: Image Books, 1983).

Another essential pattern of discernment is learning the gracious application of the Ten Commandments to our lives. These laws bring health and vitality to those who follow them, and we can quickly memorize them and apply them to our life situations. Instilling a knowledge and tendency to follow the Ten Commandments should be central to the ethical teaching of the church. We should be more concerned that the Ten Commandments be learned and followed by ordinary Christians than that they are posted in public buildings. The concern that adherence to the Ten Commandments will lead to legalism is simply not valid. Legalism is an innate tendency in humankind, and we will tend to subvert any system of grace into legalism because, in our pride, legalism emphasizes our importance. The Reformers deeply understood that a proper emphasis on the Ten Commandments would continually make people aware of their sin and continually draw them to the Savior while providing wise guidance for corporate and personal living.

On morning retreats, space can be provided for people to reflect on their lives in solitude and to seek the prayer and counsel of elders and other wise persons in the church. The path of wisdom is hard to walk alone; the book of Proverbs reminds us that the counsel of others can provide wisdom and guidance. In informal and semiformal ways, churches should let people know that there are opportunities to pray and to seek the counsel of those who will bring an independent perspective and some years of life experience to bear on the struggles and decisions they are facing. The church also needs to model a Scripture-based and prayerful decision-making process in times of ministry planning.

Service days and mission trips are excellent ways of introducing people to the joy of service and showing them agencies and strategies that do creative ministry in the community. A friend who has led several trips to rebuild houses in storm-damaged areas has remarked that the best spiritual formation takes place on a twenty-hour van ride. The power of community combined with tangible, hands-on, community-based care for the poor in the context of prayer and worship can help people discern avenues of service.

Jesus Invites Us to Weep as a Godly Response

As a young Christian, I was nurtured in a faith tradition that subtly communicated that to be increasingly emotionally disengaged is a mark of spiritual maturity. The hidden curriculum of this discipleship orientation emphasized that emotions could not be trusted, and we would do well to follow the example of Paul and Jesus, who did not display emotions. Somewhere along the line, we simply overlooked passages that speak of Jesus's and Paul's humanity and the reality of their emotions. Jesus's humanity is imaged in his emotional states. In his ministry, we see a full range of human emotions and physiological responses.

Jesus experienced hunger and weariness and profound fatigue. He suffered and displayed raw human feelings. He was angered by stubborn hearts (Mark 3:5) and felt deep compassion for the crowds that followed him (Matt. 9:36; 14:14). He was moved to tears at the death of his friend Lazarus (John 11:35) and yet experienced joy in the Spirit at various times (Luke 10:21). He was overwhelmed with sorrow in the garden of Gethsemane (Matt. 26:37–38; Mark 14:33–34); Luke records that he agonized as he fervently prayed and was so moved that "his sweat became like great drops of blood falling down on the ground" (Luke 22:44; cf. Heb. 5:7). And finally, at the agony of the cross, he felt forsaken by God and expressed that anguish in the cry "My God, my God, why have you forsaken me?" (Mark 15:34).

Jesus's example teaches us that weeping is often the most appropriate response to the brokenness we find in the world. His view of God's providence and care did not hold him back from entering into the sufferings of others with deep empathy, even to the point of tears. Similarly, Paul describes his ministry in Ephesus as one of visiting houses and marked by tears. One of the gospel responses to the brokenness of the world is allowing ourselves to enter into the sorrow (the groaning of creation) and to weep over how things are not the way they should be. Because of God's providence and rule, Christians have a reason to hope, but we also have a reason to be sorrowful because we know that this groaning is not what God intended. The sorrow of the world is not an accident; the pain of the world represents a marring of God's good creation.

How can we foster weeping? (1) Do not try to fix everything. At times, the most sensible response is to weep and pray. (2) Honor empathetic emotional responses as appropriate and truthful. (3) Learn to enter into the sufferings of others with a desire to love, not to fix the problem, fully aware that sometimes the problem will not be fixed on this side of eternity. (4) Ask the Lord for the gift of tears.

Responding through a Life of Integrity

One of the unique teachings of Jesus involved his confrontation of hypocrisy. As I mentioned earlier, Jesus essentially coined a new ethical construct. The Greek word *hypokrisis* (hypocrisy) was a term for acting. Jesus publicly confronted the deceptive acting in his religious community in which a person's heart and values and actions do not align and in which a person seeks to manipulate others by giving a false impression of himself or herself. Exposing hypocrisy and the lack of integrity in leaders was a concern for Jesus. Once we have moved to a place where we routinely live with our lives and souls out of sync, it becomes difficult to receive the feedback that is necessary to live a gospel-oriented life. Three invitations of Jesus summarize the essence of gospel integrity.

The first great invitation for living with integrity is the call of Jesus for us to avoid hypocrisy (Matt. 7:5). We often practice hypocrisy unknowingly, and it is a spiritual disease that kills our souls. Its essence is when we put on a front and seek to show ourselves as someone we truly are not. Jesus warned about seeking to show off spiritually so that we appear to be more pious than we are: "Be careful not to practice your righteousness in front of others to be seen by them" (Matt. 6:1 NIV). Perhaps our financial giving is made public, or we engage in veiled theological boasting, or we talk about our theological beliefs and give the impression that they guide our lives more than they actually do. In our times, hypocrisy often shows up in demands for blanket tolerance that, if actually applied, would leave a person incapable of discerning right from wrong and good from evil. The great disciplines that help to safeguard one from hypocrisy are practices of living in secret what one lives in public and guarding oneself against boasting. Integrity is akin to a foundation for the spiritual life. Integrity alone does not constitute a spiritual or righteous life, but it forms the foundation that allows a life of integrity to be built that will not end up tilting and collapsing on itself.

The second invitation is in the Golden Rule: "In everything do to others as you would have them do to you" (Matt. 7:12). This speaks of a basic, ethical life orientation in which we always imagine ourselves to be subject to the ethical requirements we place on others. We do not ask people to do what we would not do. The Golden Rule strikes at an entitlement mentality that would have us believe we are somehow so uniquely wounded or so uniquely in need of attention that we can demand of others what we would never deliver ourselves.

The third invitation comes in Jesus's call for us to keep our word (Matt. 5:37). We are to be people whose word can be counted on. I know from painful personal experience that we do not achieve this by merely pledging to speak the truth; it also requires soul-searching and reflection on what is so valuable to us that we are willing to lie so that we are not deprived of it. Personal inner peace and tension-free living can become idols; they are often valued in churches far more than truth-telling. We need to be people who tell the truth and who are committed to keeping our word.

Before moving to the last *R* (*relating*), a bit of review may be useful. *Responding* is our construct for appraising how we view what we have received and what we remember over time. The purpose and intent of our response are to render service to our Lord and those around us. Service to others is possible only as we access Christ and his work on our behalf and as we focus on God's transforming grace. Our actions and thoughts toward others demonstrate our service to the Lord. Responses toward others and the Lord depend on each other and cannot be separated.

For Further Reading

Baxter, Richard. *The Reformed Pastor*. 1656. Reprint, Edinburgh and Carlisle, PA: Banner of Truth, 1974. A classic work concerned with the spirituality and practice of the pastor's personal life and ministry to others.

Farnham, Suzanne G., Stephanie A. Hull, and R. Taylor McLean. *Grounded in God: Listening Hearts Discernment for Group Deliberations*. Harrisburg, PA: Morehouse, 1996. A brief, helpful work that includes theoretical foundation and practical method for cultivating intentional listening and prayerful discernment with groups.

Hays, Richard B. *The Moral Vision of the New Testament: Community, Cross, New Creation: A Contemporary Introduction to New Testament Ethics*. San Francisco: HarperSanFrancisco, 1996. A comprehensive exposition of the ethical agenda of the New Testament.

Hestenes, Roberta. *Turning Committees into Communities*. Colorado Springs: NavPress, 1991. A refreshing call to get around the usual divide between task groups and community groups.

Liechty, Daniel, trans. and ed. *Early Anabaptist Spirituality: Selected Writings*. Classics of Western Spirituality. New York: Paulist Press, 1994. A good selection of sources that emphasize the need for Christians to be engaged in compassionate service.

McNeill, John Thomas. *A History of the Cure of Souls*. New York: Harper & Brothers, 1951. A well-regarded study of the history of pastoral care.

Peacock, Barbara. *Soul Care in African American Practice*. Downers Grove, IL: InterVarsity, 2020. A book that explores the deep connection in this tradition between the private devotional life and responding to the needs around us.

Thurman, Howard. *Jesus and the Disinherited*. 1949. Reprint, Boston, MA: Beacon, 1997. A classic reflection on Jesus's message for the poor and disenfranchised. Martin Luther King Jr. carried a well-worn copy of this book in his pocket during the Montgomery bus boycott.

Torrance, James B. *Worship, Community, and the Triune God of Grace*. Downers Grove, IL: InterVarsity, 1996. A careful study of the theological and practical implications of a trinitarian stance in worship, prayer, sacraments, and gender concerns; includes operational definitions of *person, individual, community,* and *society.*

Wolterstorff, Nicholas. *Educating for Responsible Action.* Grand Rapids: Eerdmans, 1980. A reminder that Christian education must cultivate tendencies to live out kingdom values.

SIX

Relating

Spiritually Enriching Relationships of Love and Service

And let us consider how to provoke one another to love and good deeds.

Hebrews 10:24

The test of the character and quality of our relationship with God is measured by the character and quality of all other relationships.

John H. Westerhoff III[1]

In corporate worship the lives of Christians are formed and transformed, Christian identity is conferred and nurtured.

Debra Dean Murphy[2]

What role do our relationships play in spiritual formation? Who are we to relate to? Our Creator designed us to live and grow in relationship with him and in human community. Other people are among the most important sources of God's grace in our lives.

1. *Spiritual Life: The Foundation for Preaching and Teaching* (Louisville: Westminster John Knox, 1994), 1.
2. *Teaching That Transforms: Worship as the Heart of Christian Education* (Grand Rapids: Brazos, 2004), 16.

How do we do this? We need to seek out spiritually enriching relationships of love and service. We should put ourselves in places such as small groups and service units where the formation and growth of these relationships are encouraged. We need to invest in community.

What stance does this require? A commitment to fellowship and a profound recognition that we need the church far more than the church needs us.

The biblical way of life is decidedly centered on others. Christian service is a pathway of great joy and not one of self-annihilation. Our service begins by giving ourselves to God. All Christian service starts by acknowledging God's claim on all our property, talent, and time. We serve God in our worship, our giving, our study, and our concern for others. Springing from a heart given to God, service always involves doing. The doing may be kind words, time spent with another, using our skills in service, or teaching, but in any event, the servant, like Jesus, goes about doing kind and good deeds.

Corporate Celebration and CSF: An Opening Note

Essentially mysterious but entirely accessible, the sacraments are pure genius for teaching us what we need to know and, paradoxically, what we can never know about our relationship with God. . . . In every case, the first thing they teach us is that we do not worship God alone. We need other people in our lives to feed us and forgive us, to touch us and bless us and strengthen our resolve. There are no solo sacraments. We need one another.

Barbara Brown Taylor[3]

Christians have every reason to celebrate, and our worshipful celebration is the central forming event in our community life. The single most important event in our spiritual formation is participating in worship that evokes awe, draws forth a loving response to others, and leaves us certain that isolated individualism is not compatible with the gospel. We are loved by God and adopted as his children. The new spiritual life we have received, the continuing redemptive work of God, and the very beauty of God should call forth our celebration. In celebration, we strengthen one another through our corporate rejoicing. The doxology of God's people is an end in itself and bears healing fruit. Many struggling individuals have found themselves strengthened and their life vision renewed simply by experiencing the celebration of God's people.

3. *The Preaching Life* (Cambridge, MA: Cowley, 1993), 66.

When reading the Gospels, we are struck with how central celebration was to the life of Christ. Paul goes so far as to command us to "rejoice in the Lord always" (Phil. 4:4). Celebration is not merely a feel-good, group-building activity; instead, it should be a response to God's gracious deliverance of us. So the celebration called for here is one of celebrating the jubilee that Christ has given us. We might speak of this as having parties for a purpose in which we seek to enjoy one another and remind ourselves of the great gifts God has given us.

The Power of Relationships for CSF

> Ultimate reality is a community of persons who know and love one another. That is what the universe, God, history, and life is all about. . . . We believe the world was made by a God who is a community of persons who have loved each other for all eternity.
>
> Timothy Keller[4]

> If you have read this far in the book, you will not be surprised by my three-word summary of positive psychology: *Other people matter.*
>
> Christopher Peterson[5]

> The seventy-five years and twenty million dollars expended on the Grant Study points . . . to a straightforward five-word conclusion: "Happiness is love. Full stop."
>
> George Vaillant[6]

The statement above by George Vaillant is his summary of the Grant Study, which he oversaw for three decades at Harvard Medical School. This longitudinal study of Harvard undergraduate men ran in conjunction with the Glueck Study, a study of a cohort of disadvantaged inner-city male youth who grew up in Boston neighborhoods between 1940 and 1945. The men were evaluated at least every two years through questionnaires and personal interviews. For a female longitudinal comparison group, the Grant Study selected ninety women from the Stanford-Terman Study, which began in 1922. The findings of the Grant Study are rich and identify several factors associated

---

4. *The Reason for God: Belief in an Age of Skepticism* (New York: Dutton, 2008), 226.
5. *A Primer in Positive Psychology* (Oxford: Oxford University Press, 2006), 249.
6. Quoted in Scott Stossel, "What Makes Us Happy, Revisited," *The Atlantic*, April 24, 2013, https://www.theatlantic.com/magazine/archive/2013/05/thanks-mom/309287.

with healthy aging. The current director, Robert Waldinger, and the previous director, George Vaillant, emphasize the outsized role relationships play in mental and physical health. For example, Vaillant asserts, "A good marriage at age 50 predicted positive aging at 80. But surprisingly, low cholesterol levels at age 50 did not."[7] And Waldinger sums up the study's main point as "Good relationships keep us happier and healthier. Period."[8]

Christopher Peterson was one of the leaders in the positive psychology movement. With Martin Seligman, he developed an assessment of virtues associated with human flourishing that has been taken by over eleven million people and is available in more than forty languages.[9] One of the findings of their massive research projects looking at character strengths and human flourishing is the importance of relationships. They found that good character supports good relationships. Peterson writes, "Character is sexy, and there is a reason that it is sexy. Good character makes relationships of all sorts possible, including romance but also friendship and the relationships that matter at school or at work, around the neighborhood, and of course in the family."[10] I have taken their unremitting emphasis on the importance of relationships to heart by making the strengthening of relationships a priority and seeking to include people who find themselves isolated. In CSF, relationships matter; an excellent, simple starting point for a CSF program is intentionally fostering deep spiritual friendships for church members of all ages.

CSF is most healthy when it takes place in a context marked by strong and vibrant relationships. These relationships provide the background and support for transformation to occur. Healthy relationships can furnish a sense of belonging, models to emulate, encouragement, esprit de corps, and positive expectations. Many educators have observed the power of a strong relational context to foster openness and encourage change. However, the more teaching-centric and performance-oriented churches tend to dismiss the relational focus as unnecessary or even counterproductive. They are sadly wrong: their emphasis on efficiency has blinded them to an invisible but genuinely essential aspect of CSF.

---

7. George E. Vaillant, *Aging Well: Surprising Guideposts to a Happier Life from the Landmark Harvard Study of Adult Development* (Boston: Little, Brown, 2002), 13.

8. Robert Waldinger, "What Makes a Good Life? Lessons from the Longest Study on Happiness," YouTube video, 12:47, filmed January 2016 in Brookline, MA, TED Talk, https://youtu.be/8KkKuTCFvzI.

9. "About," The VIA Institute on Character, accessed July 10, 2020, https://www.viacharacter.org/about.

10. Christopher Peterson, *Pursuing the Good Life: 100 Reflections on Positive Psychology* (New York: Oxford University Press, 2013), Kindle Loc. 1262.

Encouraging Formational Relationships

One cannot despise oneself and truly love God or the neighbor.

Ray S. Anderson[11]

The link between emotional health and spiritual maturity is a large, unexplored area of discipleship.

Peter Scazzero[12]

Part of our yearning for heaven is a yearning for a whole and open relationship in which we are fully known and understood. When things are set right, we will stand before God and, for the first time, be fully known by someone and yet not afraid because "there is no fear in love. But perfect love drives out fear, because fear has to do with punishment" (1 John 4:18 NIV).

We live in a remarkably future-oriented culture. We are a culture of savers and planners and people who only uneasily enter into the present moment, except for brief hedonistic retreats into mindless activities. We are impatient when it comes to seriously reflecting on the past. At a friend's suggestion, I have begun to ask students in my classes to list their great-grandparents' first and last names, and I have yet to have a student identify all their great-grandparents. The sobering thought is that we live just two generations away from extinction in the collective memory. There are wonderful benefits of a future orientation regarding its support of long-term research and careful planning about public works projects. However, an excessive focus on the future robs us of some of the deepest joys we were designed to know. It makes it hard for us to dwell in the present time—the time where we meet and enjoy God.

The spiritual life requires that we step out of the future orientation, where we ask, "What does this present activity do for me in terms of the future?" and simply live our current moment. We get a sense of the difference between a future orientation and a present orientation when we think about friendships in our culture. A straightforward definition of friendship says, "Friends are the people we waste time with." Think about a brief commercial encounter that seems unending. The actual time spent is not the issue as much as our perception of its value and necessity and what we are receiving from this meeting to help us meet our goals. Yet we eagerly prolong pleasant conversations with friends and leave pleasant gatherings far later than we

11. *Self-Care: A Theology of Personal Empowerment and Spiritual Healing* (Wheaton: Victor Books, 1995), 106.
12. *The Emotionally Healthy Church* (Grand Rapids: Zondervan, 2003), 18.

had planned because we enjoy spending time with friends. At some level, we can enjoy friendships only when we enter into the present and simply enjoy the reality of talking and sharing and supporting one another. For a little while, we lose track of time.

The deep joy promised in the gospel is available only if we learn to switch out of a driven, future orientation and are willing to waste time with God. To have a sense of the joy of coming home and being known. To feel God's embrace. To enjoy the pleasure of his company. Part of the dynamic of the spiritual life is forming and deepening one's friendship with God. God desires to be our friend! He wants so much for us to live in relationship with him that he chose to die rather than live without us as friends. As I began to learn to sit quietly before God, I began to experience God's caress. With this experience of God's tender love, I began to find in Scripture a whole new emphasis on God's extravagant and alluring love. Words like Zephaniah's beautiful picture of God quieting us with his love and rejoicing over us with singing (Zeph. 3:17; cf. Isa. 62:5) have become favorites of mine. On my best days, I increasingly see that if indeed "God is love," then he can respond to me only out of love.

Community First, Growth Second

Faith and the life of faith are communal before they are individual.

                                                                    Craig Dykstra[13]

People need two sorts of relationships to grow: the divine and the human. . . . No matter what the issue or struggle, relatedness must come first.

                                                        Henry Cloud and John Townsend[14]

A friend of mine, José, relocated with his family to a distant city. From our brief communications, I sensed that they were not settled. In a phone call, I heard that the move had not gone well. The move, the new job, and the new house all came with more problems than they had anticipated. When I inquired about how they were doing on finding a church, I heard, "It's going okay. All we need is a place where we'll be fed." My friend had confessed to me that he was lonely, that his wife often cried over the loss of friends and family, and he thought that all he needed from church was "to be fed."

---

13. *Growing in the Life of Faith: Education and Christian Practices*, 2nd ed. (Louisville: Westminster John Knox, 2005), 39.

14. *How People Grow: What the Bible Reveals about Personal Growth* (Grand Rapids: Zondervan, 2001), 81.

Is this a consummate consumer orientation to church? When one comes to get a commodity—preaching and teaching—with little thought of personal engagement, it dramatically diminishes one's openness to the real formation the church can offer.

The conversation with José was like so many I have had over the years. He was young, married, and successful, but his life showed signs of stress and loneliness. He and his wife were many states removed from their parents and extended family. At a church social event, he opened up to a friend about his wife nagging him about his long work hours, his ineptitude with the children, and his weekly Saturday golf game. His friend encouraged him to join a small group with his wife and assured him that they could find friends and support there. I talked with José some time later. Aware that things had worsened in his marriage and his emotional state, I inquired about how their small group was responding to this. "Oh, we stopped going after a few weeks," he replied. "We weren't getting anything out of it; it didn't help us at all, and it was a real nuisance to get a sitter for the kids."

We need to be aware that no single program or spiritual activity will be a means of healing grace for everyone. Perhaps José's friend had made it seem like all he had to do was show up, or maybe the experience revealed a quick-fix mentality. There must be a willingness to engage—a willingness and desire to love—that makes grace available in these settings.

We know the maxim "If you pursue happiness, you'll never find it." We discover happiness as the by-product of other pursuits. Happiness will forever elude us when we pursue it directly. Likewise, we generally find healing and support in community when they are not our primary aim. Much hope and healing can come through participation in authentic Christian community, but only if we invest ourselves in the community and relate to it in a receptive way. As Robert Bellah and his colleagues ask, "Are friends that one makes in order to improve one's health really friends enough to improve one's health?"[15] We generally find help and healing through community when we are willing to commit to being part of community, period. The commitment to others does begin to put us in a place where we are more open to the healing and change that communities truly offer.

Spiritual formation is concerned with facilitating spiritual change in people. People change most readily when they are in environments that foster change as they learn to live out their unique-communal life calling. Such

---

15. Robert Bellah, *Habits of the Heart: Individualism and Commitment in American Life* (Berkeley: University of California Press, 1985), 135.

Evangelism, Discipleship, Mentoring, Spiritual Guidance, and Psychological Counseling

Evangelism is the ministry that introduces a pre-Christian to Jesus Christ and launches the new convert on a lifelong spiritual journey. The essential message of evangelism is, "Here is what you must do to become a child of God." Evangelism focuses on issues of sin, conversion, and trust in Christ as Savior and Lord. Every Christian helping ministry builds on this foundation.

Spiritual formation concerns the shaping of our lives after the pattern of Jesus Christ. It is a process that takes place in the inner person, whereby the Spirit reshapes our character. Many Scriptures describe this lifelong spiritual formation process, including 2 Corinthians 3:18; Galatians 4:19; Ephesians 4:13, 22–24; Colossians 3:9–10; and 1 Thessalonians 5:23.

Discipleship is the ministry that seeks to teach new believers essential Christian beliefs and also to train us in practices that are normal in the unfolding spiritual journey. Richard V. Peace, a professor at Fuller Theological Seminary, tells of being discipled by a program that included church attendance, Bible reading, believing the right things, prayer, and witnessing. "We did pretty well at the *knowing*, okay at the *doing*, but the whole question of *being* was fraught with difficulty. The real issue was internal. Something else was needed." Peace concludes that in order to *become*, true disciples of Jesus will benefit greatly by supplementing helpful, short-term discipleship programs with lifelong patterns of spiritual formation and direction.

Mentoring is the process whereby someone who is more experienced at a given skill teaches, models, and imparts essential knowledge, skills, and strategies to someone less experienced. The spirit of the mentoring relationship is that the mentor imparts these things freely in order to help the protégés attain goals that are their own. It is not mentoring, but something else, if we try to re-create people in our image or to accomplish goals that are ours, not theirs. Gordon Shea describes a mentor as one of those special people in

environments supply both support and challenge, and participants accept community responsibility as a way of life. We think of being responsible for others and of allowing others to care for us. There is a shift from independence to healthy interdependence. We begin to let go of our fear of self-disclosure, vulnerability, and revealing our weakness. Commitment is upheld instead of being feared as binding or controlling.[16]

16. Julie A. Gorman, *Community That Is Christian*, 2nd ed. (Grand Rapids: Baker Books, 2002), 16.

life who, through their deeds and words, help other people move toward the fulfillment of their individual potential.

Spiritual guidance refers to any help given individually or in a group that advances the process of spiritual formation. The essential message of spiritual guidance is, "Together, we're going to pay prayerful attention to God's gracious working in your life."

Spiritual friendship is the most basic ministry of spiritual guidance in which two or more friends—on a relatively equal basis—support, encourage, and pray for one another on their journeys.

Spiritual counsel refers to the occasional helping ministry in which a godly Christian offers focused help to another person who seeks to know God and his will. One may offer spiritual counsel through a personal conversation, letter, or sermon.

Spiritual direction refers to the ministry of soul care in which a gifted and experienced Christian helps another person to grow in relationship with and obedience to God by following the example of Jesus Christ. Spiritual direction is a highly personalized ministry, respecting individual life histories, temperaments, levels of maturity, and vocations. The goals of spiritual direction are threefold. In the area of knowing, the spiritual director helps the directee understand God's will as revealed in Scripture and illuminated by faithful spiritual writings. In the realm of being, the director prays for the transformation of the directee's inner world after the image of Christ. In the realm of doing, the director encourages the directee to faithfully live out the gospel in the power of the Spirit.

Psychological counseling is the ministry that seeks personality growth, resolution of inner conflicts, and more efficient interpersonal functioning. This kind of counseling is initiated by an anxiety-laden problem or crisis, advances through personal discovery and growth, and ends with the resolution of the presenting problem. An important healing factor is the client-counselor relationship.[a]

a. Adapted from Bruce A. Demarest, *Soul Guide: Following Jesus as Spiritual Director* (Colorado Springs: NavPress, 2003), 35–41. Used by permission.

The Importance of Various Relationships in CSF

When we listen to people's journeys of faith, we cannot help but recognize other people's presence and impact in these stories. The old adage is right: "People are God's method. The church is looking for better methods; God is looking for better people."[17] Most of us can attest to God's persistent

17. Adapted from E. M. Bounds, *The Complete Works of E. M. Bounds on Prayer* (Grand Rapids: Baker, 1990), 447.

practice of taking people who were not much "better"—but available—and growing them into better people through whose lives God could work. The people who enter our lives for our spiritual good relate to us in a variety of roles. Some are mentors. Generally, these are people older than we are who have had more experience in the faith and who come alongside us for a season, giving some direct guidance as to how to follow Christ more closely. At times, mentors or examples may not even be aware of the impact they are having. For example, certain authors have shaped my life in significant ways.

There are also spiritual friendships. These are marked by more reciprocity in the relationship and may go on for decades or mark a special season, especially in times of transition such as college or military service. The key words for these relationships are *sharing* and *support*. Family members provide another important source of spiritual guidance. Whether through parents, siblings, grandparents, or aunts and uncles, we are influenced spiritually in our families, often in quite positive ways, through godly role models who care for us, love us, and pray for us. Finally, we need to mention what we would simply call those serendipitous encounters. Usually, these are memorable moments when a stranger speaks or models, often unknowingly, a word that gives shape to our current situation and guides us in our spiritual lives.

Part of the task of leaders in spiritual formation is to encourage the formation of spiritually challenging and supportive relationships in the Christian community. This is a call not for some grand social engineering scheme of trying to match people up but rather for cultivation of a climate in which spiritually healthy relationships can flourish and are valued. It is also essential that leaders give attention to what types of relationships seem available to persons at different places on their spiritual journey.

For example, I have spoken with many people who feel spiritually forsaken: to them, God is silent and distant. Generally, these people believe that there is no one in their church to turn to at such a time. Church leaders can do informal audits by asking what resources are available for these different parts of the journey. What wise and healing relationships are available to those in a dark night? Who can help disciple a new Christian? What resources are available to the adult Christian who is growing weary in service? How intentional are our efforts to identify and encourage spiritual directors? In what ways are we training the congregation as a whole about steps to take and people to contact when someone is feeling disconnected? How are we speaking openly to these issues so that people are not blindsided by the ebb and flow of spiritual experience?

Taking Time to Honor Relationships

Time surely does not guarantee positive relationships, but without time, they cannot develop and mature into deep, spiritually forming relationships. In parenting, we make a distinction between quantity and quality of time, the premise being that a few hours of focused attention may be worth more than many hours of distracted mutual presence. While that distinction may be a bit dubious, we need to see that there are differences in the types of time we spend together in a church. In practice, we discover that in parenting and fellowship, quality times often show up unannounced in the middle of quantity times. Announcing to our children or fellow believers that we are about to focus solely on quality time for the next hour may be greeted with less than enthusiastic approval. The question is, Are we eager and willing to inject or derive quality from our times together? To get a sense of how the quality of our time in community varies, consider the following examples:

Task time. Many churches carry out their work through small committees or task groups. It is possible to work side by side with people week after week and not know much about them. You may find yourself completely surprised when a struggle in their life surfaces in another context, because during the task time there were no opportunities to expose that area of struggle.

Large gathering time. Whether in business meetings or worship services, most churches are going to call people together to meet at times when the focus is not primarily on making connections but on conveying information or on some stated spiritual end. After such a meeting, a friend quipped that all of us had our elbows together but our hearts apart.

Large social time. These gatherings provide an opportunity for people to connect with acquaintances and meet new people on a personal-affinity basis. They are opportunities for people to talk and share their lives and catch up on news with one another.

Midsize congregational time. These gatherings intentionally form relational groups that number less than 150 people and may consist of the congregation of the church or a selected subgroup of the congregation. Often there is an emphasis on teaching, worship, and spiritual formation activities. There is an opportunity for people to engage with one another at a personal level in a context of prayer and worship.

Small formational study-group time. Small groups meeting in a home or comfortable environment, where people have made a commitment to study and pray together, provide an opportunity for in-depth sharing and support.

Spiritual friendship time. These may be one-on-one meetings with a peer or respected spiritual mentor or meetings with a small prayer group. The people are committed to Christ and one another. Meeting together, they urge "one another to love and good deeds" (Heb. 10:24).

The purpose of the above list is to remind us that the effects of time together are going to be different depending on how the time is spent. A person whose entire time in the Christian community is spent in large, impersonal gatherings is going to leave with the knowledge and orientation that were provided in that group but is going to lack the kind of interpersonal support and challenge that are found in smaller formation groups. Likewise, a person who is simply in a small formation group is going to lack the connection with the larger body of Christ and will miss some of the opportunities for worship and proclamation that can occur in such venues. A minimum quantity of time is necessary to be really engaged in the task of community formation, but it is also important that we experience community in a rich variety of ways.

Another important consideration that comes into the time equation of spiritual formation concerns our time orientation. As previously mentioned, we in North America are a very future-oriented lot. We tend to measure our lives in terms of productivity and think of time as something to be saved and spent. For many of us, we are able to identify who our friends are by recognizing that they are the small subset of people we are quite willing to "waste time with." But our rigid connection to a future-time orientation can limit our ability to truly engage in community. There is much practical wisdom in the longtime Christian practice of sharing meals together, because eating a meal is one thing that pulls us out of our future orientation and causes us to dwell for a time in the present. It is only when we are in the present that we can enter into the spiritual realm and engage in true friendship activities.

Formation Takes Place in Relationships

The secret of all life-giving relation to others, and of all that is social, lies in the fact that the primary other for a human being, whether he wants it or not, is always God.

Dallas Willard[18]

18. *Renovation of the Heart: Putting on the Character of Christ* (Colorado Springs: NavPress, 2002), 185.

We have many people who are passionate for God and his work, yet who are unconnected to their own emotions or those around them.

Peter Scazzero[19]

Formation takes place in life. Our classes, small groups, reading, and worship equip us to respond well to the formational events of our lives. Most of the deeply forming events of our lives will come in the midst of relationships. All the Rs of formation are important, but relating has unique power both to show our formation (Are we patient in the face of interpersonal tensions? Do we display long-suffering love? Do we exhibit relational integrity?) and to form us (through the forming power of love, the "rocks my world" effects of a mentor, the soothing effects of a parent). Relating is where the rubber of formation teaching meets the road of life.

Connection refers not only to the development of spiritual friendships and interpersonal bonds that allow formational relationships to operate but also to a deep commitment to the reality that "two are better than one" (Eccles. 4:9). People who care for us and hold us accountable are a means of grace. This level of connecting is encouraged when churches affirm that relationships are vital to spiritual growth. "Truth-model" churches, which place the emphasis exclusively on learning truth to change, occasionally downplay the value of relationships. We need to underscore the place that spiritual friendships and supportive relationships can have in our nurture and seek to foster their presence in our communities. Jesus calls us to become more and more dependent on God and increasingly interdependent with other people. Interdependent relationships are one of God's means of helping us become more and more dependent on him. Never support the false dichotomy that drives a wedge between knowing God and being in relationships with people. The two invitations in the greatest commandment make our relationships with God and people inseparable.

Those seeking to foster spiritual formation in churches need to encourage interpersonal connection, but there must also be an emphasis on learning to follow Jesus's wisdom in relationships. Jesus's invitation to us to live a life of love is not simply a call to benign acceptance and tolerance. Love calls us to seek the best for another; it calls for wisdom, self-awareness ("First take the log out of your own eye" [Luke 6:42]), knowledge, empathy, and the ability to discern the heart rather than mere appearance. True love requires training and practice. In a society filled with interpersonal pain, the church must offer "Love 101" as part of its spiritual formation. Believers must model and teach love.

19. *Emotionally Healthy Church*, 37.

Jesus Invites Us to Extend Hospitality

> Just as the human need for hospitality is a constant, so, it seems, is the human fear of the stranger.
>
> Ana María Pineda[20]

In both word and deed, Jesus invites his followers to show hospitality. In the Gospels, Jesus was the frequent recipient of hospitality (Matt. 13:1, 36; Mark 1:29–31; 14:3–9; Luke 7:36–39; 10:38–42; 14:1–6; John 2:1–10). He also clearly extends hospitality in his mass feedings (Matt. 14:15–21; 15:32) and especially at the Last Supper (John 13), when he serves as the host who provides the space and food and breaks social convention by washing the feet of his guests.

The early church took to heart Jesus's invitation and placed special emphasis on showing hospitality to strangers. Opening the fellowship of reading and interpreting Scripture and prayer to friends and strangers widens the circle of fellowship and breaks down barriers that previously left strangers on the outside. Three scriptural lists of virtuous actions highlight hospitality to strangers (Rom. 12:13; 1 Tim. 5:10; Heb. 13:2). Additionally, one of the qualifications of a church leader is a hospitable nature (1 Tim. 3:2; Titus 1:8).

The call for hospitality goes beyond simply entertaining. Hospitality is a practical outworking of the call to love and creates a space for formation. Creating a space for food, spiritual conversation, and the warmth of acceptance is so important to our formation. The New Testament writers first gave these commands in cultures where hospitality was already a social norm. How much more we need this urging today, when we treasure privacy and acknowledge that "we are short not only of tables that welcome strangers but even of tables that welcome friends."[21]

Keeping Relational Commitments and Handling Conflict

> The calling of community is to lure people off the island onto the mainland where connection is possible and to provide it.
>
> Larry Crabb[22]

20. "Hospitality," in *Practicing Our Faith: A Way of Life for a Searching People*, ed. Dorothy C. Bass (San Francisco: Jossey-Bass, 1997), 31.
21. Pineda, "Hospitality," 32.
22. *Connecting: Healing for Ourselves and Our Relationships; A Radical New Vision* (Nashville: Word, 1997), 38.

A spiritual friend is a sensitive, caring, open, flexible person of faith and prayer who listens well and maintains confidentiality.

John H. Westerhoff III[23]

Lifestyles and choices that love and value people more than things is the litmus test of faith.

Adele Ahlberg Calhoun[24]

Certain relational activities have more spiritual leverage in the way they affect our souls. Keeping and honoring relational responsibilities should be gospel-driven priorities in our lives. Scripture understands justice largely as a matter of carrying out a relational responsibility. These relationships extend beyond immediate friends and family and include the family of God: those whom the Bible calls our neighbors, our nation, and our environment. When considering spiritual formation, we place an emphasis on relational responsibilities because doing so is an important ethical principle and because honoring or breaking them uniquely affects our souls.

The church's preoccupation with sex comes, in part, from the wisdom that sexual transgressions, which violate our relational commitments, have a significant power to deform the soul. Paul warns, "Run from sexual sin! No other sin so clearly affects the body as this one does. For sexual immorality is a sin against your own body" (1 Cor. 6:18 NLT). Chastity speaks about the discipline of living and relating to other people so that we see them primarily as persons, not as objects of sexual fantasy or manipulation. Our sexuality is a good and perfect gift that we need to celebrate. Nevertheless, we need to discipline ourselves in Christian community so that we do not sexualize our interactions in ways that distract us from our spiritual tasks. At the practical level, this means that we need to control the wandering eye, avoid flirtation, and be careful about our dress and demeanor so that we can relate to one another as brothers and sisters in Christ with full integrity.

Compassion complements the previous mark of responding. Here we are called to care for one another, but even more important, the community looks outward. Some of my most memorable times of community building have been when the church worked together to show compassion for others. Community forms at its deepest not when people are simply seeking to form

23. *Spiritual Life*, 69.
24. *Spiritual Disciplines Handbook: Practices That Transform Us* (Downers Grove, IL: InterVarsity, 2005), 195.

Insights on Forgiveness

Forgiveness takes brokenness seriously and affirms that guilt is real but also that guilt is not the last word. The possibility of forgiveness is rooted in the character and actions of God. Forgiving is not forgetting. . . . Forgiving is not excusing. . . . Forgiving is not ignoring. . . . Forgiving is not necessarily to offer unconditional trust.

Along the way to accomplishing forgiveness, you will need to: (1) Consider how you were forgiven. (2) Be realistic. Name the sin against you for what it truly is. Limit your expectations of what will result from forgiveness. (3) Share the pain (Isa. 53:4; Matt. 8:17; Gal. 6:2). (4) Accept the time forgiving may take. (5) Understand what it means to "forgive and forget." God cannot forget our sins in the sense that he loses them from his memory. By forgetting them, he must mean that he sets aside the punishment we deserve. So, when we "forget" the offense done to us, it means we will not in the future "use" the offense as reason to punish the offender. (6) Finally learn ways to break the chain of self-enslavement to bitter thoughts.

For healing to occur, our perceptions must be brought into line with reality, with truth. The essence of this reinterpretation of my hurt is seeing those who hurt me as separate from what they did to me and *seeing myself as more than my wound.*

To forgive is not necessarily to extend unconditional trust. Additionally, I must realize that the perceived value from the empowerment that anger seems to give me must be put in perspective with the possible ultimate cost to my own spirit of abiding malice (Heb. 12:15).

relationships as an end in themselves but when enlightened task groups aim at showing compassion for the surrounding community.

In the context of an ongoing ministry of teaching the Word, we need specific instruction because we are a forgetful people; we must continually remind each other of God's love. We are also a highly prejudiced people, and we must continually train each other to set aside our racial prejudices and our innate tendency to assign persons to a certain status. We also need to remind people that God will work in their life circumstances, if invited, and to emphasize the importance of learning to handle conflict as a true peacemaker. We need to give the call to love God and neighbor both as a challenge and as a lived reality that brings support and safety. Without the challenge, we often will retreat to self-protective strategies that make it difficult for us to give and receive love.

The other set of difficulties in forgiveness is in receiving it. The hard-work miracle may be hard to believe as a miracle. Who qualifies for a miracle? The answers and solutions may lie in following three steps: (1) Realize the hidden motives you may have in fearing to rest in God's sheer mercy. (2) Remember the tactics of the enemy of your soul's peace and learn how to overcome them. (3) Reexamine the reality and integrity of the forgiveness provided for you in Jesus Christ.

I also need to realize that a *refusal to accept forgiveness can be a form of idolatry and pride.* Boldly put, am I such a unique exception in the world that I can handle my redemption better than God?

In his accusations, *the devil always points us away from Christ*, to get us either to excuse self or to dwell on self. On the other hand, the Holy Spirit points us to Christ, and if he convicts of sin, he also seeks to convince us of grace. Satan twists Scripture. Satan confuses doctrine. How do we meet his accusations? (1) Address the power of sin instead of the shame of sin. Study what it is doing to you more than how it makes you feel (Rom. 2–8). (2) Work to keep your conscience clean through confession (Acts 24:16; 1 Tim. 1:19; Heb. 9:14). (3) Fix your eyes on the evidences of grace in your life, past and present. (4) Share your struggle over guilt with another believer, and ask that friend to pray for your assurance of forgiveness. (5) Above all, realize that Satan cannot accuse you, a Christian, before God! God may convict you of sin in order to bring you to confession and cleansing, but he will not listen to the accusations of Satan and change his mind about your salvation (Rom. 8:33–34).[a]

a. Adapted from David G. Benner and Robert W. Harvey, *Understanding and Facilitating Forgiveness,* *Strategic Pastoral Counseling Resources* (Grand Rapids: Baker, 1996), 33–83. Used by permission.

Church conflict ranges from interpersonal irritations, based in pride and pettiness, to deep-seated ideological conflicts; from genuine differences between high-minded people over allocating scarce resources for a good cause to systemic patterns of institutionalized conflict. Handling conflict well was certainly one of Jesus's major concerns, and every New Testament epistle addresses it. Gracious accountability is a witness to the gospel. Years ago, I bumped into a woman who had been involved in restorative church discipline. She thanked me profoundly for being part of a very difficult, grace-filled church discipline process that brought her to repentance and brought sanity and health to her life. The process involved accountability and forgiveness, both vital aspects of church life. Forgiving is a powerful witness to our personal and corporate ability to recognize the forgiveness that we have received and our ability to multiply it by extending it to others.

"The experience of forgiveness makes us forgiving. Once we see ourselves as people who need God's mercy, we will be more likely to show mercy to others."[25]

Offense and conflict are inevitable and come in all shapes and sizes. The bottom-line questions should point first to the reality of the resources available in the love and sovereignty of God and then to the difficulties of particular cases. Our churches need to guide groups and individuals through reconciliation that is grounded in the grace that has been received in the gospel of Christ. Jesus sternly summarized the parable of the unmerciful servant: "So my heavenly Father will also do to every one of you, if you do not forgive your brother or sister from your heart" (Matt. 18:35). As we forgive and extend mercy, we relate as Jesus has invited us to do. This makes the gospel evident to us and to all within our circle of influence. Here the power of the gospel shines because forgiveness is often extremely difficult—and in an individualistic, preoccupied culture, some even consider it impossible.

To implement this R of *relating*, we need to realize that people often resist the kind of formative relationships that are truly essential. These relationships require vulnerability and expose us to the challenge of connection and the disappointment that comes whenever we have extended ourselves in love. As leaders in formation, we are not able to—nor should we try to—manipulate things so that people experience formative relationships. However, we do have a responsibility to do all that is in our power, through prayer and diligent work, to create a climate that supports formative relationships.

Community Disciplines

The spiritual health of a community is crucial to spiritual formation. A community's spiritual health can be encouraged by members practicing community disciplines as a means of being open and transparent before God. This corporate life is important, for communities as well as for individuals, and must embody humility. The reality of the Lord's promise, "My grace is sufficient for you, for power is made perfect in weakness" (2 Cor. 12:9), is true for churches. We practice the disciplines because they allow us to access the grace and strength needed to cultivate the community we want. God builds true community through grace, which we access through our disciplined, grace-filled living.

25. Gerald Sittser, *A Grace Disguised: How the Soul Grows through Loss* (Grand Rapids: Zondervan, 2004), 147.

The disciplines needed for grace-bathed community are those of abstinence (practices of giving up or abstaining from a destructive pattern such as gossip), empowerment (practices like confession, in which we actively embrace truth that will guide), and discernment (practices that allow godly wisdom a central place in our communities). Historically, many communities have found it useful to develop a "community rule of life" that provides concrete guidance about how to live together in a grace-oriented way. Wise groups consult and learn from the experiences of previous generations. Spiritual formation is not a wheel for us to reinvent, but it is a badly neglected part of the vehicle that we need to grease. In their own traditional documents and history, many denominations can find the outlines for community rules. From the ancient monastic rules, the catechisms of the Reformation, and the journals of Wesley to the "new monastic" movement and contemporary Christian colleges' and camps' statements of community standards, sources of insight and wisdom abound. Confession, participation in church life, secrecy, and the avoidance of gossip are common elements of a community rule.

Confession

Confession is a basic discipline in the spiritual life, not for us to dread but for us to accept as a good gift. The old maxim that tells us "There is no stronger sin than the sin that remains hidden" is indeed true. There is also a place for us to offer confession and find accountability among other Christians. In some circles, people fear confession because of abuses that have taken place, but this does not diminish the Bible's call for us to confess to one another and its spiritual importance: "Therefore confess your sins to one another, and pray for one another, so that you may be healed" (James 5:16). The reality of these abuses should encourage us to train others for this pastoral ministry and to be very wise in how we encourage the practice of confession in our congregations.

Participation in Church Life

Jesus said, "For where two or three are gathered in my name, I am there among them" (Matt. 18:20). Christ is present with us as we gather, and in fellowship we can have an experience of the Lord's presence as we engage with one another for spiritual growth. At its heart, fellowship is a commitment to be with one another through the thick and thin of things and to recognize the importance of using our giftings in such settings. Earlier we talked about the God of formation, and we identified the force of entropy that is constantly seeking to tear us apart. Adam was not complete without Eve (Gen. 2:18), and, sadly, sin isolated him from Eve and from God. Jesus came to restore our relationship with God and to create the possibility of a new community. We see in the book of Revelation that at the end of history there will finally be perfect fellowship among the saints of God.

Secrecy

Secrecy refers to the discipline that Jesus advocated in terms of our giving money and care. Secrecy works in tandem with confession; confession highlights the level of openness we seek with each other, and secrecy emphasizes the care with which we treat each other's confidences. In community groups we often hear of needs, and sometimes it is quite appropriate for us to respond in public ways as we join together to help someone. But at times, it is also important for us to keep our responses confidential, which may protect the dignity of the person who is receiving help and certainly protects us from vainglory. This is an important discipline that deserves clear, sustained instruction. We can encourage the practice of secret help without making it the sole means by which we show compassion in our community. This is best left to individuals' discretion, as they realize that in a particular situation the person receiving aid and they themselves will benefit most when it is given in secret.

Avoidance of Gossip

Society generally understands gossip as the spreading of rumors and misinformation. Consequently, I have heard sincere persons justify their gossiping by saying, "It was true, so it is not gossip." From a Christian perspective, gossip is the public revelation of another person's sins, generally for self-oriented reasons. Gossip tears at the fabric of community and is part of a long list of community vices that we need to set aside and guard against. Paul pointed to these when he wrote, "I fear that there may perhaps be quarreling, jealousy, anger, selfishness, slander, gossip, conceit, and disorder" (2 Cor. 12:20).

The church is Christ's body on earth. When Jesus confronted Paul on the Damascus road, he questioned his persecutor: "Saul, Saul, why do you persecute me?" (Acts 9:4). What a remarkable identification with the church! To persecute the church is to persecute Christ. Paul uses the natural impulse to care for one's body to show Christ's care for the church: "For no one ever hates his own body, but he nourishes and tenderly cares for it, just as Christ does for the church" (Eph. 5:29). As we consider the church and spiritual formation, we must remember that spiritual formation is always an outflow of the church following Christ. When formation is made a preliminary goal or a means to an end—"We follow Jesus so our kids will turn out okay"—we obtain neither the formation we seek nor a church that lives out Christ's values and serves as his hands and feet on earth. Julie Gorman writes, "True community issues out of a realization that God has placed us and held us together as he wants. . . . Community becomes God's nurturing, caring, revealing, supportive means of displaying himself as a personal, relational being in our culture."[26]

Attributes of the Forming Community

A church in which God reigns, in which the kingdom of God is manifest, will demonstrate five attributes: meaningful worship, compassionate service (in and outside the church), fellowship, public witness, and disciple making. These attributes do not appear in isolation; they function in harmony, reinforcing each other.

Meaningful Worship

The church was born at Pentecost by the Holy Spirit's power when the disciples gathered together to worship. The book of Acts regularly describes the church as a vibrant worshiping community. The believers broke bread, gathered at the temple, sang, rejoiced, and prayed. They were grateful to God for their salvation, and when they gathered together, they ascribed to him worth and honor. The church was born in worship, and, likewise, at the consummation of this age, the church will give itself over to the worship of God (Rev. 7:9–17). Faithful servants will worship God alone. We respond to God's grace with gratitude, and his character draws us to worship. The worship of the church is also formative. Doxological formation should make us less likely to bow before the idols of money, power, and security instead of the one living and true God.

Compassionate Service

God has called Christians to be instruments of his compassion and service in the world. We love God wholly in worship, and we love our neighbor in service. The model of such service is Jesus, who "came not to be served but to serve, and to give his life a ransom for many" (Matt. 20:28), and who "emptied himself, taking the form of a slave, being born in human likeness. And being found in human form, he humbled himself and became obedient to the point of death—even death on a cross" (Phil. 2:7–8). This example of service guides the church as it ministers to and provides care for its members

26. Gorman, *Community That Is Christian*, 15.

and as it strives to address the sources of injustice, oppression, and degradation in our aching world. In service, the church uses all the gifts and resources it possesses as it seeks to minister to the entire person.

Fellowship

At Pentecost, three thousand people turned to Christ. Luke tells us that "they devoted themselves to the apostles' teaching and the fellowship, to the breaking of bread and the prayers" (Acts 2:42 ESV). This crucial verse captures the church's initial life and cuts through a false dichotomy that pits teaching against fellowship. In the grammatical structure of this verse in the original language, both "the apostles' teaching" and "the fellowship" have a definite article, which marks them as of parallel importance. These three thousand new converts were *proskartereō* (devoted), which implies "to attend constantly" or "busy oneself with," to "the fellowship" and "the apostles' teaching." This fellowship and attention to teaching were done with deliberation. The Revised English Bible's rendering captures this well: "They met constantly to hear the apostles teach and to share the common life, to break bread, and to pray" (2:42). Our common life as Christians is the context and one of the chief means of CSF. In terms of fellowship, safe fellowship is implied, and I must stress the importance of leaders taking child safety seriously. Please do not fall into the misunderstanding that "it can't happen here." Spiritual deformation is one of the bitter fruits of child abuse and sexual abuse in the church. Church leaders need to be realistic about the real threat of these forms of sin in their places of worship and put in place appropriate safeguards.

Public Witness

The church in which the Lord reigns has a message of joy and hope that we must tell a troubled world: the message of divine-human reconciliation and true freedom through Jesus Christ. Loving God and neighbor, in its deepest sense, leads us to share the good news with our neighbor. Witness must be in both word and deed. The faithful church confirms the validity of its spoken and written message by living out its doctrines and showing forth a contagious love. Jesus indicates that outsiders can legitimately test the truth of our message by our actions: "Everyone will know that you are my disciples, if you have love for one another" (John 13:35). Christ here asserts that true love is to be the mark of the Christian community, and he assures us that its presence will be a powerful witness. "Jesus turns to the world and says, 'I've something to say to you. On the basis of my authority, I give you a right: you may judge whether or not an individual is a Christian on the basis of the love he shows.'"[27]

Disciple Making

Finally—and most important for CSF—the church has the responsibility of discipling its members and supporting the discipleship of all Christians. Loving God and neighbor comes full circle when the neighbor joins us in loving God and neighbor as a fellow disciple. The church is to develop individuals who will "lead a life worthy of God" (1 Thess. 2:12), who will bear witness through their lifestyle of gentle obedience to Christ and imitation of his character. Jesus's disciples exhibited just such obedience to and imitation of him. Recall that when the disciples of John the Baptist noticed that Jesus's followers did not fast, they went to Jesus and asked, "Why do we and the Pharisees fast often, but your disciples do not fast?" (Matt. 9:14). Here we see that Jesus's disciples had patterned their lifestyle after their Teacher. This is the heart of discipleship. A disciple's thoughts and deeds reflect those of their master. Like Jesus's first disciples, we should pattern our behavior after our Master and seriously study the curriculum for Christlikeness. (See "The Great Invitations of Christ" in chap. 2.) Then, with Paul, we will be able to say, "Be imitators of me, as I am of Christ" (1 Cor. 11:1).

It is in answering Jesus's invitations to love and obey God and to love one another by doing what naturally flows from those two invitations that we give evidence of having *received* grace and gospel, *remembered* those blessings, *responded* to them, and *related* to others in a manner directed by them (the four *R*s). Our goal is spiritual formation that, by the receiving of God's grace and the empowering of the Holy Spirit, moves a curriculum for Christlikeness from a teaching approach to a living, breathing, gospel-directed life of shared community. This mission will fill our deepest longings for home and holiness. The journey is one for us to take together and to engage in with an eye to our eternal home because going it alone or seeking out other temporary homes will never satisfy. We belong together in our Father's house.

For Further Reading

Augustine. *Love One Another, My Friends: St. Augustine's Homilies on the First Letter of John; An Abridged English Version.* Translated and abridged by John Leinenweber. San Francisco: Harper & Row, 1989. A book with a simple and

27. Francis A. Schaeffer, *The Mark of the Christian* (Downers Grove, IL: InterVarsity, 1970), 13.

attractive writing style that invites readers to follow the path of love in their relationships.

Bellah, Robert. *Habits of the Heart: Individualism and Commitment in American Life*. Berkeley: University of California Press, 1985. A book, now a bit dated, that in its day startlingly revealed the pervasive individualism in modern American life and the resulting alienation and isolation.

Bonhoeffer, Dietrich. *Life Together*. Translated by John W. Doberstein. New York: Harper & Row, 1954. A compelling and now classic exploration of faith in community.

Hauerwas, Stanley, and William H. Willimon. *Resident Aliens: Life in the Christian Colony*. Nashville: Abingdon, 1989. A book that explores the ramifications of discipleship and ethics for a church that considers itself "a colony of heaven" in an ever-changing, secular culture.

Pohl, Christine D. *Living into Community: Cultivating Practices That Sustain Us*. Grand Rapids: Eerdmans, 2012. A wise and rich reflection on the practices that can sustain Christian community.

Schaeffer, Francis A. *The Mark of the Christian*. Downers Grove, IL: InterVarsity, 1970. A book that argues that love is to be the distinctive mark of the Christian and the church.

Snyder, Howard A. *The Community of the King*. Downers Grove, IL: InterVarsity, 1977. A practical guide for church life based on the relationship between the kingdom of God and the church.

Spener, Philipp Jakob. *Pia Desideria*. 1675. Reprint, Philadelphia: Fortress, 1964. A historic call to honor the priesthood of all believers.

SEVEN

High-Impact Practices

Proven Community Practices
That Foster Formation

By "Christian practices" we mean things Christian people do together over time to address fundamental human needs in response to and in the light of God's active presence for the life of the world.

Craig Dykstra and Dorothy Bass[1]

When we pay attention to practices, we are likely to notice the significance and beauty in small acts of grace and truth.

Christine Pohl[2]

Always we begin again.

John McQuiston[3]

The Importance of Gracious Practices

Time and again in this book, I have made the point that God loves us with an everlasting love and desires us to live as his beloved. And while that is the

---

1. "A Theological Understanding of Christian Practices," in *Practicing Theology: Beliefs and Practices in Christian Life*, ed. Miroslav Volf and Dorothy Bass (Grand Rapids: Eerdmans, 2002), 18.
2. *Living into Community: Cultivating Practices That Sustain Us* (Grand Rapids: Eerdmans, 2012), 7.
3. *Always We Begin Again: The Benedictine Way of Living*, rev. ed. (New York: Morehouse, 2011).

reality, we often live without a clear awareness of God's affection for us. In this chapter, I will pick up themes that I wrote about earlier and suggest some evidence-based practices that help us live as God's beloved. If through this book I could affect one change in the church, it would be to move leaders from thinking that "tellin' is spiritual training" to training people in actual practices. I suggest some high-impact practices in this chapter, and I want to underscore that these should be selected through a process of discernment. What does your particular church need to practice at this particular time?

Christians have given attention to spiritual formation throughout the entire history of the Christian church. Their practices have varied widely depending on the leaders and the situation. In the book of Acts we see people formed through worship, service, prayer, mentoring, conflicts, and teaching and preaching. This formation enabled them to be bold witnesses for Christ in a hostile environment and to be known for their countercultural love and compassion.[4] The desert elders of the third and fourth centuries developed very sophisticated patterns of formation that enabled them to demonstrate the radical call of the gospel.[5] During the sixth century, Benedict of Nursia sought to regularize the formation of those in his charge through the use of a comprehensive, formation-oriented rule that was intended to allow monasteries to serve as "a school for the Lord's service."[6] Centuries later, Martin Luther advocated an approach to the interpretation of Scripture (prayer and meditation on the text in the context of the trials of our life) that adapted monastic practice for any sincere believer.[7] John Wesley fostered meetings of different types in which small groups of people could support one another in the pursuit of holiness of heart and life.[8] In the twentieth century, Byang

---

4. Joel B. Green, "Doing Repentance: The Formation of Disciples in the Acts of the Apostles," *Ex Auditu* 18 (2002): 1–23. For surveys of spirituality and spiritual formation in Scripture and history, see Glen Scorgie, ed., *Dictionary of Christian Spirituality* (Grand Rapids: Zondervan, 2011); Richard J. Foster, *Streams of Living Water: Celebrating the Great Traditions of Christian Faith* (San Francisco: HarperSanFrancisco, 1998).

5. A brief overview of themes in desert spirituality and sanctification can be found in Henri J. M. Nouwen, *The Way of the Heart: Desert Spirituality and Contemporary Ministry* (New York: HarperOne, 1991); Douglas Burton-Christie, *The Word in the Desert: Scripture and the Quest for Holiness in Early Christian Monasticism* (New York: Oxford University Press, 1993); Luke Dysinger, *Psalmody and Prayer in the Writings of Evagrius Ponticus* (Oxford: Oxford University Press, 2005). Dysinger shows how the devotional use of the Psalms was perceived as a spiritual remedy.

6. Benedict of Nursia, *Rule of Saint Benedict in English*, ed. Timothy Fry (Collegeville, MN: Liturgical Press, 1982), 18.

7. See "Preface to the Wittenberg Edition of Luther's German Writings," in *Luther's Works*, ed. J. Pelikan, H. C. Oswald, and H. T. Lehmann (Philadelphia: Fortress, 1999), 34:287.

8. D. Michael Henderson, *John Wesley's Class Meeting: A Model for Making Disciples* (Nappanee, IN: Evangel, 2016); David Watson, *The Early Methodist Class Meeting: Its Origins and*

Kato saw that spiritual formation in Nigeria required that Christians get past their "theological anemia" through the development of a robust, theologically grounded Christianity.[9] Karol Wojtyła (who later became Pope John Paul II) courageously led the church in Poland in the face of Communist opposition, and when the authorities sought to construct Nowa Huta as a model workers' town without a place for worship—the first such town in Polish history—he creatively held open-air services in the community.[10] He forcefully stated that Christianity, not Communism, is the true protector of the poor and oppressed. He modeled the importance of fighting creatively and responsibly for what is right. Through fellowship, Scripture, public trials, and private meditation, leaders in the Christian church sought to encourage formation into maturity.

Dallas Willard rightly reminds us again and again that attitude alone is not sufficient for true spiritual formation: Scripture, history, and common sense all teach us that God uses *means* of grace to communicate grace. The means of grace are those relationships, practices, situations, and such through which the Holy Spirit works to restore the image of Christ in individuals and communities.[11] Some means of grace can be considered *primary*—basic to the Christian faith in Scripture and tradition. These include Scripture reading, prayer, trials, compassionate action, Christian fellowship, and the celebration of the sacraments or ordinances of the church. Other means of grace such as solitude, journaling, prayer walking, and observing a rule of life can be considered secondary: helpful to many but not basic for all.

One important means of grace is Christian fellowship. CSF is character-istically *relational*. While there may be a rare person who matures simply by means of private devotional disciplines, the Christian faith is fundamentally about love (love God, love neighbor), and thus formation in this faith in-volves relationships of various sorts. It is perhaps most accurate to think of

Significance (Eugene, OR: Wipf & Stock, 2002). The emphasis that Wesley placed on genuine religion can be seen in John Wesley, "A Plain Account of Genuine Christianity," in *John and Charles Wesley: Selected Prayers, Hymns, Journal Notes, Sermons, Letters and Treatises*, ed. Frank Whaling (New York: Paulist Press, 1981), 121–33.

9. Mark Noll and Carolyn Nystrom, *Clouds of Witnesses: Christian Voices from Africa and Asia* (Downers Grove, IL: InterVarsity Press, 2011), 81.

10. George Weigel, *Witness to Hope: The Biography of Pope John Paul II* (New York: Cliff Street Books, 1999), 188–90.

11. See Donald G. Bloesch, *Essentials of Evangelical Authority*, vol. 1, *God, Authority, and Salvation* (San Francisco: Harper & Row, 1978), 208–12; Charles Hambrick-Stowe, *The Practice of Piety: Puritan Devotional Disciplines in Seventeenth-Century New England* (Chapel Hill: University of North Carolina Press, 1982); Howard Thurman, *Disciplines of the Spirit* (Richmond, IN: Friends United, 1963); Richard J. Foster, *Celebration of Discipline: The Path to Spiritual Growth*, 3rd ed. (San Francisco: HarperSanFrancisco, 1998); Adele Calhoun, *Spiritual Disciplines Handbook: Practices That Transform Us*, rev. ed. (Downers Grove, IL: InterVarsity, 2015).

community as both an aim and a means of CSF. As an *aim*, authentic, loving community is what God is after, what most clearly expresses the image of Christ. Francis Schaeffer captures this well: "The Christian really has a double task. He has to practice both God's holiness and God's love. . . . Love—and the unity it attests to—is the mark Christ gave Christians to *wear* before the world."[12] In God's gospel the outcome is not merely sanctified individuals but a holy people, the bride of Christ. As a *means* of CSF, the body of Christ is a primary context through which the Spirit of God guides and matures us. It is the context where God's transforming grace is uniquely available.

At the same time, we recognize that God also uses trials as a means of grace. "Consider it pure joy, my brothers and sisters, whenever you face trials of many kinds," James exhorts, "because you know that the testing of your faith produces perseverance. Let perseverance finish its work so that you may be mature and complete, not lacking anything" (James 1:2–4 NIV). Our trials come in "many kinds" (personal weaknesses, interpersonal conflicts, unfortunate circumstances, oppressive structures), and we understand them best when we receive them not as passive victims but rather as co-participants in a transformational event. Reformer John Calvin, in the section "Bearing the Cross" in his *Institutes of the Christian Religion*, describes a number of ways in which sufferings facilitate formation: "By communion with him the very sufferings themselves not only become blessed to us but also help much in promoting our salvation. They lead us to trust in God, they enable us to experience God's faithfulness, they train us in patience and obedience, they restrain our unhealthy indulgence, and they correct our transgressions."[13]

We must remember that many Christians throughout history faced some form of persecution, and the presence of persecution deeply influenced their patterns of formation. Formation in Christ in the midst of trials and persecutions is not a shallow "surrender to the will of God." Each trial of each kind (involving voluntary or involuntary brokenness) invites us to a fresh kind of perseverance that, given time, will bear the fruit of Christian maturity.[14]

12. Francis Schaeffer, *The Mark of the Christian* (Downers Grove, IL: InterVarsity, 1970), 21, 35.

13. John Calvin, *Institutes of the Christian Religion*, ed. John McNeill, trans. Ford Lewis Battles (Philadelphia: Westminster, 1960), 2:702. See also Diodochus of Photike, "On Spiritual Knowledge and Discrimination: One Hundred Texts," no. 94, in *The Philokalia*, trans. G. E. H. Palmer, Philip Sherrard, and Kallistos Ware (London: Faber & Faber, 1979), 1:291. Richard Baxter describes how pastors are to practice pastoral care in the midst of trials to facilitate parishioners' spiritual growth. Richard Baxter, *The Reformed Pastor* (Carlisle, PA: Banner of Truth, 1974).

14. See Alan Nelson, *Broken in the Right Place* (Nashville: Nelson, 1994), 27–28; Siang-Yang Tan, *Shepherding God's People: A Guide to Faithful and Fruitful Pastoral Ministry* (Grand Rapids:

As with the other distinctive features of CSF, dangers lurk on either side of our approach to the means of grace. If we ignore the community or the practices God provides, claiming our sanctification simply by verbal assent or trusting that the Spirit will act apart from means, then we flirt with an unhealthy quietism. On the other hand, if we place too much emphasis on community or practices, we can fall into either an anxious striving or a pharisaic legalism. Consequently, authentic CSF requires a delicate balance between contentment and longing. Too much contentment leads to complacency; too much longing leads to a crisis of trust. This theme is poetically expressed in Proverbs: "Give me neither poverty nor riches, but give me only my daily bread. Otherwise, I may have too much and disown you and say, 'Who is the LORD?' Or I may become poor and steal, and so dishonor the name of my God" (30:8–9 NIV).[15]

Disciplines, community engagement, and trials all function as means of grace. How we intentionally, habitually relate to them provides appropriate environments within which the Spirit of God transforms the church. Likewise, we live out our formation through patterns of thought, feeling, and life that embody the work of God appropriately in the circumstances of our ordinary lives as individuals and communities. We "work out" through means what God "works in" through means (Phil. 2:12–13).

Learning to rest in God's love is going to require change on our part, but that does not mean we have to subject ourselves to a kind of New Year's resolution Christianity—a Christianity in which we make a commitment, hold to it for a while, forget to do it, discover our lapse, and sit in our despair. No! While the change we are invited to does involve some ordinary means of change, it has an important distinction: we are being asked by a loving friend to change our way of relating to him. He is inviting us to grow in our friendship, and he is with us as our ever-present teacher, mentor, guide, and Lord who welcomes us into a change-producing new community. In conversation with him, we can ask, "How can I keep you in mind right now? What can I do to be present and loving right now?" It is a bit like help from a friend who knows the ropes and can guide us in a new situation. Yes, relationally based spiritual change is very different from a New Year's resolution—you have a

---

Baker Academic, 2019), 34. For a classic example of formation through the trials of personal faithfulness to the gospel message, see John Woolman, "Journal," in *The Journal and Major Essays of John Woolman*, ed. Phillips P. Moulton (Oxford: Oxford University Press, 1971), 21–192.

15. In developmental psychology the need for a person to experience both support and challenge to move beyond a comfortable homeostasis is well documented. Two volumes that bring that theme to Christian discipleship are Nancy J. Kane, *Stages of the Soul: God's Invitation to Greater Love* (Chicago: Moody, 2019); James E. Loder, *The Logic of the Spirit: Human Development in Theological Perspective* (San Francisco: Jossey-Bass, 1998).

coach, a community, and an empowering presence that draws you to a better way of being.

When I was in college, I went to the business office one day to cash a check. When the clerk stepped away briefly, she left open a file that exposed the financial misdeeds of a student who was something of a campus celebrity. I had never liked the guy, and here was evidence of his financial shenanigans. I headed off to lunch with every intention of letting my new information shape my lunchtime conversation, but as I walked across the campus quad, I had a distinct impression: "Don't gossip." It was an unmistakable word—a word that had authority—and with reluctance I decided to obey. As I got closer to the dorm and my imagination savored the delight of gossiping, I got a follow-up message: "This is really important." I didn't gossip at lunch, and not gossiping became a spiritual focus for the next six months; my obedience there paid great dividends.

We now turn to some practices that can help us open ourselves to God's love and direct our attention to that which should be honored and obeyed. They are presented as personal spiritual practices, but the pastoral wisdom of the church and empirical findings on personal change indicate that these practices are best learned in a community context where you can see them modeled. That sets them in a proper theological framework and points us to community engagement, not just personal change. Practices such as Bible reading and intercessory prayer are key too, but the practices discussed below are high-impact practices that generally are learned only through community practice. In time, one may experience many of these as personal practices, but they are best begun with the help and support of others.

Spiritual conversations. We are formed in community in a host of ways. We see faith modeled, we are mentored by authors whom we will never meet, we receive grace through Word and Table, and much good comes to us in spiritual conversations. It is easy to develop habits of conversation in which sports, politics, and media dominate what we talk about. Those topics are well and good in their place, but community spiritual formation needs spiritual conversations.

Gratitude. This practice involves acknowledging the presence of goodness and beauty in our lives that did not come through our own work. It is cultivated by pausing to notice the presence of gifts and grace in our lives. There are simple practices that help establish this disposition. Most involve simple cataloging of the good things present in our lives that we perceive to be gifts.

Guarding the heart. A person facing a tough choice might lament the difficulty of the decision by exclaiming, "I need the wisdom of Solomon to figure this out." Solomon, whose name has come to symbolize wisdom, encountered the Lord at Gibeon, and when God offered him his choice of gifts, Solomon chose "a discerning heart" (1 Kings 3:9 NIV). This choice symbolized the early Solomon, whose judgment was praised and who composed and collected thousands of proverbs and songs (4:32). And yet the story of Solomon does not end well. By the end of his life, Solomon had compromised himself spiritually and had fallen into an unsustainable, lavish lifestyle that necessitated burdensome taxes and virtual enslavement of part of his population. Where did Solomon go wrong? The official history tells us that "as Solomon grew old, . . . his heart was not fully devoted to the LORD his God. . . . His heart had turned away from the LORD, the God of Israel, who had appeared to him twice" (11:4, 9 NIV). The immediate cause of this was the foreign wives he married as part of his treaty obligations. With those treaty wives came their foreign gods.

The story of Solomon's loss of direction illustrates the importance the Bible places on the heart. The biblical writers understood that our hearts direct us. The heart was seen as the seat of what we would call the mind, the will, and the emotions. We guard and protect what is valuable to us. We walk our children to school, lock our cars, and choose complex passwords all in an effort to protect what we value. And to this list we should add our hearts. Proverbs tells us, "Above all else, guard your heart, for everything you do flows from it" (4:23 NIV). The proverb's message is that this guarding is very important. The Hebrew word for *guard* gives the sense of "more than anything that needs to be guarded—guard your heart." The word found here is used elsewhere for guarding creatures that must be restrained, like a prisoner or monster of the deep (Lev. 24:12; Job 7:12), which communicates the importance of the task. Since we are "above all else" to guard our hearts, how can we do this?

The elders of the desert set purity of heart as the goal of their spiritual lives, and they recognized a deep potential connection between the heart and Scripture. Abba Moses, for example, in a conversation with John Cassian in the fourth century, summarized the life of the desert by saying, "Everything we do, our every objective, must be undertaken for the sake of this purity of heart. . . . For this we must practice the reading of Scripture, together with all the other virtuous activities, and we do so to trap and to hold our hearts free of harm of every dangerous [addiction] and in order to rise step by step to the high point of love."[16]

16. John Cassian, *Conferences*, ed. Philip Schaff, Nicene and Post-Nicene Fathers, Second Series (Peabody, MA: Hendrickson, 1994), 41. I substituted *addiction* for *passion*, which seems to better convey Cassian's meaning.

Notice that the reason to seek purity of heart is for the sake of love. The desert fathers desired to love God and others fully and knew that this required attention to the affections and thoughts of their hearts. One of the most loving things we can do for others is to take the time and effort to seek after our own purity of heart.

Paying attention (mindfulness). On many levels this is a fundamental move in the spiritual life. We need to pay attention so we can see what we should be grateful for, we need to pay attention to what we are thinking about so we can guard our thoughts, and we need to pay attention so we can be present in prayer and Bible reading. There are practices we can employ that help us grow in our ability to appropriately focus.

Self-compassion. Many of us say things to ourselves that we would never say to a friend. We can berate and tear ourselves down. We do this to motivate ourselves, but we know that if anyone else said such things, it would absolutely demoralize us. We need to work and engage with the Holy Spirit in working out our salvation, and negative self-talk should not be a part of our striving. We'll look at practices that help us bring the grace of Christ, rather than our biting self-criticism, to our struggles and disappointments.

Meditation. We all mull over things, replay events, and think about things that are valuable. The old adage that our god is what we think about when we are alone is very true. Meditation is the deliberate process of directing our thoughts away from worries to the Scriptures and God's beauty. By doing so, we reshape the contours of our souls.

Unceasing prayer. A metric used in the early church to mark spiritual progress was the practice of continual prayer. These Christians took seriously the call in Scripture to constantly turn to God in prayer and saw the disposition of turning to God in prayer as a way of guarding one's heart. We are shaped by what we dwell on throughout the day.

Spiritual Conversations

The less people think about God, the less they talk about God.

Barna Group[17]

One of the most basic means of spiritual formation in the church is conversation. A teacher asking a child about what they enjoy at school and helping them see that their interests reflect how God made them, a youth sponsor

17. Barna Group, *Spiritual Conversations in the Digital Age: How Christians' Approach to Sharing Their Faith Has Changed in 25 Years* (Ventura, CA: Barna Group, 2018), 83.

taking a high school couple out for coffee to talk about their relationship, a congregant having a conversation with a pastor about the sermon—these are some of the most basic, persistent, and helpful tools of formation.

Yet spiritual conversation is something we need to encourage. Elders and church leaders can model the practice to others. What we really have to offer to others in ministry is not our skills or learning but Jesus. And one way we offer Jesus to others is by talking about him and his work and the reality of his presence in and among us. In the United States, spiritual conversations are rare. "Fewer than one in 10 talks about God, faith, religion or spirituality even once a week (8%)—and only an additional 15 percent do so once a month."[18]

Puritan pastor Richard Baxter wrote this about the importance of spiritual conversations: "I have found by experience, that some . . . persons, who have been so long unprofitable hearers, have got more knowledge and remorse of conscience in half an hour's close discourse, than they did from ten years' public preaching."[19] The Puritans thought that spiritual conversations— *conferences*, as they called them—are essential to the spiritual formation of Christians. They saw Malachi 3:16 as pointing to the practice of such conversations and noted that the Lord takes pleasure in such occupations: "Then those who revered the LORD spoke with one another. The LORD took note and listened, and a book of remembrance was written before him of those who revered the LORD and thought on his name."

J. I. Packer, who styled himself as a twentieth-century Puritan, wrote in his book on Puritan spirituality of the importance of spiritual conversations.

Whereas to the Puritans communion with God was a great thing, to evangelicals today it is a comparatively small thing.

The Puritans were concerned about communion with God in a way that we are not. The measure of our unconcern is the little that we say about it. When Christians meet, they talk to each other about their Christian work and Christian interests, their Christian acquaintances, the state of the churches, and the problems of theology—but rarely of their daily experience of God. Modern Christian books and magazines contain much about Christian doctrine, Christian standards, problems of Christian conduct, techniques of Christian service—but little about the inner realities of fellowship with God. Our sermons contain much sound doctrine—but little relating to the converse between the soul and the Saviour. We do not spend much time, alone or

18. Barna Group, *Spiritual Conversations in the Digital Age*, 7.
19. Richard Baxter, *The Reformed Pastor* (Carlisle, PA: Banner of Truth, 1974), 196. See also Joanne Jung, *The Lost Discipline of Conversation: Surprising Lessons in Spiritual Formation Drawn from the English Puritans* (Grand Rapids: Zondervan, 2018), 39–43.

together, in dwelling on the wonder of the fact that God and sinners have communion at all; no, we just take that for granted, and give our minds to other matters. Thus we make it plain that communion with God is a small thing to us.[20]

Packer suggests that there is little spiritual conversation today because our faith is increasingly abstract. I am sympathetic to his diagnosis, but I think it is also true that we have so privatized our faith that we feel it almost rude to "inquire of one's soul." I had a colleague who for years used to greet me with the query, "Brother Wilhoit, how goes it with your soul?" That simple question, asked with genuine sincerity, led to helpful spiritual conversations.

Years ago, as a graduate student, I had a conversation with an academic who was seeking to bring to the church what he knew about Jean Piaget's cognitive development work. He was new to thinking about applying his scholarly world to areas of faith. I asked him what he thought Piaget would suggest about faith development, and he said, "He'd want us to create a religiously rich environment." When I asked how that could be done, he said simply, "You've got to talk about it." And that is about all there is to say: encourage spiritual conversations.

In the past several decades a number of programs and organizations have arisen to promote renewal in churches. I have seen the benefit of these programs and been involved in leading them. Though these programs are diverse, they share at least two outcomes. First, the participants come to experience the reality of the gospel more deeply, seeing the depth of God's love for them and the reality of their own sin and its effects. And second, the participants become comfortable with having spiritual conversations with each other. I have seen that outcome in churches that used programs as diverse as the Ignatian spiritual exercises and the Sonship program.[21] A friend of mine whose job took him into numerous churches mentioned that he could tell when a church had been through the Sonship program because people had a shared language for talking about their faith and seemed more ready to have spiritual conversations. The community context provides support for spiritual conversations that would not be as likely without this support.

20. J. I. Packer, *A Quest for Godliness* (Wheaton: Crossway, 1994), 215–16.
21. An overview of the Ignatian exercises can be found in this accessible volume: William A. Barry, *Finding God in All Things: A Companion to the Spiritual Exercises of St. Ignatius* (Notre Dame, IN: Ave Maria, 1991). An overview of the Sonship program can be found in Bob Thune and Will Walker, *The Gospel-Centered Life* (Greensboro, NC: New Growth, 2011).

Gratitude

All prayer is essentially an act of gratitude.

David Steindl-Rast[22]

May the moment find you eager and unafraid, ready to take it by the hand with joy and with gratitude.

Howard Thurman[23]

Over the past several decades, many researchers have devoted attention to answering the question "What practices and perspectives significantly enhance our well-being?" There are a number of contenders. One that always makes these researchers' short lists is gratitude. Now, gratitude is more than just a practice; it is a virtue—a learned way of responding with thankfulness to the good things we find in our lives. The practice of gratitude always involves community because it begins by acknowledging the goodness in one's life and then includes acknowledging that some of the sources of this good lie outside oneself.[24]

Cultivating gratitude through gratitude practices is quite simple. Research has shown that keeping a gratitude journal or daily remembering the good things in one's life can measurably increase the presence of gratitude in one's life and boost one's sense of well-being. We should seek to be grateful people because that is a natural response to the gracious way God has dealt with us and because of the good gifts he has given us. "We have been given possession of an unshakeable kingdom. Let us therefore be grateful and use our gratitude to worship God in the way that pleases him, in reverence and fear" (Heb. 12:28 NJB). The side benefits of this grateful response to God include a heightened sense of well-being, a decreased likelihood of depression, improved health, enhanced relationships, and better discernment.[25]

Gratitude encompasses thankfulness, but it goes beyond being thankful just for specific things or blessings. Gratitude includes a general wonder at

22. *Gratefulness, the Heart of Prayer: An Approach to Life in Fullness* (New York: Paulist Press, 1984), back cover.

23. *Meditations of the Heart* (Boston: Beacon, 2014), 139.

24. Robert Emmons, *Thanks! How Practicing Gratitude Can Make You Happier* (New York: Houghton Mifflin Harcourt, 2008), 4–6.

25. For reports on research about the positive benefits of gratitude and related topics, see Emmons, *Thanks!*; Robert A. Emmons and Michael E. McCullough, eds., *The Psychology of Gratitude* (New York: Oxford University Press, 2004); Sonja Lyubomirsky, *The How of Happiness: A New Approach to Getting the Life You Want* (New York: Penguin, 2008).

the goodness of God's universe and quiet, awe-struck amazement at the pervasiveness of his grace in our lives. One of the foremost gratitude researchers, Robert Emmons, captures the breadth of gratitude when he says it is "a felt sense of wonder, thankfulness and appreciation for life."[26] It is our recognition that we are the recipients of wonderful, abundant, and completely undeserved goodness and that many things have entered our lives for which we cannot rightly claim responsibility.

I can testify that our theology provides a foundation for being grateful, but it is also very easy to live with a disconnect that allows us to affirm the goodness of God but live lives marked by complaining and cynicism. If good theology necessarily led to gratitude, seminaries would be places of immense gratitude, and such is not typically the case. My journey into gratitude began as an experiment. I was interested in the scientific studies that were being done in the area of positive psychology and was reading the literature on gratitude practices. The research was compelling in both how easy it seemed to be to boost one's gratitude and the benefits doing so had in so many areas of life. I decided to try keeping a gratitude journal, and the practice was humbling. My first foray into journal keeping showed me how entitled and cynical I had become. I am afraid I had to start very small—I was grateful for good roads, long runs, the beauty of spring flowers, my family. It took me a while to include other people (I had settled into subtle patterns of cynicism) and to build the courage to speak of God acting in love and goodness to me. But oh, how this practice healed my heart.

Gratitude involves seeing and naming. We have to pause from the rush of life to see and savor the good things we have been given. We pause to notice the tartness and texture of our first bite of a crisp fall apple, and we slow down to enjoy the emerging buds of an early blooming dogwood. I, at least, need to go a few steps further and name what I am experiencing, study its texture, and marvel at its richness. Part of growing in gratitude involves savoring these gifts so that we marvel at their richness and find the multiple ways we can be thankful for what we have.

Cultivating gratitude is also an important way of guarding one's heart. Gratitude protects one from a sense of deprivation. During my years providing pastoral counseling, I have observed that a sense of deprivation—a focus on what one lacks and on those thoughts that keep one from this desired good—is a slippery slope to relational sins, addictions, and bitterness of heart.

26. Robert A. Emmons and Charles M. Shelton, "Gratitude and the Science of Positive Psychology," in *Handbook of Positive Psychology*, ed. C. R. Snyder and Shane J. Lopez (New York: Oxford University Press, 2002), 460.

Living with a sense of deprivation and a spirit of entitlement is a fertile field for sensing that one has a right to act out in a sinful way. Many Christian leaders I have spoken with who compromised their ministry through sinful patterns—whether these harmful acts were sexual, financial, or an abuse of power—confessed to entering these patterns with a sense of deprivation and often with a resentment of someone (spouse, children, board members) who seemingly deprived them of what they thought they "needed." I have learned that people find it difficult to step away from this sense of deprivation. Sometimes the utter brokenness that follows being caught eventually leads to a deep gratitude for what they had. Cultivation of gratitude has the power to drive away a sense of deprivation.

Throughout his letter to the Colossians, Paul warns them about the dangers of false teachers. He tells them of his prayers and work on their behalf. He does this "so that no one may deceive you by fine-sounding arguments" (Col. 2:4 NIV). He goes on to suggest ways they can guard their hearts from false teaching. They are to continue to develop their sense of being united to Christ, follow his teaching, and live "overflowing with thankfulness" (2:7 NIV). Overflowing with thankfulness—being deeply grateful—is the way to guard our hearts from the deceptions of the enemy of our souls.

Practices That Foster Gratitude

Naming Five Good Things

A couple of decades ago I was introduced to this practice. Two roommates were struggling with the cynicism that can come with a college education. Dismayed at how critical they had become, they geared up to reclaim their earlier, wide-eyed openness to God. They committed themselves to naming and writing down on a poster ten good things they found in each day. Sadly, I tried it out and found it too tough—little did I realize how a PhD and years in the academy had left me deeply entitled and chronically critical.

The research is in, and the practice of naming between three and five good things you experienced during the day (things that did not come about through your own efforts) boosts your sense of gratitude and overall well-being. It is best to tie this to another well-established practice—like the commute home from work, a reflection on the day as you head to bed, an evening family meal at which everyone names a gift from the day. I mentally say, "What are the gifts I received today?" And then I allow my day to play back before me. I stop the replay when I notice a gift, I savor it briefly, and then I restart the playback.

Redemptively Remembering the Bad

My wife and I began redemptively remembering the bad spontaneously. We noticed that when we shared our stories with others, we often chose to emphasize what we had gained through various losses. Concerning one event, we found ourselves finding comfort in Joseph's assessment of his brothers' conspiracy against him: "You intended to harm me, but God intended it all for good" (Gen. 50:20 NLT). Joseph is speaking of how God used his brothers' actions to further redemptive history. Our comfort came through the affirmation that God can take human evil and use it redemptively in a believer's life. God's redeeming of what happened does not mitigate the evil of what happened but allows the believer to benefit from it in deep and lasting ways.

To practice this, you need to reflect on a time of loss, illness, betrayal, or confusion. As you think about the event, ask yourself, "What good has come from this? How have I been strengthened by this? Are there gifts, like a new friendship, reconciliation in a family, or a new perspective on life, that came from this?" We seem to be wired to focus on the bad and take little notice of what we gained through hard times. This exercise does not ask you to excuse another party or deny the original pain but to look for what you gained. It may be helpful to do this over several days or weeks and to briefly record in a journal what you discover.

Keeping a Gratitude Journal

I have not been a consistent journal keeper. I routinely log life metrics like fitness goals and daily activities, and I process my thoughts on paper during times of discernment, on retreats, and for a daily examen, but I do not journal day in and day out. So I was a bit dismayed when I read in the research about the power of journaling to cultivate gratitude. Gratitude was something I desired, but journaling seemed like a very unwelcome path to get there. I decided to try it, and the results were astonishing. There have been few spiritual activities that I undertook that have made such a positive and noticeable improvement in my life. I found myself noticing things throughout the day that I could record and began eagerly awaiting going home in the evening so I could write them down. Now I am an avid recorder of gratitude items but still not a regular journal keeper.

Find a way and a place to write down things for which you are grateful. I use a simple spiral-bound notebook, but digital or analog is also fine; just find a system that works. I write at the top of the page "Gifts." Then I review the day or week and write down good things that have entered my life independent of my effort. Sometimes patterns develop, like a focus on natural beauty at a change of season, or on family during the holidays. A time of focused gratitude can help deepen one's spirit of appreciation.

Here are some ways to deepen the practice:

- Try to be specific. What was it about a server's attention at lunch that made you grateful? What is it about your child's appreciation that leaves you so grateful? Being specific helps keep gratitude from being abstract and makes it more tangible and real.
- For a week, seek to find things to be grateful for in an area of your life that tends not to generate items for your list—perhaps work or people at church.
- An old gospel song tells us to "Count your many blessings, name them one by one." Number each blessing and perhaps set a goal such as finding five hundred blessings by the end of this summer.
- Avoid fatigue. For the first several months of my gratitude journaling, I recorded items every morning and evening. After a while this began to lose its luster, and out of fear that I might tire of recording these items, I scaled back to logging items a couple of times a week. You need to find a schedule that keeps you looking for gifts but is not so frequent that the task becomes ordinary or burdensome.

Savoring Experiences

Savoring an experience involves taking time after a significant event to relish what just happened. It can be as simple as pausing in the car after a great meeting with a friend to offer a prayer of thanks and to sit with the realization that you are deeply cherished by your friend. When our children returned from an important school trip, we stopped at a coffee shop on our way home to savor what they had experienced before the rush of being back home overwhelmed that time of sharing and making memories. Don't wait until the pictures are neatly organized or printed to do this. Take time after an event to name what went well, what was special, what you and others enjoyed—not in a lessons-learned sort of way but in the mode of childlike delight.

Not Defending Yourself

Not defending yourself is not a direct gratitude practice. Instead, it helps make room for gratitude. It is a simple practice in which you commit to allowing God to be the vindicator of your reputation. What this means is that you agree with yourself not to defend or explain your actions. So, you arrive late for a lunch with a friend and you apologize for being late and keeping them waiting, and you leave it at that—no mention of the heavy traffic or the train that held you up. If they ask for an explanation of what happened, you tell them, but you keep it simple and respectful.

How does this relate to gratitude? The practice trains us to see that God is at work in our lives. He will protect our reputations. We don't need to bore people by blathering on and on about what impeded our performance. It also subtly shifts the focus away from ourselves and allows us to see the gifts in our lives.

Here are some suggestions for practicing not defending yourself:

- Commit to doing this practice for a defined period of time. I suggest beginning with a week.
- Notice certain contexts where the group culture or your own insecurities make this practice particularly difficult.
- When you know that politeness will dictate that you acknowledge your mistake, decide ahead of time how to acknowledge the mistake without making excuses.
- Notice what lessons you learn. I observed how habitual defending and explaining myself had become. I became aware of how fragile my sense of self was.

There are not many commands in Scripture involving things we are always to be doing. Being grateful is one of them: "Give thanks in all circumstances; for this is God's will for you in Christ Jesus" (1 Thess. 5:18 NIV). It is God's will that we are to be constantly grateful. Science and the Scriptures both conclude that being grateful is the gate to a more other-oriented and flourishing life. And gratitude is a very effective way of guarding our hearts from a sense of deprivation and the enemy's spiritual lie that God is not for us. Through the liturgy, teaching, and special services of the church, we are reminded of the importance of gratitude and learn practices that cultivate it.

Thoughts direct our lives. That is the message that comes from the early Christian spiritual writers. As they looked into their own hearts and listened to the stories of the men and women who came to them for spiritual guidance, they noticed the important role thoughts play in shaping our lives. We hold, in our thoughts, a way of seeing and being in the world. The community plays a crucial role here by elevating the importance of the heart and one's interior. We know the problem of religious hypocrisy that can be fostered in churches that emphasize simply looking good.

Converts to Christ discover new ways of thinking. Sometimes we are oppressed by our thoughts: patterns of perceiving, relating, and understanding can crowd out the presence of God's Spirit in our lives. At other times our thoughts bring us comfort and enable us to make tough choices and live well. An important message of the early desert spiritual masters is that we are not our thoughts. We may have thoughts that are lustful or vengeful, but we can choose to step away from them.

Paul highlights the fickle nature of our thoughts when he says, "Their conflicting thoughts will accuse or perhaps excuse them" (Rom. 2:15). He is speaking not of productive thinking—the thoughts of planning, solving a problem, or thinking hard about something—but of the mental chatter of accusations, daydreams, nursing wounds, and thoughts of anger and revenge. The desert writers remind us that it is not only the content of our thoughts that is the problem but also the presence of what they called *logismoi*: automatic negative thoughts, self-focused daydreams, and fantasies. The desert elders saw these thoughts as having a sticky quality. Like Velcro, they attach themselves to other thoughts and quickly form a train of thoughts. None of these tempting thoughts are innocent; they remove us from the here and now—where God is at work—and contain lies about our true value and God's love for us. We find God in reality—in the beauty of nature, in the gift of a friendship, in doing well the work that is before us, or in the hope of the resurrection in the midst of tragedy. We do not find God in the chatter in our heads. This ancient wisdom tells us to step back from the chatter and listen to the still, small voice of God in his Word and his world. His presence is found only in the present moment, so be mindful of this time. We should seek to have our minds carefully observe and engage in the situation at hand—living fully in the moment rather than being trapped in our "vain imaginations" (1:21 KJV).

The ancient desert elders saw these automatic thoughts as very appealing and generated by one's mind more than perceived in the real world. One of the great human freedoms is the ability to direct the focus of our attention. If we are told, "Pay attention to what you are doing," "Watch the road," or "Think about a white bear," we have a remarkable ability to direct our thinking in the short term. We find it easier to switch our focus than to maintain long-term attention. Because we are so good at switching our attention, we may operate under the illusion that willpower is all we need to continuously direct our thinking. The ancient Christian soul-physicians remind us that trying (using willpower alone) will never bring about the results that training our brains through spiritual practices will produce.

Our thoughts matter, and over time we can learn to reshape the way we think and what we focus on. Our initial attempts at redirecting our thoughts may end so poorly that we may be tempted to give up. But as difficult as this change may be, there is reason for optimism, for both the Bible and contemporary neuroscience tell us that we can reshape the focus of our attention.

The White Bear Problem

We all have thoughts we would rather not have. These may be worries, memories of painful events, or just a cringe moment that haunts us. A common strategy for ridding ourselves of these thoughts is to suppress them—to direct our minds to just not think about them. While this is a common strategy, it is not very effective.

Daniel Wegner conducted a now-famous study that measured students' abilities to suppress a thought. Participants were isolated in a laboratory and seated at a table with a microphone and a bell. They were asked to spend five minutes free associating and saying anything that came to mind into the microphone. He asked them not to think about a white bear; if they did, they were to ring the bell. On average the participants reported that they thought of a white bear once every minute. When the five minutes were over, a researcher came in and asked the participant to continue free associating but now to think of a white bear. If they thought of a white bear, they were to ring the bell and continue on. A second group of participants was given the same task, but they were told from the beginning to think of a white bear. Wegner found that the second group reported thinking less of a white bear than the first group of participants, who had tried to suppress that thought. Wegner concluded, "The people thinking about a white bear after suppressing it tended even to show an *acceleration* of white bear thoughts over time." He summarized that the attempt to suppress a thought "made them especially inclined to become absorbed with the thought later on."[27]

The limited value of suppressing unwanted thoughts was understood by the early Christian spiritual writers. The Bible does not ask Christians to suppress harmful thoughts but suggests that we redirect our thinking ("Set your minds on things above" [Col. 3:2 NIV]), cultivate a new focus ("Whatever is true, whatever is noble, whatever is right, whatever is pure, whatever is lovely, whatever is admirable—if anything is excellent or praiseworthy—think about such things" [Phil. 4:8 NIV]), and shift to a new way of thinking ("Consequently, you are no longer foreigners and strangers, but fellow citizens with God's people and also members of his household" [Eph. 2:19 NIV]).

27. Daniel M. Wegner, *White Bears and Other Unwanted Thoughts: Suppression, Obsession, and the Psychology of Mental Control* (New York: Guilford, 1994), 4.

John Cassian suggests another problem with thought suppression: it is often very willful, not grace-oriented, since it is a solution done in our own power and represents the impulse to hide rather than confess. "For just as a snake which is brought from its dark hole into the light makes every effort to escape and hide itself, so the malicious thoughts that a person brings out into the open by sincere confession seek to depart from him."[28] A Christian is greatly harmed by suppressing harmful thoughts rather than confessing them. Notice in Cassian's image that the thoughts confessed and brought into the open slither away; they cannot abide the bright lights of God's love and truth.

These elders suggest a number of strategies for reprogramming our hearts through exposure to Scripture and the grace of God. They urge us to be watchful of our thoughts. Grounded in Peter's command, "Be alert and of sober mind. Your enemy the devil prowls around like a roaring lion looking for someone to devour" (1 Pet. 5:8 NIV), they developed practical suggestions about how to be prudent in our thinking.

To step away from sticky, tempting thoughts, we need to have a ready thought alternative at hand. Again, as we have said, we are very poor at suppressing a thought (e.g., "Don't think that lustful thought. . . . I'm just not going to think that"), but we will have far more success by redirecting our attention toward something that we regard as emotionally positive. I know a pastor who travels with a picture of his family, which he always puts on the TV in his hotel room. For him, the TV is often a source of temptation, and he has learned to turn it off when the temptation arises and gaze at his family instead. In his case his family represents a source of great warmth and comfort. Begin to experiment with places where you can direct your mind when tempting or negative thoughts come. Have a place to direct your thoughts that is attractive to you—a place your mind wants to go and does not need to be dragged. It should be something stable, like a positive childhood memory, an affirmation received, a cherished person, a truth, a piece of art or music, or a place of beauty. This is advanced decision making. Troublesome thoughts will come; where can you go for refuge? Decide now.

Another proven strategy is to have a simple "arrow prayer" that you can offer to redirect your thinking: "Lord, fill me with your peace"; "Lord, come to my assistance"; "Lord, make haste to help me." During a time of trial, when I was especially susceptible to dwelling on the difficulties I faced, I turned to the prayer "Lord Jesus Christ, fill my mind with your peace and my heart with your love." For such prayers to work we need to make a firm covenant

---

28. "St. John Cassian," in *The Philokalia*, trans. and ed. G. E. H. Palmer, Philip Sherrard, and Kallistos Ware (London: Faber & Faber, 2011), 1:132.

with ourselves to turn to prayer rather than entertain negative thoughts. In the manner of Job, who says, "I made a covenant with my eyes not to look lustfully at a young woman" (Job 31:1 NIV), we should make a covenant to turn away from thoughts that we have learned to be watchful of and turn to prayer.

Evagrius wrote a book called *Talking Back* that is largely a listing of Scripture passages that one can direct at false thoughts that arise, and part of the strategy is to talk back to these thoughts.[29] A friend told me of going through an excruciating divorce as a new Christian and learning to tell herself, "Just don't go there." When thoughts arose of her unfaithful husband and his lover, she deliberately thought about her mother's faithful love. If you struggle with lustful thoughts, with gentleness and with no self-condemnation for the thought arising, tell yourself, "Lustful thoughts just take me to where I don't want to be."

Another very effective way to handle malicious thoughts is to note a thought arising and, at its first sign, label it: a lustful thought, a jealous thought, and so on. Generally, the thoughts will just pop like a soap bubble poked by a finger. Seek to be neutral in labeling the thought. It's best to mentally say, "This is a depressive thought" rather than, "I am having a depressive thought." These thoughts just sneak in. A lustful thought does not announce, "I am here to take you down the path of lust, which will end with you looking at porn and feeling great self-loathing." Such thoughts first appear as friends who want to eliminate our boredom or hurt. Unmask them by naming them, and they will usually flee. But do this with gentleness and a sense of prayerful dependence on God.

The New Testament tells a story about some brothers who in their own power were seeking to cast out demons. A demon responded, "'Jesus I know, and Paul I know about, but who are you?' Then the man who had the evil spirit jumped on them and overpowered them all. He gave them such a beating that they ran out of the house naked and bleeding" (Acts 19:15–16 NIV). We don't order our thoughts away; we name them and trust that God will hear the prayer for help that is hidden in our naming them.

Paying Attention (Mindfulness)

We know seat belts save lives. What is the spiritual equivalent of a seat belt? A simple practice that protects us from the accidents of life and makes it easier to weather life's tragedies. It seems to me that the habit of being present is

29. Evagrius of Pontus, *Talking Back: A Monastic Handbook for Combating Demons*, trans. David Brakke (Kalamazoo, MI: Cistercian Publications, 2009).

a good nominee for this designation. If we are unable to be present, we will miss much of what life offers, find it tough to engage in worship, and feel as though spiritual practices like prayer and meditation just can't be done. The habit of being present is an opening move in the spiritual life.

To take the automotive analogy a step further, what might be the spiritual equivalent of driving drunk? I suggest that overthinking or rumination is a good candidate for this designation. Rumination is the constant replaying of the negative stuff in one's life in a way that accentuates the problems and difficulties rather than looking for solutions. The word *rumination* is derived from the Latin word for "chewing over again." Ruminant animals swallow their food, then regurgitate and rechew it. Mental rumination involves a process of bringing up an issue from memory and then mulling over it at length. Rumination is not lamenting and grieving over the tragedies in one's life—that is a normal, natural, and healthy situation-based response that takes us before God. Charles Spurgeon, contrasting genuine lament with chronic overthinking and dwelling on losses, concludes that "ruminating upon trouble is bitter work."[30] People grow bitter as they ruminate, rehearse, and catalog the wrong done to them, all the while daydreaming of ways to get even and facilitate the destruction of their enemies. Rumination (brooding, introspection, overthinking) does not contribute to our flourishing, and it promotes a tendency to close one's heart to God.

While rumination is a common thought process, it is a learned behavior that can be unlearned. However, the process of unlearning requires some training and can be fostered by deep engagement with the Christian community. We'll look at some practices that can help us be more present and that strengthen our "mental muscles" so we find it easier to direct our attention.

Being Present with Love

The present moment is all we have. These gems strung together form our lives. The expression "stuck in the past" hints at the limitations of those who live in the past. Whether it be the high school football star who has not adjusted to his fading fame or the woman caught in the pain of a decades-old betrayal, living in the past does not fill life with grace and joy. We need to value and savor what is before us in this moment. Jean-Pierre de Caussade (1675–1751), in his book *Abandonment to Divine Providence*, urges us to take the present moment seriously because "we must realize that we cannot be really fed, strengthened, purified, enriched and made holy unless we fulfill

---

30. C. H. Spurgeon, *Treasury of David* (Grand Rapids: Baker, 1977), 1:170.

A Means to Mental Health

Clyde Kilby was a beloved literature professor at Wheaton College and is now well known for assembling a collection of papers from C. S. Lewis and the Inklings. He had a love for life that was contagious, and in this set of resolutions, distributed to his students, you can see how important being fully engaged in the present moment was to him.

"At least once every day I shall look steadily up at the sky and remember that I, a consciousness with a conscience, am on a planet traveling in space with wonderfully mysterious things above and about me.

"Instead of the accustomed idea of a mindless and endless evolutionary change to which we can neither add nor subtract, I shall suppose the universe guided by an intelligence which, as Aristotle said of Greek drama, requires a beginning, a middle and an end. I think this will save me from the cynicism expressed by Bertrand Russell before his death, when he said: 'There is darkness without, and when I die there will be darkness within. There is no splendour, no vastness anywhere, only triviality for a moment, and then nothing.'

"I shall not fall into the falsehood that this day, or any day, is merely another ambiguous and plodding twenty-four hours, but rather a unique event filled, if I so wish, with worthy potentialities. I shall not be fool enough to suppose that trouble and pain are wholly evil parentheses in my existence but just as likely ladders to be climbed toward moral and spiritual manhood.

"I shall not turn my life into a thin straight line which prefers abstractions to reality. I shall know what I am doing when I abstract, which of course I shall often have to do.

the duties of the present moment."[31] This mundane moment, what we call *now*, is the only time I can be present with God, and it is the only time I can be strengthened by his grace.

In *The Screwtape Letters*, C. S. Lewis imagines a correspondence between a senior demon and his understudy as they seek to win over a man's soul. The senior devil explains that "the Present is the point at which time touches eternity. . . . Our business is to get them away from the eternal, and from the Present."[32] The demons will gain the advantage if they can lure us to fantasize about the future or brood over the past. This is because, as Lewis makes clear, we meet God only in the present moment.

31. Jean-Pierre de Caussade, *Abandonment to Divine Providence*, trans. John Beevers (New York: Doubleday, 1975), 31.
32. C. S. Lewis, *The Screwtape Letters* (New York: HarperCollins, 1996), 75.

"I shall not demean my own uniqueness by envy of others. I shall stop boring into myself to discover what psychological or social categories I might belong to. Mostly I shall simply forget about myself and do my work.

"I shall open my eyes and ears. Once every day I shall simply stare at a tree, a flower, a cloud, or a person. I shall not then be concerned at all to ask what they are but simply be glad that they are. I shall joyfully allow them the mystery of what C. S. Lewis calls their 'divine, magical, terrifying and ecstatic' existence.

"I shall sometimes look back at the freshness of vision I had in childhood and try, at least for a little while, to be, in the words of Lewis Carroll, the 'child of the pure unclouded brow, and dreaming eyes of wonder.'

"I shall follow Darwin's advice and turn frequently to imaginative things such as good literature and good music, preferably, as C. S. Lewis suggests, an old book and timeless music.

"I shall not allow the devilish onrush of this century to usurp all my energies but will instead, as Charles Williams suggested, 'fulfill the moment as the moment.' I shall try to live well just now because the only time that exists is now.

"If for nothing more than the sake of a change of view, I shall assume my ancestry to be from the heavens rather than from the caves.

"Even if I turn out to be wrong, I shall bet my life on the assumption that this world is not idiotic, neither run by an absentee landlord, but that today, this very day, some stroke is being added to the cosmic canvas that in due course I shall understand with joy as a stroke made by the architect who calls Himself Alpha and Omega."[a]

a. Clyde S. Kilby, © Marion E. Wade Center, Wheaton College, Wheaton, IL. Used by permission.

Paul wrote that he had learned "to be content whatever the circumstances" (Phil. 4:11 NIV). Part of what brought him to that place was learning to set aside worry as he became mindful of the present brimming full of the eternal. I once spent the last few miles of a very hot half marathon staring at the shirt of a runner in front of me that boldly proclaimed, "I can do all things through [Christ] who strengthens me" (4:13). What a thought, doing "all things" through Christ. It is a remarkably bold statement, but in its context, it does not have much to say about running marathons and meeting various personal goals. It is Paul's proclamation after he declares that he has learned to be content. It is as if he said, "Wow, God can even bring contentment to us." The original sense is well captured in The Message version: "Whatever I have, wherever I am, I can make it through anything in the One who makes me who I am." God has yet to bless anyone except in the present moment.

While anxiety is a perennial human struggle, as seen in the number of times it is mentioned in the Bible, ours does seem to be an age that warrants the title "age of anxiety." What does anxiety have to do with cultivating a loving presence? Anxiety needs a future. Our worries are about things that might happen. When we are lovingly tending to what is present, we have less room for anxiety. In the past thirty years researchers have devoted significant attention to how the practice of mindfulness, what I call cultivating a loving presence, can help people function well and thrive in the midst of life challenges like depression and anxiety.

Mindfulness is a cultivated way of being present to ourselves and others. It includes the practice of focusing our attention and awareness on the present moment. And this present-moment attention needs to have a gentleness about it. It is not the detached observation and analysis of the laboratory. It has the qualities of a loving curiosity and a slowness to label. This diminishes prejudices and stereotyping—we really see and savor before we label.

The health benefits of mindfulness began to be studied in well-designed clinical studies in the late 1970s. The initial populations that responded well to a mindfulness intervention were those suffering with chronic pain or depression. Patients who participated in a six-week mindfulness-based stress reduction program (MBSR) experienced measurable improvement in their severity of symptoms. The promise of mindfulness in meditation received national attention when Jon Kabat-Zinn performed a study of psoriasis patients receiving ultraviolet light therapy. The patients were divided into two groups. One group listened to recordings of mindfulness instructions while receiving light therapy, and the other group went through the standard therapy that did not include the recordings. The psoriasis of the patients who listened to the guided meditations cleared significantly faster than that of the people who did not hear the recordings.[33] The pilot psoriasis study was reported on national TV, and this contributed to the growing interest in the benefits of mindfulness in medicine.

A large and growing body of research provides evidence that mindfulness changes both subjective and physiological states. Those who engage in mindfulness practices find feelings of anxiety and depression lessened, they experience greater self-compassion, they are less reactive, and they experience deeper satisfaction in their relationships. Not only does their sense of well-being improve, but their overall health also improves. Mindfulness is

---

33. Jon Kabat-Zinn, *Full Catastrophe Living: Using the Wisdom of Your Body and Mind to Face Stress, Pain, and Illness*, rev. ed. (London: Bantam, 2013), 204–7.

associated with a stronger immune system, decreased blood pressure, better sleep patterns, and changes in brain activity to a more calm and focused state of attention.

A loving, mindful focus allows us to be present and available to those we love and enables us to be in a position to open our hearts to God. As we have said before, opening our hearts to God is one of the first steps in the spiritual life. To open our hearts, we need to be present, but the continuous partial attention that afflicts so many of us prevents us from being openhearted. It turns out that a mindful orientation to life is a very sensible way to live.

While *mindful* is used a few times in English translations of the Bible (ten times in the KJV), it could easily be substituted with a synonym like *attentive*. The concept of mindfulness cannot be found in the Bible through a simple word search. The Greek word *nepsis* (meaning "watchfulness," "sobriety," or "discipline") in this verse from 1 Peter captures a significant part of what is meant by mindfulness: "But the end of all things is at hand: be ye therefore sober, and watch unto prayer" (4:7 KJV). It places an emphasis on guarding the perimeter of one's mind/heart and on being careful about what one permits into one's heart, and that is the first move in mindfulness.

A number of passages call us to observe and constrain our thought life through a loving focus on the present moment. The quiet and humble child-like faith in Psalm 131 reflects mindful attention on God—the child's loving attention to his mother is a picture of our life before God. Jesus's picture of the futility of worry in the Sermon on the Mount shows worry to be a kind of mindless preoccupation with material needs at the cost of trusting God (Matt. 6:25–34). Jesus's admonition "Do not judge" (7:1) contains a call to nonjudgmental mindfulness. He is aware that we are constantly assessing people and assigning them labels of "high status" or "low status." He wants his disciples to be discerning, but he calls them to be less prejudiced and more open to what is actually going on. Ultimately, our faith honors our lived experiences, and mindfulness supports our being fully engaged with these experiences. Israel not only heard God's declaration of care but experienced his deliverance as well: "With your hand you drove out the nations and planted our ancestors; you crushed the peoples and made our ancestors flourish" (Ps. 44:2 NIV). We are invited to experience God and his goodness: "Taste and see that the LORD is good; blessed is the one who takes refuge in him" (34:8 NIV). The mindless person who devotes only fleeting, partial attention to the spiritual dimension is ill-equipped to experience God in worship and in the everyday realities of life.

Cultivating Loving, Full Attention

The tendency to be more fully present is a habit that can be learned, and it is best learned in community. Like any new habit, it does not come easily. We will need to practice this new way of being. It is not just enough to want it; we must engage in practices that will cultivate this way of being present. It's a bit like swimming: we learn to swim only by swimming, and we learn mindfulness only by disciplining ourselves to be present.

Three Breaths

One of the simplest ways of grounding ourselves in the present moment and stepping back from the chatter in our heads is to pause several times throughout the day and take three slow breaths. You might want to set an alarm or post some notes to remind you. All you need to do is just pause what you are doing and slowly exhale through your mouth and then inhale through your nose three times. Slow down and focus on your breath; observe and feel it in your nose, belly, or chest.

Taking three breaths might not seem like much of a spiritual practice. To be sure, it is not as explicitly God-oriented as prayer or meditating on Scripture. Think of it as mental fitness for spiritual activities, a bit like weight training for an athlete. If you can't quiet your inner voice, you can't show up for prayer.

A few things can help deepen this practice:

- Really pay attention to how the breath feels in your body.
- Think of this as taking a brief vacation from yourself—you are hitting the reset button.
- Pay attention to your posture; adjust your body so that it is open and dignified as you sit, stand, or walk.
- Try experimenting with some small changes in your breathing pattern. For example, lengthen your breathing or attach a phrase to your breathing—for example, breathing out, "I release my cares," and breathing in, "I receive life."
- Begin with a simple prayer: "Here I am," "Lord, I reset my compass," or "Quiet my racing mind."

Mindful Walking

Here is a practice that may not take any additional time. As a way to start, designate a walk that you take regularly, like walking from the parking lot into work or walking to the bus, as a mindful walk. Choose to notice just your walking while you walk. Feel your feet on the pavement; notice your feet lifting and your knees bending. Focus on what you are experiencing. This is not the time for a mental essay on walking or a replay of past walks. As your mind wanders, which it will, gently return it to noticing your walking without mentally scolding yourself. What you are doing is developing mental muscles that enable you to bring your thinking back to what you want to think about. To do this, you'll need to walk by yourself and without distractions like a phone or music.

A few things can help deepen this practice:

- You might want to set aside a time to do this as a formal practice. Find a place where you can walk slowly back and forth for about twenty feet. If you can, find a place where you don't need to be concerned with other walkers or feel that you have to explain what you are doing. Set a timer (start with five minutes).
- Do this in your church, chapel, or worship space. Remind yourself as you start that you are walking in the presence of God.
- Try exaggerating your movements or walking very slowly to see if that makes it easier to focus on your walking.

Sitting Meditation

Scientific evidence shows that the practice of sitting meditation can help people become more mindful and less reactive. The process is simple, but after years of practice, one will still feel like a neophyte. Here are four steps that will get you started.

First, pray and dedicate your time. Sitting meditation is like bicep curls for your brain. You are training it to be more focused and to help you be less controlled by the thoughts and voices in your head. With any practice that involves spiritual openness, it is wise to dedicate the time to God and ask for his guidance and protection as you meditate. This also gives you an opportunity to tell God why you have come—to become less anxious, to be more loving and less reactive, and to quiet your anxious mind. Consider using a simple prayer like, "Lord, guard my heart and my mind as I sit here before you. I am sitting here to learn to be more skillful in how I think and to grow in my ability to be more lovingly present."

Second, find a comfortable sitting position. Begin by using a chair with a straight back and sit with your spine straight and your feet on the floor. Set a timer. This lets you enter into the time of meditation with a simple contract with yourself—I'll do it for five minutes.

Third, focus on your breathing. Pick a spot to notice your breath (nose, belly, or chest). This is not about altering your breathing but about finding a place where it is easy and pleasant to feel your breathing.

Fourth, return to your breathing. Here is where the training begins. As your mind wanders from focusing on your breathing, gently return your focus. When you notice that you have stopped feeling your breath, it is important to simply return to feeling it without any self-critical comments. The power of this practice lies in the act of noticing and correcting your inattention.

When the timer rings, end your session without scoring it. You will see the effects when you have an encounter with someone who normally pushes your buttons and you return a kind word. It takes time for this practice to work its magic; you just need to keep at it, even though you don't feel like a meditation superstar. If this was easy to do, you wouldn't need to do it. You practice what is hard, like an athlete, to get better in an area of struggle—in this case, staying focused on the good.

Here are a couple of things to keep in mind:

- The purpose of sitting meditation is for you to gain greater control over your thoughts. The goal is not to empty your mind (that's impossible) but to quiet it and learn to focus it.
- The research that showed the positive effects of this practice for anxiety, pain, and depression involved meditating twice a day for twenty minutes each time. Begin where you can, but the dosage does affect effectiveness of this practice.

A few things can help deepen this practice:

- You may want to have a pad of paper handy so you can write down any to-dos that come to mind. Otherwise, you may find yourself meditating on "remember to buy milk" the entire time.
- Consider comfortable floor-sitting postures. Sitting on the floor and supporting yourself with your spine can help with alertness and allow you to adopt a more open and receptive posture.
- You may want to experiment with a timer on your phone or computer that will alert you at set intervals—perhaps thirty seconds into your time, midway through, and at the end.
- Consider ending your practice by reciting the Lord's Prayer or a passage of Scripture.
- Construct a simple meditation space that is free of distractions and can become "your space" for prayer and meditation.

About a year after I began practicing sitting meditation, I began to notice comments from people who came to my office. They all were variations on "It is so calm and peaceful here." The office had not changed, but I had. Through this practice, I had become more present and attentive. While meditation is often seen as an intensely private practice, it is almost always learned in a group setting, and for many of us it is best maintained by regularly attending a group that practices and supports mindfulness.

Self-Compassion

In J. K. Rowling's Harry Potter series, the protagonist, Harry Potter, comes to see that things are not quite the way he imagined.[34] A teacher who seemed to despise him turns out to be a brave protector, and Dumbledore, his strong, wise, and resourceful mentor, is debilitated by self-loathing. In their final meeting Dumbledore expresses regret for not trusting Harry and tells him how he is racked by guilt and shame. He tells Harry, "You cannot despise me more than I despise myself." Harry knows what Dumbledore did in the distant past, but he gently challenges his mentor's thoroughgoing negative self-assessment. As he respectfully pushes back against Dumbledore's harsh self-criticism, he muses, "How odd it was to sit here . . . and defend Dumbledore from himself."[35]

Understanding Self-Criticism

Dumbledore's intemperate self-criticism is very personal but not ultimately private because it shapes how he views others. It keeps him from trusting and makes him unduly risk averse toward Harry. What Rowling so exquisitely captured in her portrayal of this encounter is that we are often more critical of ourselves than a good friend would ever be of us, even if they knew the full backstory that generated our debilitating guilt and shame. The act of self-compassion is really about learning "to treat ourselves with the same kindness, caring and compassion we would show to a good friend. . . . Sadly, however, there's almost no one whom we treat as badly as ourselves."[36] We allow ourselves to get away with murder when the crime is against our own

34. Material in this section is adapted from James C. Wilhoit, "Self-Compassion as a Christian Spiritual Practice," *Journal of Spiritual Formation & Soul Care* 12, no. 1 (2019): 71–88.

35. J. K. Rowling, *Harry Potter and the Deathly Hallows* (New York: Scholastic Books, 2007), 713–14.

36. Kristin Neff, *Self-Compassion: Stop Beating Yourself Up and Leave Insecurity Behind* (New York: William Morrow, 2011), 6.

souls. But don't we have a responsibility to care for our souls? Don't we need to nurture our hearts? Don't we need to be a good and caring friend to ourselves? Showing self-compassion toward ourselves is not about boosting our self-esteem or convincing ourselves that we are better than average but about being empathetic and caring for ourselves just as we would care for a friend.

The book of Psalms opens with a portrait of the godly person. This person does not become entangled with cynics nor seek out the advice of those mired in wrongdoing. Instead, this person dwells on God's truth and leads a life of stability and fidelity. The psalmist completes the picture by saying that this person flourishes in all they do. In other psalms, we are shown over and over that the righteous person has an independence of thought. Circumstances, an enemy's taunts, and cynics' jeers don't deeply affect them because they trust in God and have learned to talk to themselves, to engage in a truth-based conversation with their soul.

In Psalms 42 and 43 we find a writer whose world has been turned upside down. He used to lead the congregation in worship but now feels discouraged, is the object of deceitful attacks, and is in physical agony. What a difficult place to be. He acknowledges the reality of his situation—the reversal of fortunes, the spiritual despair, and the biting personal attacks—yet he does not let these very real circumstances define him. In the midst of these rough seas, he knows that God is a rock that can be trusted. He asks himself, "Why, my soul, are you downcast?" And then he tells himself, "Put your hope in God" (Ps. 42:5 NIV). He is gently firm in reminding himself to take his eyes off the overwhelming circumstances and instead hope in God. For many of us, failures, sins, and disappointments are the triggers for speaking harshly to ourselves. Our failures stare us in the face. A range of shame-oriented emotions flood over us, and we lash out at ourselves. We don't decide to berate ourselves; it just happens. And the logic of self-attack seems impeccable—we screwed up, so we should be "corrected."

It is worth noting that a number of our spiritual heroes had moral and spiritual falls. These include such luminaries as Sarah and Abraham, David, Elijah, and Peter. Their failures include murder, loss of faith, and betrayal, but none of them turned to self-criticism when their eyes were opened and they saw what they had done. This is not to say they were never self-critical, but the Bible never portrays beating ourselves up as the way to deal with sin and failure. God's gracious way comes through confession and repentance, not self-criticism.

Paul is painfully aware of his own sin. He recounts that "when the blood of your martyr Stephen was shed, I stood there giving my approval and guarding the clothes of those who were killing him" (Acts 22:20 NIV). As Paul's relationship with Christ deepens, he becomes more aware of his sinfulness and calls himself the "worst" of sinners (1 Tim. 1:15 NIV). As he reflects on his struggle to live well, he describes himself as "miserable" (Rom. 7:24 NLT). Yet he does not berate himself. Instead, he urges his readers to follow his example by dwelling on "whatever is true, whatever is noble, whatever is right, whatever is pure, whatever is lovely, whatever is admirable—if anything is excellent or praiseworthy—think about such things" (Phil. 4:8 NIV).[37] And he goes as far as saying that he has given up self-judgment: "I do not even judge myself" (1 Cor. 4:3 NIV).

David gives us a profound glimpse into his thought processes as he responds to his own failings. At first, he seems to have successfully buried his crimes and misdemeanors, but through the word of the prophet Nathan, he comes to see the vileness of his sin—the adultery, betrayal, murder, theft, and deceit. He responds to Nathan by naming his sin with brokenness and repentance. He is deeply affected by his grief. He weeps, can't sleep, and feels isolated. In a way, David is the ideal penitent who cries out to God.

This is a man who had "sinned big." We find in Psalm 51 that he "repented big" also.[38] His response is humble brokenness before God. He writes of his transgressions, his iniquity, and his sin, but in this confession there is no harsh self-criticism. He suffers greatly as a result of his sin; not only does he bear the guilt for what he has done, but he also loses the child born of his illicit union. Later, the effects of his sin will manifest themselves in tensions in his family and in his faltering reign. His suffering is so intense that he feels as though God has crushed his bones (51:8). Notice what he does not say: "You're worthless. You call yourself a king? Look at the mess you made. What a loser." Instead, he focuses on God's generous fidelity toward him and recounts God's mercy, steadfast love, and abundant compassion. A self-critical spirit begins with the self and seeks to whip the self into shape; Christian self-compassion begins with the abundant compassion of God and speaks God's gracious words to the self.

Problems Caused by Self-Criticism

Paul Gilbert and Chris Irons have suggested that self-criticism has two dimensions. The first dimension is "self-directed hostility, contempt, and self-loathing." The second dimension concerns the difficulty in directing

37. Eric L. Johnson, *Foundations for Soul Care: A Christian Psychology Proposal* (Downers Grove, IL: InterVarsity, 2007), 447.

38. Nancy L. deClaissé-Walford, Rolf A. Jacobson, and Beth LaNeel Tanner, *The Book of Psalms*, New International Commentary on the Old Testament (Grand Rapids: Eerdmans, 2014), 457.

compassion inward or the "relative inability to generate feelings of self-directed warmth, reassurance, soothing, and self-liking."[39]

The gospel calls us to be people who "clothe yourselves with compassion, kindness, humility, gentleness and patience" (Col. 3:12 NIV). And that compassion should be directed both inward (self-compassion) and outward (compassion). Self-compassion is expressing the same kind of concern for our own pain and well-being as we would show for another in such a predicament. Leanne Payne directed a significant inner healing ministry for years. Her influential book, *Restoring the Christian Soul*, begins with a discussion of the virtue of self-acceptance, which she sees as foundational to well-being. She refers to self-hatred as "the traitor within when temptation comes" and calls our failure to accept ourselves the "first great barrier to wholeness in Christ."[40] Payne found through decades of ministry that self-acceptance is a virtue that needs to be cultivated for spiritual wholeness. "If we are busy hating that soul that God loves and is in the process of straightening out, we cannot help others—our minds will be riveted on ourselves—not on Christ who is our wholeness. When we hate the self, we in fact practice the presence of the old self; we are self-conscious rather than God-conscious."[41]

This theme in Payne's writings, that a negative self-focus is spiritually deleterious, is shared by many other widely respected writers in the area of pastoral care. For example, Romano Guardini emphasizes that the virtue of acceptance is foundational to spiritual growth. The maturing Christian must possess an "acceptance of what is, the acceptance of reality," which includes an "acceptance of self" and a "consent simply to be."[42] Self-criticism is seen as a refusal to acknowledge the reality of how things actually are. Adrian Van Kaam writes about how self-criticism is part of the independent impulse that leaves one isolated and self-absorbed. He writes, "An 'I can do it alone' mentality may eat away at our interiority like corrosive acid. It weakens our reliance on Christ, leaving in its wake only a sense of our own importance."[43] Henri Nouwen extensively explored the persistence of self-rejection and observed, "These negative voices are so loud and so persistent it is easy to believe them.

---

39. Paul Gilbert and Chris Irons, "Shame, Self-Criticism, and Self-Compassion in Adolescence," in *Adolescent Emotional Development and the Emergence of Depressive Disorders*, ed. Nicholas B. Allen and Lisa B. Sheeber (New York: Cambridge University Press, 2008), 209.

40. Leanne Payne, *Restoring the Christian Soul: Overcoming Barriers to Completion in Christ through Healing Prayer* (Grand Rapids: Baker, 1996), 19–29.

41. Payne, *Restoring the Christian Soul*, 32–33.

42. Romano Guardini, *Learning the Virtues That Lead You to God* (Manchester, NH: Sophia Institute Press, 1992), 25–26, 31.

43. Adrian Van Kaam and Susan Muto, *Formation Theology*, vol. 3, *Formation of the Christian Heart* (Pittsburgh: Epiphany Association, 2006), 112.

. . . The greatest trap in our life is not success, popularity, or power, but self-rejection."[44] This unified voice of pastoral wisdom regarding the deformative power of self-criticism must be accorded a hearing as we work in this area.

Self-compassion helps protect us from one of Satan's great patterns of attack on believers. While Satan was soundly defeated at the cross ("And having disarmed the powers and authorities, . . . triumphing over them by the cross" [Col. 2:15 NIV]), he is still active and a great cause of distress for Christians. He is active in his constant work of accusation (Rev. 12:10). The root meaning of his Hebrew title *Satan* is "adversary," and the Greek title *devil* means "slanderer." Zechariah paints a picture for us of this accusation orientation: "Joshua the high priest standing before the angel of the LORD, and Satan standing at his right side to accuse him" (Zech. 3:1 NIV). One of the ways Satan accuses Christians is by speaking lies to us and about us. As Jesus said, "When he lies, he speaks his native language, for he is a liar and the father of lies" (John 8:44 NIV). Satan has a stance toward us of lying accusation, and we need to counter this with a stance of godly self-compassion. The harsh words we speak to ourselves are not just our words; they are the messages of the Accuser, who, unlike our heavenly Father, actively despises us.

Practicing Self-Compassion

Self-compassion is one of those things that we need to practice if we want to have it. We won't get it through osmosis or by reading books or listening to sermons about it. We have to do it, and like any skillful way of living, we will do it badly before we do it well. Reading, listening to sermons, and talking with others about self-compassion may help us practice it, but they are not a substitute for actually doing the work.

Self-compassion is fulfilling your relational responsibility to yourself—respecting your value as being created in the image of God, honoring your gifts and God-given uniqueness, and responding with empathy for the difficulties you face. Full expression of self-compassion should include (1) empathetic, caring words, (2) a physical action that quiets and comforts, and (3) a recognition that what you are experiencing is common to humanity. To see what these three actions mean in practice, think of a time when you messed up or a tough time that was marked by conflict, bad news, pain, or struggle.[45]

I first spoke empathetic and caring words to myself during a time of confusion. I was meeting with someone and working through an issue when

---

44. Henri J. M. Nouwen, *Life of the Beloved: Spiritual Living in a Secular World* (New York: Crossroad, 2002), 31.
45. Neff, *Self-Compassion.*

my motives were challenged. The words stung. I had begun to explore self-compassion, so I spoke to myself: "Jim, this is hard. It hurts to be misunderstood." My friend continued to speak and mount the evidence that he thought proved his point. Not knowing what to say, I listened and silently spoke words of comfort to myself. The point is not to try to boost your self-esteem or challenge what is happening; it is to be a good friend to yourself by showing empathy and care.

When a friend expresses care to us, it is with their body. Whether the care is communicated through the tone of voice, a compassionate look, or a hug, our bodies are set up to receive care. We can use our bodies to comfort and quiet ourselves in the same way. When we do this, we are tapping in to the mammalian care-giving system—we are wired to respond to empathy expressed through touch, voice, and affection. Part of our expression of self-compassion should include a gesture of physical care. My preferred gesture of care is to place my hand over my heart as I speak words of self-compassion. You may find that something as simple as pausing and taking some long, slow breaths will calm you and give you a sense of being cared for.

Something common to humanity is that many of us are quite adept at catastrophizing. We can make our experience seem so terrible and so utterly unique, and with that can come a sense of aloneness—no one else has experienced what we are going through, and no one else can understand. We need to remind ourselves that while the circumstances we face may be unique, others have suffered in similar ways. Our suffering is the result of the fall and part of our shared humanity. I seek to put my situation in a broad category of human experience, telling myself, "This is hard. Others have faced betrayal and lived well." Our pain is multiplied when we perceive that our suffering and challenges are utterly unique. One of the great comforts of reading the Bible is finding ourselves in the narrative; we come to see how we fit into the universal human experiences depicted there. This is also part of the power of hearing testimonies of God's grace in church. We hear the stories of those whose struggles seem so close to our experience, and we hear that in the midst of loss, pain, and confusion, God was present. This encourages us to keep on keeping on.

God as the Master Affirmer

In speaking of self-compassion, we must also speak of opening ourselves to God's compassion. I don't want to give the impression that God's care and our self-compassion are at odds with each other. The Christian expresses compassion toward the self that ultimately comes from God, the origin of all blessings: "Every good and perfect gift is from above, coming down from the Father of the heavenly lights" (James 1:17 NIV). Through the ministry of the Spirit, our hearts are changed so that we can express compassion toward ourselves and others, and the new identity we have in Christ gives us the confidence to express compassion. We are enabled to be compassionate because of the comfort we receive from God, "the Father of compassion and the God of all comfort, who comforts us in all our troubles, so that we can comfort those in any trouble with the comfort we ourselves receive from God" (2 Cor. 1:3–4 NIV). The expression of self-compassion is one way we open our hearts to receive the love of God more fully.

Meditation

A promise is only as good as the person who makes it. It's the character of the promiser that gives the promise its value. So when we hear God promise that the person who meditates on his Word will prosper in what they do, will flourish, and will experience God's peace-inducing presence, it is worth taking notice (Josh. 1:8; Ps. 1:3; Phil. 4:7). This promise is sure and is given for our good by the one who cares most deeply for us. Few other spiritual practices receive this level of endorsement in the Bible.

When we turn to the Bible, we find about two dozen references to meditation. Most are in the Psalms, and they show us people meditating: "My eyes stay open through the watches of the night, that I may meditate on your promises" (Ps. 119:148 NIV). But they don't tell us much about how it is done. We learn that there is a strong connection between what we delight in and what we meditate on: "Oh, how I love your law! I meditate on it all day long" (119:97 NIV). We also learn that wisdom is nurtured through meditation (49:3) and that we grow in our faith and confidence in God (16:8). When we widen our view a bit and include passages that use words like *ponder* and *think*, our list greatly expands and the message is the same: meditation is one of the primary ways of refashioning our minds to highly value God and his truth.

> Happy are those whose way is blameless,
>   who walk in the law of the LORD.
> Happy are those who keep his decrees. (119:1–2)

> Then I shall not be put to shame,
>   having my eyes fixed on all your commandments. (119:6)

How can young people keep their way pure?
  By guarding it according to your word. (119:9)

I treasure your word in my heart,
  so that I may not sin against you. (119:11)

My soul is consumed with longing
  for your ordinances at all times. (119:20)

I run the way of your commandments,
  for you enlarge my understanding. (119:32)

I shall walk at liberty,
  for I have sought your precepts. (119:45)

Oh, how I love your law!
  It is my meditation all day long. (119:97)

Your word is a lamp to my feet
  and a light to my path. (119:105)

Your decrees are wonderful;
  therefore my soul keeps them. (119:129)

Trouble and anguish have come upon me,
  but your commandments are my delight. (119:143)

Let my cry come before you, O Lord;
  give me understanding according to your word. (119:169)

I long for your salvation, O Lord,
  and your law is my delight. (119:174)

This dwelling on the law is part of what is meant by meditation. But in meditation we direct our attention not just to the Old Testament law but also to that
which is good and positive. We may dwell on our love for a child or spouse, or
pause and stand in awe of something beautiful, or simply be grateful for "every
desirable and beneficial gift" that comes from God (James 1:17 Message). We
can focus on what is positive and excellent around us and relish and delight
in how God's grace is operating at this very moment in our lives and world.

A favorite picture of meditation in Scripture is that of Mary. She is perplexed and troubled by the greeting of the angel Gabriel. When the angel

announces that she will be the mother of the Messiah—"Greetings, you who are highly favored! The Lord is with you" (Luke 1:28 NIV)—we are told that she "pondered" (1:29) the message. When the shepherds came with their greeting, many heard them and ran off to spread the news, but Luke makes it clear that, by contrast, Mary carefully remembered the words and meditated on them. After Jesus's display of spiritual insight in the temple at age twelve, we are told that "his mother treasured all these things in her heart" (2:51). Of course, even before Jesus's birth, she was a meditator; her response to Gabriel, "The Magnificat," reveals a mind that has soaked in the Bible—it is filled through and through with Old Testament passages. What we see in Mary is what we find in the meditators of the Psalms—soaking in Scripture and pondering what they experience in the world, talking with God about it all the while.

The biblical authors tell us the importance and benefits of meditating, and they assume their readers understand the practice. When the term *meditation* is mentioned today, we think of something very foreign to the world of biblical authors. A friend might tell us that she is going to her meditation class, and we have the idea of meditation as something set apart from life, perhaps done in a special, quiet space. For the biblical writers, meditation took place in the midst of life and was not an activity set apart as we tend to see it. Today it is often portrayed as the entry point for a spiritual quest, but in the Bible, meditation implies that one has come to treasure and value the Word of God and find delight in the things of God—so it is for people who have gone down the road a bit with God. Finally, the focus of contemporary meditation tends to be self-improvement, while biblical meditation emphasizes gaining wisdom and following God more faithfully.

The Bible portrays meditation as a very natural and straightforward activity. We are wired to meditate—that is, to focus on what we value. The meditation valued in Scripture (Josh. 1:8; Ps. 1:2; Phil. 4:8–9) flows naturally from a heart filled with a love of and fascination with God, knowledge of the Bible, awe-filled observations of the world, and a pattern of slowing down to reflect on what is happening in one's life. We need to see that meditation in the Bible is a category, like sports. There are all kinds of sports—soccer, badminton, running, baseball—and there are all kinds of meditation—memorizing Scripture and recalling it as needed, quiet prayer while pondering a truth, recalling a biblical character's life choices as we ponder a decision, singing a Scripture-based song, praying a psalm. A bench press is a fitness activity, but it is not the only fitness activity. Memorizing Scripture and pondering it are forms of meditation, but they are not the only forms. Meditation is the habitual bringing of biblical truth and beauty into our lives.

And, by the way, we are all meditators. The Bible never commands one to meditate; it assumes that we all meditate—in the sense of thinking about what we value. What the Bible commands is the object of our meditation. We are to focus on "whatever is true, whatever is noble, whatever is right, whatever is pure, whatever is lovely, whatever is admirable—if anything is excellent or praiseworthy" (Phil. 4:8 NIV). We can see this in Psalm 19, where the writer assumes that they will be meditating and that their prayers and inevitable meditation will be rightly focused: "May these words of my mouth and this meditation of my heart be pleasing in your sight, LORD, my Rock and my Redeemer" (v. 14 NIV). In the Sermon on the Mount, Jesus portrays worry as a form of meditation (Matt. 6:25–34). We might call it negative meditation, in which one meditates on what might go wrong.

In the next section we will look at some patterns of biblical meditation, but before we do that, it is worth pausing and looking for the bright spots of meditation in your life. At what times do you pause and ponder truth in the midst of your life? If meditation is well integrated into your life, the specific times and contexts may not be noticeable. Perhaps you pray before your meals with a prayer based on Scripture. Maybe you reflect at the end of the day on what went well and measure your day by a scriptural standard. Do you find yourself singing or humming hymns throughout the day, or do you have a few stock phrases like "God is for me" that you turn to again and again? These are forms of biblical meditation. Part of our task is to take what is working well and see how it can be enhanced.

Ways to Meditate

Pair It

One of the easiest ways to build a new habit in your life is to pair it with a well-established habit or routine. Consider your morning coffee, your drive to work, a mealtime, picking up kids from school—there are things you do without fail that contain enough space for you to include a brief meditative practice. Perhaps to a mealtime prayer you could add a brief pause to be grateful for three things; that is a form of meditating on God's good provision. You'll find it much easier to pair a meditation practice with something you regularly do than to start a habit from scratch.

Meditate on Scripture as You Fall Asleep

The psalmist speaks of the practice of having Scripture in mind as he goes to sleep: "I think of you on my bed, and meditate on you in the watches of the night" (Ps. 63:6). Meditating on Scripture as you fall asleep is a simple pattern of redirecting your thinking that yields powerful results and does not require the use of "productive time." You can use a passage you read earlier in the day or a go-to verse. Some years ago, I spoke with a man whose national ministry had unraveled, and he mentioned that as things had gotten busy, he began to fall asleep with the worries of ministry washing over him rather than the truth of Scripture. Meditating on Scripture as you fall asleep is a fixed form of meditation in that it follows a timed plan and uses fixed content. This type of meditation is helpful when you need to reorient yourself, want clarity as you make a decision, need to calm and recollect yourself in the midst of life's storms, or need to be strengthened before facing a tough event.

Before you begin, find a brief Scripture passage to meditate on that can be divided into two lines. If you memorize it, it will always be available when you need it.

Next, begin the practice by observing your breathing. This simple observation is an easy way to bring your focus to the present moment and summon your attention to the meditation practice. *Hagah*, one of the main Hebrew words we translate as "meditate," denotes a distinctly bodily process, like muttering or speaking softly. Observing your breathing is a way of capturing this bodily connection.

The rhythm of breathing undergirds this entire meditation. Begin by observing your breathing for three breaths. Then tie the Scripture passage to your breathing. Inhale slowly through your nose for four counts as you think of the first line, and exhale slowly through your mouth for four counts as you think of the second line. Do this three times. End the time of meditation with a prayer.

The guide below may be helpful as you initially practice this meditation, then you can personalize it with a passage more appropriate to your life situation.

Two Truths Meditation Practice

Inhaling	Exhaling
Inhale slowly through your nose. Count 1, 2, 3, 4. Do this three times.	Exhale slowly through your mouth. Count 1, 2, 3, 4.
Praise the LORD, my soul,	and forget not all his benefits. (Ps. 103:2)
For great is his love toward us,	and the faithfulness of the LORD endures forever. (Ps. 117:2)
May I be strengthened by your love.	May I remember your benefits.
Inhale slowly through your nose. Count 1, 2, 3, 4. Do this three times.	Exhale slowly through your mouth. Count 1, 2, 3, 4.

Post a Note

In the Old Testament book of Deuteronomy, the Israelites were instructed to write the law "on the doorframes of your houses and on your gates" (11:20 NIV). The law was to be ubiquitous, ever present before their eyes. A generation ago, the homes of Christians contained plaques with Bible verses or embroidered Bible verses hanging on the wall, and we are poorer for having abandoned that practice. Here the idea is to fill your living spaces with the Word of God so that you are reminded to dwell on good things. Often the things we see regularly affect us the most. The presence of Scripture verses can help draw you back to important truths. Place index cards with Scripture passages in your home, car, and workplace, rotating them so they have an inviting newness.

Memorize Scripture

Memorizing longer passages of Scripture affords a great opportunity to meditate in a rich and powerful way. And memorizing is something that can very effectively be encouraged in the church. In an age of ubiquitous books and electronic texts, it is easy to dismiss memorization as a relic of bygone days, but we relate differently to memorized text—we have *acquired* it, and it is available at all times and places for recall and pondering. Recite a passage to yourself, out loud whenever possible. Pay attention to what comes to mind—a truth or an image—and then return to the words. Stay with the passage for a while, repeating it and asking questions.

Read and Write

Another practice of meditation involves reading Scripture and writing down important insights. Find a reading plan that will take you through significant portions of Scripture over a year's time. Choose a plan that is realistic for your life patterns and allows you to read at the beginning of your day. Commit to finding a word, phrase, or image each day that seems important to the passage and your life. Write this down on a piece of paper and put it in a place you will remember it—in your pocket or stuck to your dashboard or refrigerator. I prefer writing things out by hand with some underlining and stylized text, but many find that doing this digitally keeps what they've written in their view throughout the day, especially when they make it the lock screen on their phone or a reminder on their computer. Each time you notice what you've written, pause, take three breaths, and ponder what it says. Savor the truth.

These practices of meditation allow us to fulfill Paul's command to "let the word of Christ dwell in you richly" (Col. 3:16). What we give our attention to shapes our brains. When we redirect our attention to worthy topics, we slowly begin to develop new neural pathways that make a loving and God-focused disposition more natural.

Unceasing Prayer

A related practice that often springs from the soil that is worked through meditation is unceasing prayer. As our hearts are trained to turn to truth, not ruled by passions, we have greater freedom about where we set our minds: "Set your minds on things that are above" (Col. 3:2).

Unceasing prayer is an important spiritual practice and one that should be taught and encouraged. Paul considered this practice so important that he wrote about it to four communities: the Romans, Ephesians, Colossians, and Thessalonians. It appears to have been a regular practice for Paul, and he urges other Christians to do it too. He discusses it matter-of-factly, conveying that he considers it possible and does not regard it as an advanced or optional practice. I don't think he would have kept calling those early believers to "pray constantly" if it was not something they could do. In fact, Paul says that praying always is God's will for you: "Rejoice always, pray without ceasing, give thanks in all circumstances; for this is the will of God in Christ Jesus for you" (1 Thess. 5:16–18). God's will—his desire for us—is that our lives are marked by gratitude, rejoicing, and prayer.

We catch a glimpse of Paul's own practice when he says that he is "always offering prayer with joy" for the Philippian church (Phil. 1:4 NASB). He reminds the Colossians that he is "praying always" for them (Col. 1:3 NASB), and he sends a similar message to his friend Philemon: "I thank my God always, making mention of you in my prayers" (Philem. 4). What does it mean to pray always? It means that prayer is a regular, recurring, sustained, unabating, steadfast, disciplined, unwavering practice. It should be like eating or sleeping, going to work or playing—a regular part of our lives.

When we hear the call to ceaseless prayer, we may imagine that means prayers will arise spontaneously. Prayers do arise spontaneously but not continually. As Anne Lamott reminds us, our spontaneous prayers are generally prayers of "Help," "Thanks," or "Wow." These are good prayers, but these types of prayers punctuate our lives more than fill them.[46]

46. Anne Lamott, *Help, Thanks, Wow: The Three Essential Prayers* (New York: Riverhead Books, 2012).

Life will bring us crises that evoke the God-ward "Help," moments of gratitude when "Thanks" wells up in our hearts, and those times of stunning beauty when we stand dumbstruck and silently say, "Wow." However, much of life does not evoke those prayers. If we think that prayer will just magically fill in the cracks, it won't.

One of the most basic ways that churches teach unceasing prayer is by raising it as a possibility. This comes through testimonies and the casual comments of leaders as they describe how they seek to fill their lives with prayer. There are a number of well-established ways to introduce unceasing prayer:

> Books. A number of spiritual classics present this practice; these include Brother Lawrence's Practicing the Presence of God and Frank Laubach's Letters by a Modern Mystic.[47] Such books provide compelling stories about how the authors adopted this pattern of prayer, making it seem attainable. Virtually every Christian tradition has authors who have experienced the joy of unceasing, prayerful fellowship with God.
>
> Training programs. This is probably one of the disciplines in which we need to realize that "when the student is ready, the teacher will arise." We can make teaching on this subject available for students who feel drawn to living more intentionally in God's presence.
>
> Groups. Churches can provide an ongoing weekly or monthly group for directed prayer, perhaps for an hour, aimed at cultivating an awareness of God.

We are united with Christ in our new birth and indwelt by the Holy Spirit. An emphasis on our union with Christ makes all teaching on unceasing prayer a Christocentric activity and keeps unceasing prayer from becoming a mere skill or spiritual attainment.

Luke introduced a parable on prayer with the words, "Then Jesus told them a parable about their need to pray always and not to lose heart" (Luke 18:1). Those words are good to keep in mind as we think about praying always. Jesus asks us to pray, and he realizes that it is easy to give up. Therefore, ask your ever-present teacher and Lord how to do it: "Jesus, you prayed throughout your life. Teach me right now how to be prayerful in this situation." And then listen and learn.

47. Brother Lawrence, Practicing the Presence of God (Old Tappan, NJ: Revell, 1973); Frank Laubach, Letters by a Modern Mystic (Westwood, NJ: Revell, 1937); Thérèse, The Autobiography of Saint Thérèse of Lisieux: The Story of a Soul, trans. John Beevers (Garden City, NY: Image Books, 1957).

Conclusion

Christian Spiritual Formation is important. It is important for fulfilling the broad mission of the church. It is important for channeling the compassion of Christ. It is important for nurturing and giving expression to authentic Christian worship. There is a wealth of accumulated pastoral wisdom regarding best practices of formation, and every specific context deserves an appropriately tailored approach to formation. We grieve when we see pastors crumble under the tyranny of the urgent, compelled by the need to "pull off this program" and make their church work. The practices in this chapter are supported by biblical reflection, pastoral wisdom, and in many cases empirical research, so they can be rightly deemed high-impact practices. But they should be shared with churches by leaders who have experienced their power. C. S. Lewis, grumbling about attempts to bring novelty into worship services, quoted someone who quipped, "I wish they'd remember that the charge to Peter was Feed my sheep; not Try experiments on my rats, or even, Teach my performing dogs new tricks."[48] Our call is to discern what is needed at this time and what the Spirit would have us offer to the beloved church.

For Further Reading

Charry, Ellen T. *God and the Art of Happiness*. Grand Rapids: Eerdmans, 2010. A book that explores a biblical vision of happiness and human flourishing through a comprehensive theological survey.

Hanson, Rick. *Just One Thing: Developing a Buddha Brain One Simple Practice at a Time*. Oakland: New Harbinger, 2011. A book with a Buddhist orientation that sets forth well-documented practices with clarity.

Kaczor, Christopher. *The Gospel of Happiness*. New York: Image Books, 2015. An application of positive psychology on the cultivation of Christian virtues.

Kraegel, Irene. *The Mindful Christian: Cultivating a Life of Intentionality, Openness, and Faith*. Minneapolis: Fortress, 2020. A book that provides an overview of the principles of mindfulness and easy-to-follow practices.

Lyubomirsky, Sonja. *The How of Happiness: A New Approach to Getting the Life You Want*. New York: Penguin, 2008. A clear presentation of empirically grounded practices designed to cultivate the good life.

Peterson, Christopher. *Pursuing the Good Life: 100 Reflections on Positive Psychology*. New York: Oxford University Press, 2012. A clear presentation of practices for flourishing.

48. C. S. Lewis, *Letters to Malcolm: Chiefly on Prayer* (New York: Harcourt Brace Jovanovich, 1963), 5.

Peterson, Christopher, and Martin Seligman. *Character Strengths and Virtues: A Handbook and Classification.* New York: Oxford University Press, 2004. A compilation of the key virtues found to contribute to human flourishing.

Worthington, Everett L. *Humility: The Quiet Virtue.* West Conshohocken, PA: Templeton, 2007. A clear statement of the foundational value of humility and the practices that foster it.

APPENDIX

Assessment Questions

My purpose has been to set forth a curriculum for Christlikeness grounded in the gospel and the grace that it makes available. Without a constant appropriation of the grace extended, it would be foolish to pursue such an involved and demanding purpose as imitating Christ. Grace sets us on our way and accompanies us to the finish. The framework for this curriculum is the lifelong practice of *receiving*, *remembering*, *responding*, and *relating*. These are verbs, not nouns. These categories call for believers to take action and to do so in the ordinary circumstances of everyday life. The four *R*s invite us to intentional activity, to live out—in both the public and the most private aspects of daily life and thought—the wise invitations of Jesus to kingdom living. The goal of Christlikeness has been well articulated by Dallas Willard:

> This process of "conformation to Christ," as we might more appropriately call it, is constantly supported by grace and otherwise would be impossible. But it is not therefore passive. Grace is opposed to earning, not to effort. In fact, nothing inspires and enhances effort like the experience of grace.
>
> Yet it is today necessary to assert boldly and often that becoming Christlike never occurs without intense and well-informed action on our part. This in turn cannot be reliably sustained outside of a like-minded fellowship. Our churches will be centers of spiritual formation only as they understand Christlikeness and communicate it to individuals, through teaching and example, in a convincing and supportive fashion.[1]

1. Dallas Willard, "The Spirit Is Willing: The Body as a Tool for Spiritual Growth," in *The Christian Educator's Handbook on Spiritual Formation*, ed. Kenneth O. Gangel and James C. Wilhoit (Grand Rapids: Baker Books, 1994), 225.

As we work with this curriculum, it will be necessary to take some time for evaluation and planning. Are we getting it? Are we doing better or worse? Why? What has helped and what has hindered our work with the curriculum? The questions in the following section are intended to assist us in the process of self and group evaluation regarding our progress in *receiving, remembering, responding,* and *relating.* I have constructed the questions to use the terms *we* and *our church* to facilitate a group assessment setting.

If spiritual formation is the mission of the church, then thoughtful evaluation is necessary to ensure that we are carrying out the mission as our priority. Since any curriculum for Christlikeness takes concerted resolve, we should understand that assessments are profoundly difficult due to the human vulnerability to self-deception and blind spots. Here it is immensely important not to rush. Be open to the work of the Holy Spirit, pray, and plead for the grace and humility to see what God sees.

The two sets of questions that follow are designed to look at the formation process from two distinct perspectives. Each perspective is important in evaluating the formational ministry of a church regarding the presence of the four *R*s.

Examining the Four Main Components of the Curriculum for Christlikeness

Receiving: Where Do People Receive God's Grace and Love?

In what ways does our church encourage the application of the gospel to everyday situations?

How do we encourage the cultivation of awe for God's beauty, mystery, or wonder?

Which corporate disciplines support our longing for God and for Christlikeness?

Where and when do people receive grace in our church?

Where do we cultivate the desire to receive God's love?

Remembering: Where Are People Encouraged to Remember Who They Truly Are as Children of God and Whose They Truly Are?

Where do we practice spiritual remembering through testimony, journaling, and thanksgiving?

Where are learners receiving a comprehensive presentation of the Bible?

How well is our overall curriculum teaching people to actually adopt Jesus's lifestyle?

Where are they learning to practice the spiritual disciplines that marked Jesus's life?

How well are we teaching people to live out the great invitations of Jesus? Review the list of the invitations below and list places where we are teaching people to live these out.

Invitations to Steward Christ's Gospel

- Jesus invites us to tell people about the good news and make disciples.
- Jesus invites us to practice discernment.
- Jesus invites us to a life of integrity.
- Jesus invites us to use our money wisely.
- Jesus invites us to practice detachment.

Invitations to Extend Christ's Compassion

- Jesus invites us to pray for and bless others.
- Jesus invites us to keep relational commitments.
- Jesus invites us to a life of compassion for the poor and marginalized and to the elimination of prejudice.
- Jesus invites us to weep—a call to empathy.
- Jesus invites us to handle conflicts well and to forgive one another.
- Jesus invites us to extend hospitality.

Invitations to Worship

- Jesus invites us to worship and to celebrate the sacraments.
- Jesus invites us to create a space for God through solitude.
- Jesus invites us to use our bodies in prayer and worship.

Invitations to Think Rightly about God

- Jesus invites us to depend more and more on God and his grace.
- Jesus invites us to the joy and freedom of practicing spiritual disciplines.
- Jesus invites us to study and meditate on Scripture.
- Jesus invites us to repentance and to draw close to God and himself.
- Jesus invites us to believe he is who he claims to be.
- Jesus invites us to a life of learning.

Responding: In What Ways Do We Foster a Disposition to Be People of Love and "Right Living"?

Where do we provide specific training to live well in relationships? in families? at work?

Where do we provide training in Christian conflict resolution?

Where do we help people learn to set aside racial and ethnic prejudices?

Where do we help people learn to be good stewards of creation?

Where do we equip people to evangelize?

Relating: Where Do We Provide Opportunities to Grow in and through Relationships?

In what ways does our community support an attitude or outlook of brokenness before one another and before God?

Where do we show hospitality to one another? Where do we show hospitality to the stranger?

How well do we discipline or confront known patterns of sin within our church?

Assessing Where Formation Happens in the Church

These questions are a parallel way of evaluating the formational patterns and programs in a church or ministry. Here the focus switches to look at resources for the journey.

Goal: provide rich, formative opportunities for all stages of the Christian life.

Evaluative task: identify life phases that are under-resourced.

Process: observe the experience of a church member at each of these stages on the spiritual journey. Then brainstorm a description.

1. New Christians

   What education or discipleship program is in place to train a new believer? In what ways does the program reflect the curriculum of Christlikeness in the ordinary aspects of individual lives?

   How do we fold new believers into the fellowship of the larger group?

   Do we give new believers service opportunities that match their abilities and maturation?

When new believers ask hard questions or seek to change the status quo, how do we respond?

How well are we doing at providing mentors for new Christians?

2. Christians struggling with addictions, temptations, crises, grief

Where in our church do we allow or encourage the troubled to share their brokenness and tell their stories?

How does our church respond to these admissions of need, both initially and over the long term?

In what ways and by whom are the struggling or broken identified and cared for?

Where are the struggling or troubled allowed to contribute or serve within our church?

What is our protocol for referring the troubled to professional help or community services?

3. Christians struggling with doubting

Where in our church do we allow or encourage a doubter to ask difficult and disturbing questions?

In what ways does our church seek to engage with the ordinary day-to-day lives of doubters?

How do we identify and care for doubters?

In what ways do we assure doubters that we still accept and value them?

What are the usual long-term outcomes for those who have come to our church with difficult questions? Do these individuals usually stay or disappear over time?

What resources are available in the form of books, sermon tapes, or other study materials for doubters?

4. Christians experiencing a dark night of the soul

What efforts are we making to instruct all members of our church regarding the dark night of the soul?

Is there a conscious effort on the part of the leadership to watch for cases of spiritual depression and spiritual dryness among themselves? among those for whom they care?

What is our general attitude and response to those who express that they fear they are losing their faith?

What methods do we make available to answer the questions and concerns of those in this condition?

5. Christians wearied by the ordinariness of faithfully following Jesus

In what ways do we review and assess the educational curriculum of the church for freshness and effectiveness?

What kind of vision do we have to inspire long-term, faithful members?

How do individuals or small groups usually present their visions or challenges to the larger group?

How does the larger group usually respond to the visions or challenges of individuals or small groups?

6. Christians in need of restorative discipline

In what ways do we approach an individual or group of individuals and motivate them to cooperate with restorative discipline?

When restoration requires reconciliation between two members within the church, who usually initiates discussions—the offended party, the defending party, or a leader who has a heart that sees and responds to trouble in early stages?

How do we incorporate accountability into a restorative process?

Remember that prayer is our leading ally for the work of assessment. In prayer we can find rest from our striving and be strengthened in God's love. As R. A. Torrey has instructed, "God does not demand of us the impossible. He does not demand of us that we imitate Christ in our own strength. He offers to us something infinitely better. He offers to form Christ in us by the power of his Holy Spirit. And when Christ is thus formed in us by the Holy Spirit's power, all we have to do is to let this indwelling Christ live out his own life in us, and then we shall be like Christ without struggle and effort of our own."[2]

2. R. A. Torrey, *The Person and Work of the Holy Spirit*, rev. ed. (Grand Rapids: Zondervan, 1974), 123.

Scripture Index

Subject Index